W9-BQZ-146

communication skills
in the
organization

communication
skills
in the
organization

Gary T. Hunt

California State University, Los Angeles

PRENTICE-HALL, INC.

Englewood Cliffs, New Jersey 07632

Library of Congress Cataloging in Publication Data

HUNT, GARY T
  Communication skills in the organization.

  Bibliography: p.
  Includes index.
  1. Communication in organizations. 2. Communica-
tion in management. I. Title.
HD30.3.H86   658.4'5   79–11620
ISBN 0–13–153296–0

© 1980 by Prentice-Hall, Inc.
Englewood Cliffs, New Jersey 07632

Printed in the United States of America

10 9 8 7 6 5 4 3 2 1

Editorial/production supervision and interior design by Joan L. Lee
Cover design by Allyson Everngam
Manufacturing buyer: Harry P. Baisley

PRENTICE-HALL INTERNATIONAL INC., *London*
PRENTICE-HALL OF AUSTRALIA PTY. LIMITED, *Sydney*
PRENTICE-HALL OF CANADA, LTD., *Toronto*
PRENTICE-HALL OF INDIA PRIVATE LIMITED, *New Delhi*
PRENTICE-HALL OF JAPAN, INC., *Tokyo*
PRENTICE-HALL OF SOUTHEAST ASIA PTE. LTD., *Singapore*
WHITEHALL BOOKS LIMITED, *Wellington, New Zealand*

to Albert and Dovie

contents

vii

PART TWO

interpersonal communication

three

Good Listening:
The Key to Communication Comprehension, 63

six

Supervision:
Achieving Dynamic Leadership
Through Communication, 157

xi

PART FOUR

written communication

nine

Writing:
Developing Effective Messages, 257

xii

preface

Organizational communication has become an important area of study in many colleges, universities, and industrial training programs as scholars and managers realize that the manner in which organizational members communicate affects the success (or failure) of an organization's external and internal operations. Good organizational communication results from many factors. The structure of the organization must allow messages to be sent easily and efficiently. Newsletters, reports, and meetings must readily transfer information among units and departments. Further, the leadership of the organization must sense the potential communication problems which arise daily and work to solve them. But the most critical factor in organizational communication is the communication behavior of the *individual.* This book was written about that individual and the communication challenges he or she faces as a member of an organization.

In the past five years, many good books have outlined the way communication works in organizations. They have explained the theoretical basis of organizational communication. It is not this book's purpose to concentrate on theory. Instead, it will provide guidance on *how to communicate* in an organizational setting.

Part one introduces the nature of organizations and the communication process. In part two, communication within the organization is separated into specific person-to-person communication skills: listening, interviewing, participating in small groups, and supervising. Part three develops the planning and implementation processes that lay the foundation for effective public communication in the organization. The focus turns in part four to writing as a communication skill. Part five completes the discussion of interpersonal communication by describing the methods that an organization can use to train its members to communicate.

Each of the book's ten chapters ends with a relevant case study. The case depicts a "real life" situation, followed by guidelines for analysis that provide a structure for review and discussion. The cases, along with the examples within the chapters, encourage the student and manager to draw defensible conclusions and applications about communication within organizations.

As both a teacher of organizational communication and a consultant/trainer to many organizations, I have attempted to bring both the academic and the practical to this book. Hopefully, each perspective has enriched the other.

Many people made greatly appreciated contributions to this book. The original concept came from discussions with Professor John Makay of The Ohio State University nearly five years ago. Many of John's ideas remain in the final version. Brain Walker, formerly of Prentice-Hall, Inc., was a thoughful and knowledgeable editor. Joan Lee was extremely competent and cheerful as a production editor and all of her suggestions improved the final product. Raymond Gleason, formerly a graduate student at Cal State, Los Angeles, contributed much of the research for chapters three and ten. Many of the ideas presented here were first tried out on students at Cal State, Los Angeles, and on members of many organizations throughout Southern California. These thoughtful people offered refinements and criticisms that shaped the final manuscript. Jonathan and Michael Hunt provided many socioemotional rewards. As did "Wichita." And, finally, I would like to acknowledge the 32 years of love and understanding provided by the two people to whom this book is dedicated . . . my parents.

communication skills
in the
organization

introduction

PART ONE

understanding
the organization

For the rest of your life, you will be involved with many types of organizations. Consider a day in the life of Bill Brown, a guy who could be your next-door neighbor.

Bill's clock radio wakes him up with the latest news at 7 A.M. The news is being broadcast by a radio station *organization*.

While Bill is scraping butter across his piece of toast, he receives a telephone call. In using the telephone, Bill is interacting with a system developed and operated by a public utility *organization*.

Bill realizes that he is running late. He dresses hurriedly and dashes out to meet his car pool. Designed to meet the needs of its members, the car pool is also an *organization*.

Bill and his co-workers arrive on time at the paper plant where they are employed. The plant, too, is an *organization*. In fact, the paper plant is really many organizations in one. Bill's department, quality control, functions very much like a small, self-contained organization. The plant contains about 30 other departments that also function as separate organizations. All of these separate units, however, belong to the larger organization—*the plant*.

After a full eight hours in the plant, Bill comes home in the car pool. He suggests to his wife that they go out to a restaurant for dinner. The restaurant is run as an *organization* that exists to feed its customers.

After dinner Bill and his wife head for the bowling lanes, where their league is playing in a tournament. The bowling league is another *organization* created to serve the recreational needs of bowlers.

Bill's league wins the tournament. They decide to celebrate by stopping by the local tavern for a beer. The tavern is another recreational *organization*. After the second beer, Bill's wife suggests that they go home to the kids. The Browns themselves, operate as an *orga-*

chapter one

nization. Any typical family functions very much like the many organizations Bill has been involved with, directly or indirectly, during his routine day.

In almost every social encounter, *we are influenced by one or more organizations.* Organizations enable us to achieve many of our goals. We earn our living, enjoy our recreation, receive an education, and worship through organizations.

This book is about the communication behavior demonstrated by the members of organizations. How do people communicate in the organization? What types of communication skills are important for effective participation in the organization? Communication may be defined as the *sending and receiving of information* among people.[1] It involves the spoken word and the written word as well as the nonverbal aspects of information sending. We will consider four communication skills: speaking, writing, listening, and analysis.

This first chapter examines the nature of organizations and their impact upon humans. First, we will learn what organizations are. Next, we will discuss the things that organizations have in common. Finally, we will study the things that organization routinely do. This treatment of the nature of organizations is intended to provide you with a clear understanding of the way in which organizations operate. You need to know this before you can learn about and develop communication skills for use in organizations.

what organizations are

Organizations are unique. In this part we are going to learn why. Let us examine some of the most important characteristics of the organization.

Organizations Are Dynamic

Like human beings, organizations are dynamic. They are ongoing, ever-changing, constantly forced to meet new challenges. They are continually adapting to rapidly varying conditions in their *environments.*

For example, consider the situation of the private liberal arts college in the United States. Private colleges have traditionally been identified as schools for the rich. On the other hand, public colleges and

---

[1] A. Sanford, G. Hunt, and H. Bracey, *Communication Behavior in Organizations* (Columbus, Ohio: Charles E. Merrill Publishing Company, 1976), p. 12.

universities have been seen as middle-class schools, where families of moderate income could afford to send their children. However, as economic conditions have changed, many private colleges have had to make drastic changes to stay in business. Costs associated with higher education have risen rapidly. Private colleges have tried to attract applications from less affluent students. They have suggested that the bright, capable, middle-class young person—with some help from the family, a part-time job on campus, and a partial scholarship—can probably afford to attend a private college. In short, they have had to appeal to new constituencies in order to survive.

The public colleges, on the other hand, have found themselves enrolling many students from affluent families, because these families no longer had enough money to send their children to the best private colleges. As economic conditions fluctuate, the rules for these organizations have changed. To survive, they must be dynamic enough to adapt. Otherwise they will probably find themselves out of business.

There are four important ways in which an organization must remain dynamic.

CHANGING MARKETS Organizations must be dynamic enough to meet changing markets. Since most organizations market some type of product or service, they must be sensitive to their potential customers' changing attitudes and predispositions. If there is no market for the organization's product, the organization will not survive.

An organization that produces an intricate computer system for the nation's space program will stay in business as long as it can sell its product to the government. But if it cannot sell its product to the government because of cutbacks in the space program, it might find a market for its computers in the transportation industry. However, to meet the requirements of this new market, the organization must remain adaptable and flexible.

CHANGING ECONOMY All organizations need financial resources to remain in business. Therefore, economic conditions are a crucial influence on the operations of the organization. Organizations must pay attention to almost every facet of the economy.[2] The availability of money for expansion, resources to use as raw materials, and the cost of labor all play an important role in the development of the organization. In our society, most things cost something. To be able to exist, the organization must be prepared to pay whatever it takes to stay in

[2]H. Hicks, *The Management of Organizations: A Systems and Human Resources Approach*, 2nd ed. (New York: McGraw-Hill Book Company, 1972), p. 12.

operation. The family organization that cannot meet its financial obligation must file for bankruptcy just like the large corporation in the same situation. Organizations must remain dynamic to adjust to changing financial conditions.

CHANGING SOCIAL CONDITIONS   Since all organizations depend on human talents and initiative, they must remain dynamic enough to adjust to changing social conditions. If social conditions change, the organization must change too.

The employment of public school teachers in the 1960s and 1970s illustrates this point. During the 1960s, there was a tremendous growth in our population. Schools were expanding so rapidly that unlimited growth almost became a policy for many communities and school districts. Colleges of education worked diligently to turn out enough school teachers to meet the new demands. Even mediocre teachers found jobs. Then something happened. Zero population advocates encouraged people to stop having four or five children and to be content with one or two. Suddenly there were not enough children to fill the classrooms. However, there were more than enough trained school teachers. Any school that had an opening for a teacher was deluged with applications. The *supply* of teachers outweighed the *demand*. Educational organizations changed to meet these new conditions. Instead of hiring teachers with little experience and only limited success in college, they could now be highly selective in the types of teachers they employed. Personnel practices had to change to allow the organization to operate in a buyer's, instead of a seller's, market. This required a degree of flexibility. In summary, dynamic organizations are those which pay attention to changing social conditions.

CHANGING TECHNOLOGIES   For an organization to be successful, it must be able to accomplish a particular job. This job is called its *task*. The methods that an organization uses to accomplish its task are called *technologies*. Technologies change drastically over very brief periods of time.

Consider the way in which an organization pays its employees. Up until a few years ago, payroll was a major job of the bookkeeping department. Numerous clerks and bookkeepers would work many hours to insure that payroll checks were properly recorded and dispersed. However, sophisticated programs now exist that enable an organization to disperse and record payroll by computer. This frees many hours of human time.

Research and development departments work hard to keep organizations informed of new technologies. But, in order to learn about, acquire, and implement them, the organization must remain dynamic.

Organizations Are Informed

All organizations need information to survive. It is by exchanging information that one part of an organization learns about the duties and activities of another part. Some prominent organizational theorists have defined organizations primarily as information processing units.[3] Without exchanging information, organizations do not have the knowhow to change raw materials into final products.

What exactly is meant by the phrase *exchange of information?* Consider the case of a typical college fraternity. This fraternity has a number of subgroups called standing committees. Each standing committee operates more or less autonomously. However, for the fraternity to function effectively, each standing commitee must share its information with the others. This can be done in several ways. Perhaps all of the chairs have a weekly meeting to report on their respective committees' activities. Perhaps information is transferred during the regular fraternity meetings. Perhaps the committee members compare notes informally during class and at other fraternity activities.

As the standing committees share information, support, and compete with each other, important relationships develop among them. Without these relationships among subgroups, organizations cannot be successful. The maintenance of these relationships depends on the mutual exchange of information.

It is equally important for the organization to obtain information from its *environment.* Important events that occur *outside* are crucial to the internal operations of the organization. If an organization needs capital to build a new factory but cannot get it because the economy is tight, problems develop. If an organization continues to make a product that no one buys because it has been declared illegal, that organization cannot continue to operate. If an organization depends on a particular skill to make its product, and if people who possess this skill are not available in the labor marketplace, the organization will suffer.

[3]C. Perrow, "Hospitals: Technology, Structure, and Goals," in *Handbook of Organizations,* ed. J. March (Chicago: Rand McNally College Publishing Company, 1965), p. 324; K. Weick, *The Social Psychology of Organizing* (Reading, Mass.: Addison-Wesley Publishing Co., Inc., 1969), p. 101.

To prevent situations such as these from arising, the organization must acquire information that exists in the environment and transmit it internally. If it has no member who can do this, the organization will find itself in trouble.

The communication skills of individual members—perception, listening, planning, organizing, and presenting—are all essential to the organization. This book tells how these skills can be developed and improved. For now, it is enough to know that the transfer of information—within the organization and between the organization and its environment—is vital to the health of the organization.

Organizations Are Purposeful

Organizations are *groups of people who associate together for a common purpose*. This is what distinguishes organizations from other social phenomena. Any group of people who coordinate their behavior to achieve a goal may be said to be operating as an organization.

Most organizations exist to do a particular thing. Educational organizations exist to train young people. Voluntary organizations exist to help others. Service organizations exist to provide a service to those who need it. Religious organizations exist to promulgate their own brand of gospel. The goal of an organization is the thing that the organization exists to do.

In order to achieve its goal, the organization behaves in ways that individuals within the organization believe will achieve that goal. Organizations can said to be purposeful to the extent that (1) all members of the organization share the same goal for that organization; (2) everyone agrees as to which behaviors will best help to achieve that goal; and (3) everyone is willing to manifest the appropriate behaviors.[4] If members disagree about the appropriateness of the goal or the most viable method for achieving it, problems will arise.

Individual members of the organization must perceive the meaningfulness of the goal and its importance to themselves before they will work hard to achieve it. Occasionally, for a variety of reasons, members will disagree with the primary goals of their organization. These people will sometimes even act in ways that are *counterproductive* to the organization's goals. The worker who thinks that his organization is polluting the environment may believe that his very work is injurious to others. Instead of spending his time working (goal-accomplishing behavior), this worker may avoid his job as often as he can. He may even

---

[4]A. Sanford, *Human Relations Theory and Practice*, 2nd ed. (Columbus, Ohio: Charles E. Merrill Publishing Company, 1977), p. 178.

lobby his co-workers into avoiding their jobs. The worker's activities then become a hindrance to the goals of the organization.

Organizations differ widely in purposefulness. But the degree of purposefulness does depend on the extent to which individual members believe in and accept the organization's goals.

Organizations Are Structured

In order to accomplish their objectives, organizations normally establish rules, codes, and hierarchical (or reporting) relationships. The rules, codes, and relationships become the organization's *structure*. The last time you visited an office or factory, you may have noticed a linear diagram of the official reporting relationships in the organization. This is the firm's *organizational chart* (see figure 1–1). The organizational chart is one part of the organization's structure.

The concept of structure may be illustrated using the example of the typical college or university. The student is taught by a faculty member who operates within the rules laid down by the university. If the class is to be taught three times a week, and is so described in the catalog, the teacher will teach it three times a week. If grades are to be reported to the registrar two weeks after the last day of classes, the teacher will turn in the grades at that time. The department chair is assigned to enforce the university's rules for faculty members. Faculty members rank below the chair in the hierarchy and report to the chair. The dean supervises all the department chairs. He or she is responsible for the overall management of the college. Deans report to the vice-president of academic affairs. All vice-presidents report to the president. The president administers the university within the guidelines established by the board of trustees, to whom the president reports. *Thus, the typical university is a compilation of rules, guidelines, and hierarchical relationships that allow it to operate within its charter or mandate.*

Every organization has a structure. Some have rigidly defined and complex structures; others have loose or simple ones. Structure enables the organization to standardize work procedures and to specialize the tasks associated with the production processes. Normally, an organization will develop a structure that helps it to do its task as well as possible.

Sometimes the structure, which is established primarily for the good of the organization, comes into conflict with the good of the individual. When this happens, it is difficult for the individual to work hard to achieve the organization's goals.

In summary, structure—or official rules, codes, and relationships —helps the organization to control its own destiny.

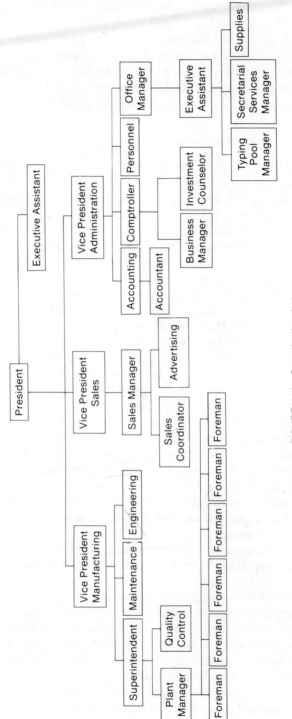

FIGURE 1-1 Organizational chart

A Review

Let us review the characteristics of organizations. Organizations are *dynamic* and *active*. Organizations require the *transfer of information* internally and the transfer of information *between the organization* and *the environment* to survive. Organizations differ from other social phenomena in that they exist to *accomplish a particular objective*. Thus organizations can be said to be purposeful. Finally, to enable the organization to accomplish its goal, it must have *rules* that will enable it to *control itself* and *its environment*. These rules are called *structure*.

At this point, you should have some idea of what organizations are. Now let us see what all organizations have in common.

what organizations have in common

All organizations have certain things in common, whether the organization is General Motors or the Walnut School first-grade class. In this part, we will examine four of these common attributes: human resources, know-how, energy, and environment. This discussion should enable you to draw some parallels among the organizations you are likely to encounter.

Human Resources

Although its sounds simplistic, it is nonetheless true that all organizations are made up of people. People manage organizations, people do the work of organizations, and people provide the knowledge that organizations use to grow and develop. People's individual communication skills are essential to an organization's operations. Organizations might actually be defined as *collections of people who have bound together for a common purpose*. People provide the energy to accomplish the tasks of the organizations.

DECISION MAKING In recent years, some organizations have developed sophisticated techniques—computer programs, management information systems, and simulations—to help them in the process of decision making. But mechanical techniques can only provide the necessary information. It is still individuals, or groups of individuals, who have the final responsibility for making decisions. As individuals make good decisions, the organization will grow and prosper. As individuals make bad decisions, the organization will stagnate.

Communication skills are very necessary in the decision-making process. To make a good decision, one must first be able to secure the kind of information one needs. One must then synthesize and interpret this information. Finally, one must be able to transmit the results of the decision to the appropriate places in the organization's hierarchy. All of these skills involve communication. Decision making is one area in which organizations depend on human resources for survival.

GROWTH AND DEVELOPMENT The organization that is not moving ahead will eventually die. Normally organizations grow through the development of new technical specialities and markets and the development of human talents. The secretary who is hired primarily as a clerical worker but eventually gains a management position is helping not only herself or himself, but the organization as well. As its people grow, so grows the organization. Sometimes organizations try to foster and encourage this growth through training programs and promotional opportunities. Other times, individuals themselves gain knowledge and expertise without official sanction. An example would be the first-line supervisor who returns to the community college to earn credits toward a degree.

As individuals gain new talents and new sophistications, they become increasingly valuable to the organization. It is sound management practice to try to keep these people.[5] Money that the organization spends today on training its personnel should be more than repaid tomorrow through their added knowledge.[6]

Communication skills play an important role in the development and growth of human resources. Supervisors and managers must be able and willing to tell their subordinates about the opportunities for growth. This information must be transmitted in such a way that it is understandable to organizational personnel. These individuals must be able to comprehend the importance and relevance of the growth opportunities *to them.* In this way, communication helps insure that organizational personnel are fully trained and ready to meet tomorrow's problems.

TASK EXPERTISE An organization may be viewed as a series of structured tasks that must be accomplished in order to achieve a purpose. These tasks may be very similar or quite different, but they are all interrelated.

Consider a typical baseball team. For this organization to achieve

[5]Sanford, *Human Relations Theory,* p. 96; W. French and C. Bell, *Organizational Development* (Englewood Cliffs, N.J.: Prentice-Hall, Inc., 1974), p. 72.
[6]R. Beckhard, *Organizational Development: Strategies and Models* (Reading, Mass.: Addison-Wesley Publishing Co., Inc., 1969), p. 76.

its purpose (to win), certain tasks must be done. For example, there must be strong pitching. In fact, this particular task may be subdivided even further. There must be both strong left-handed and strong right-handed pitching. There must also be a good infield and a strong outfield. There must be a good catcher. The team must be strong on defense (catching the ball) and strong on offense (hitting the ball). Even if the team is strong on the field, success will come only if it is equally strong in the dugout. There must be a good bench of players ready to replace the regulars on the field. A group of dependable relief pitchers is necessary, should the starters falter. Above all, there must be good management. Some *one* individual must be responsible for inserting players, changing pitchers, and so forth. If any one task in this organization breaks down, the team will not win. This analogy holds for just about every organization.

Generally, it is people who perform the tasks in an organization. However, because people have thoughts, attitudes, and feelings, they sometimes fail to accomplish their tasks. Tasks are accomplished when people (1) know what to do and (2) want to do it. Occasionally an individual will know what to do but will not want to do it. For example, a baseball player may know how to play center field well, but because he believes he is underpaid, he may not *want* to do the job. Sometimes the opposite also happens—an individual may want to do the job but does not know how. For example, it might be possible to call up a player from the minor leagues who sincerely *wants* to play center field. But he may not have the skill to do the job. Thus, both lack of desire and lack of talent can prevent tasks in organizations from being accomplished.

Organizations can develop training programs to give the individual expertise in a particular task. Communication skills play a vital role in developing task expertise. Good communication skills help trainers to explain methods and techniques clearly. These skills also help trainees to understand and apply what they hear in training programs.

The problem of motivation is a more difficult one. Here communication enables the organization to explain to individuals *why* they should accomplish the task. Information about the potential rewards of accomplishing a task can also be communicated. This, too, may increase motivation.

COMMITMENT Organizations often ask and sometimes expect contributions "above and beyond the call of duty." Consider the case of the business executive who will spend 18 solid hours working on a report, the minister who spends five nights a week calling on the sick, or the college professor who spends every weekend in his study working on a textbook. These are examples of the kind of devotion that some people bring to their jobs. As one rises in the hierarchy, the organization increasingly begins to expect (and sometimes even to demand) this kind of commitment. People render it for a variety of reasons. Some people truly love their job and would rather work than do anything else. Some people want to get ahead and see this kind of commitment as a way of doing so. Some people see their own personal goals as being linked to those of the organization, so that by giving this kind of commitment, they are really working for themselves.

The area of commitment has not yet been thoroughly investigated in the research. It is the author's opinion, based on observation, that many important tasks get accomplished only through unlimited commitment to one's job and to one's organization.

Communication skills are important in developing commitment. Managers must offer reasons why subordinates should be committed. Information about the benefits of commitment should be exchanged. As people perceive the rewards of commitment, they may well begin to demonstrate it.

Know-How

Organizations transform raw materials *(inputs)* into products *(outputs)*. This ability we call *know-how*. It is one attribute that can be used to distinguish among organizations. The Timex Corp. has the know-how to produce wristwatches at a low cost to the customer. Harvard University has the know-how to transform high school students into college graduates. Know-how takes many forms.

In the agrarian society that characterized the United States in the nineteenth century, the transmission of know-how was a fairly simple task. Each father would take the time to teach his son how to run the family farm. There really was no need to keep elaborate records or to develop sophisticated training programs. Basically, know-how was transmitted by word of mouth.[7]

But transmission has become complicated as organizations have become complex. It would not make sense for the older employees of General Motors, say, to try to communicate their know-how to the younger employees by word of mouth. You would never be sure that the automobile you bought off the showroom floor was properly assembled. Perhaps the person who was supposed to put together the axle did not get the word from his predecessor that the axle must be attached with four bolts instead of two. Today's customer would hardly be happy

[7]Hicks, *Management of Organizations*, p. 121.

if contemporary organizations decided to transmit know-how in this way.

Most organizations spend large sums of money to develop and refine their existing know-how through various types of research and development ("R and D") programs. As organizations expand their know-how, they increase their chances of success. They can use their know-how to produce a particular product at a lower cost than the competition. They can also use their know-how to produce a better product than the competition. Occasionally organizations use their know-how to produce a product that no one else makes.

Communication is vital to the transfer of know-how. Individuals in the organization must be able to develop the programs and techniques by means of which know-how is transmitted. Manuals, guides, and code books are often used to record and transmit know-how. So are many sophisticated training and growth programs. Orientation and indoctrination techniques are also used by older employees to transmit know-how to newer ones. The people who direct these programs must be skilled in communication. They must be able to present information in ways that make it meaningful and interesting to new members of the organization. Otherwise this know-how will neither be transferred nor understood. As people gain the task expertise considered in the previous section, they are contributing to the know-how of their organization.

Energy

Organizations, like people, need energy to function effectively. This energy is supplied by their members.

CONTROL As we have seen, the organization is always changing. This does not mean that the change is always random. There may well be an element of random change, but normally change will be controlled and planned.

One of management's main jobs is to control and direct human behavior. People sometimes demonstrate random energy, and this may have to be controlled. But the mechanical energy of an organization must be controlled as well. The work unit that uses two cents' worth of electricity to manufacture a product worth one cent will not stay in business. By controlling random energy, the organization eliminates the waste of human and mechanical resources. Thus, controlling energy in this context means making sure that most effort is purposeful.

Organizations that can control energy can sometimes initiate change before they are forced to do so by existing conditions. These organizations are said to be *proactive,* able to control their own destiny. A proactive organization is a leader in its field.

RESPONSIVENESS As conditions change, the organization must be able to project a complete, coordinated, appropriate response. It must have the energy to provide this response. The more dynamic and controlled the response, the greater the likelihood of successful change.

Consider the example of a growing suburban school district. The community around the school district is expanding rapidly. This necessitates a dramatic, coordinated response from the three organizational subunits of the district headquarters. The academic staff must develop the curriculum and programs that the growing number of students will demand. The business staff must find locations for new schools and the means to pay for them. The personnel staff must acquire new teachers to fill the new classrooms. Each subunit must keep the others informed of its activities in order to avoid duplication. Thus each subunit contributes to a single, coordinated response to a changing condition—the growth of the school district.

When an organization cannot coordinate its response to changing conditions, much effort and energy is wasted. Here again communication is important. People in key positions must be able to detect and interpret the need for change and communicate this need to the decision makers in the organization. These decision makers must be able to listen to and interpret the messages that are sent to them. If members of the organization lack communication skill, they will probably not respond effectively to change.

Environment

We have referred several times to the concept of organizational environment. Environment is one of the most important concepts in the theory of organizations.

The organization may be diagramed as a series of arrows inside a circle (figure 1–2). But operating outside the circle are political, economic, natural, and technological pressures. These *external* variables constitute the environment. They influence what goes on *inside* the organization. Consider the following illustration.

Let us assume that a given organization produces canned peaches to be sold in supermarkets. Obviously, the organization has the mechanical procedures to produce the peaches in a systematic way. However, there are certain external elements that will influence the organization. In the economic realm, the cost of raw peaches and sugar will affect the internal functions of the organization. In the technological realm, technical advances will speed up the transportation time from orchard to plant. Improved peach-growing techniques will also have an important

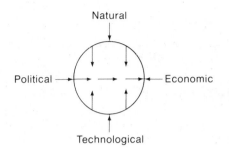

Natural

Political → Economic

Technological

FIGURE 1–2 Influence of environment

influence. In the political realm, a state legislature may tax farmland heavily or pay farmers subsidies for not growing peaches. In either case, the supply of raw materials will be reduced. Finally, natural climatic conditions such as rain, sunshine, storms, and drought will help determine the available supply of peaches.

Not every event that occurs outside the organization will influence it, of course. But a limited number of particular events will influence the organization significantly. These events are called the organization's *relevant environent*.[8] In the foregoing example the weather in the Northeast would be of little importance because very few peaches are grown there. The weather in the Southeast is very important, however, because a great many peaches are grown there. The weather in the Southeast would be part of this organization's relevant environment.

It is through the communication skills of its members that an organization defines and monitors its relevant environment. Since an organization cannot possibly keep track of everything, some kind of selection process must take place. People who listen, read, talk, and analyze decide which events must be observed. Good, perceptive people who can judge which events are likely to influence an organization enable that organization to operate successfully within its environment.

what organizations do

We have just discussed four things that all organizations have in common. Similarly, all organizations do certain things. They have certain *functions*. In each of these functions, the interpersonal communication skills of the individual members play an important role. Let us consider four of the most important things that organizations do.

[8]J. Thompson, *Organizations in Action* (New York: McGraw-Hill Book Company, 1967), p. 94.

17

Organizations Acquire Things

All organizations tend to acquire things. These things may be buildings, land, factories, and financial holdings. They may be files, records, guidelines, and written materials. They may even be such intangibles as history, reputation, image, and community regard. Occasionally an organization will acquire things it does not need, such as unnecessary regulations and meaningless rules. Organizations sometimes acquire things they would rather avoid at all costs, such as a bad community image ("They don't care about people," "They're polluting the rivers," "Most of their players are quitters").

Some organizations acquire things that are very valuable, such as a young, committed work force, a clean factory, or a reputation as a progressive firm. Most often organizations acquire many things that are worthwhile and a few things that are not. The members' task is to help the organization determine which things are going to be valuable and which things should be avoided as potential hazards. This is primarily a communications activity, as we shall see in the following example.

Consider a college basketball organization (team). The coach knows that he needs to acquire things: good high school *players* who can handle college-level work, a top-flight national *schedule* playing against good teams, and *reputation* as a spirited and competent team. At the same time, the coach wants to avoid certain things: high school players who flunk out of college, high-pressure alumni who try to pay inducements to players, and slipshod training and practice procedures. The coach is forced to walk a very narrow line. He must try to acquire the things he wants while avoiding the things he does not want.

At first, this may seem like a rather easy task for an organization. But it's not all that simple. The organization must have people who can collect information about potential hazards. To collect information, members must interact in a wide variety of contexts. In the example of the college basketball team, the coach who talks only to a potential recruit's high school coach, while avoiding the boy's high school teachers, counselors and, most importantly, his parents, is probably neglecting valuable sources of information. Communication among people who are gaining information about things in the environment and within the organization helps the organization to determine which things should be acquired.

Organizations Develop Responsibilities and Duties

As organizations acquire and avoid things, they begin to develop responsibilities and duties. With minor exceptions most organizations attempt to operate within some kind of ethical standard. This means

18

that an organization must live up to the standards it has established for itself as well as to the standards of society. These standards provide the organization with a special set of responsibilities, which may or not be related to the product it makes.

In small communities, the largest employer, like it or not, is responsible for the economic well-being of the community's citizens. If for some reason the employer is forced to lay off part of its work force, it risks the community's wrath. Even worse, the people who are hurt by the layoff may take out their frustration and disappointment through acts of vandalism against the organization's property. As the employer has economic duties, the school board has a duty to educate the community's young. If reading scores are down or math test results drop, the school board may be blamed, even though it may not be at fault.

Certain responsibilities are mandated by law ("Don't pollute," "Provide safe conditions for workers," "Hire more minorities"), and it is not difficult to measure the degree to which the organization has complied with them. Other responsibilities are subtle ("Treat customers fairly," "Help build a new YMCA," "Buy from local merchants"), and it is sometimes hard to ascertain what they are. Should we approve a land trade? What political posture should we maintain? Should we contribute money to this new program? Questions of this type are not easily answered, but the answers are crucial to the well-being of the organization.

Often a particular organization will be judged by how well it has fulfilled its responsibilities to the community rather than by the quality of its product. Corporate image may depend, not on the production line, but rather on the company's willingness to meet its community and social obligations. Organizations do develop these obligations, clear-cut or obscure, and must try to meet them.

Organizations Produce Things

The main function of an organization is to produce things. The "thing" is the product of the organization. All organizations have products. Some are obvious: for example, General Motors produces cars. But the Junior League also has a product. It takes young women and "makes" them into committed public service volunteers in their communities. The Boys' Club in your town has a product. It attempts to take young men and "produce" well-rounded, healthy adults. Your community hospital takes in sick people and (usually) discharges people who are well. If the Boys' Club has half of its members arrested for damaging automobiles, or the community hospital finds itself discharging sick people who have to go to other hospitals to get well . . . both have a *production* problem.

Some organization theorists[9] diagram an organization as shown in figure 1–3. As you can see, the organization consists of things modifying the condition of raw materials. The modification consists of the *processes* of production in the organization. Industrial engineers and management experts spend much time attempting to refine and modify these processes to produce a product rapidly and cheaply.

To produce a greeting card requires high-quality ink, paints, engraving, and printing techniques. But the most important skill in the manufacturing process is the art ability and technical expertise of the printer. The printer is the one who must match all of the other production processes to turn out good-looking greeting cards. The process might be improved in a number of ways. The manufacturer might be able to obtain some high-quality paper from a supplier. A new chemical discovery would enable the manufacturer to develop better and more colorful inks. Or the experienced printer might be given additional training to help him or her to do a more efficient job. But the final goal of all of these undertakings is to produce the best possible product at the lowest possible cost.

The effective production process depends on accurate information. People must obtain and transmit information to keep the improvements coming. If a breakdown in the engraving process occurs, the printer must be able to diagnose it and transmit information to the maintenance department for repair. Managers must become aware of new products or processes that could help the greeting card firm. Information about these things must be transmitted within the organization. In addition, information must be sent to employees that makes them *want* to produce greeting cards. The success of the production processes, then, depends on good communication skills. Without good communicators, the organization could not continue to produce a good product.

[9]Thompson, *Organizations in Action,* p. 12; Weick, *Social Psychology or Organizing,* p. 11.

FIGURE 1–3   Simple systems view of organizations

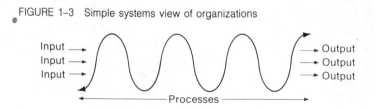

Organizations Affect and Are Affected by People

Organizations affect and are affected by people. It is people who guide, manage, direct, and cause growth within organizations. People provide the impetus that gives organizations new ideas, new programs, and new directions. Actually, people *are* the organization.

On the other hand, people, both customers and members, are affected by the organization. Most of us will spend about 50 to 60 percent of our adult working time as members of organizations. Under normal circumstances, we will tend to take on the special characteristics of these organizations. If we work in a bank, we will probably grow increasingly concerned about detail and finances. If we work in a grocery store, we will probably become sensitive to people's food-buying habits and the way in which they spend their money. If we drive a truck for a living, we will probably gain an appreciation of the open road and a dislike for discourteous drivers. The point should be clear. We begin to manifest those psychological and social tendencies which are associated with our job.

Organizations influence us in still other ways. Television organizations influence what we watch. Newspaper organizations influence what we read. Construction organizations influence where we live. Automobile-manufacturing organizations influence what we drive. Hospital organizations influence the treatment we receive when we are ill. All of these areas of influence are important to us. We must have the skill to interact with and respond to organizations.

But the influence process works both ways. To repeat, people also influence organizations. The success of an organization can be a function of the quality and abilities of its members. Consider the case of a high school football team. The success of the team organization, e.g., the number of wins the team accumulates, is a product of two influences: the quality of the players and the ability of the coach. In short, the team's success depends on people.

This chapter has emphasized the human aspects of the organization deliberately. To continue to grow, organizations must recruit the best talent available to fill their particular needs. In addition, organizations normally offer training programs and techniques to develop talent already in the organization. Organizations must also grant members freedom to develop as individuals, so that they can take on the characteristics of successful members.

Why go to all this trouble? you may ask. Because people with unique communication skills will eventually direct the organization. People who are very skilled at analysis, planning, listening, speaking, and perception will rise in the hierarchy. As they rise, they will take on more responsibility and more duties. *Good communicators are much more likely to benefit their organization than are poor communicators.*

This book is about those communication skills which enable the individual to influence his or her organization. In the next part of this chapter, we will briefly examine some of these skills. Later in the book, entire chapters will be devoted to the most important principles involved in communication skills for organizations.

some important communication skills

Some important skills enable the individual to *participate* effectively in the daily operations of an organization. Five types of communication behavior most often seen in the organization are interpersonal communication, small group skills, leadership skills, public communication, and written communication.

Interpersonal Communication

When two or more people interact, they are engaging in *interpersonal communication.* Much of the communication that takes place in the typical organization is of this kind. Interpersonal communication often takes place in the two-person, or interviewing, format. When the boss sits down to evaluate an employee in a formal appraisal, it is normally done in an interview. When a member of an organization approaches a fellow employee and asks advice on a particular topic, this, too, is likely to be done in an interview. When the boss reports on the progress of the department to a superior, again this is done in an interview.

Many important decisions are made in the interview. For example, decisions to hire, fire, spend money, or accept a proposal normally involve some form of interviewing. Interviewing involves those skills which one needs to interact successfully in both formal and informal conversations with one or two people.

Small Group Skills

The small group is almost as important to the organization as the interview. Over the past few years, organizations have encouraged their members to participate in decision making.[10] Younger managers

---

[10]D. Ewing, "Who Wants Corporate Democracy?" *Harvard Business Review,* 49, no. 6 (November/December 1971), 12–28.

especially seem willing to have their subordinates help administer the organization. Normally, this participation occurs in small group discussions of the current issues. Many of the principles presented in chapter four, which deals with the interview, are also important in the small group. Other principles of communication are specifically relevant to small group interaction. Such contemporary group techniques as the task force, the executive committee, the management team, team management, employee-centered supervision, and growth groups are all used in small group communication. These and other approaches are presented in chapter five.

Leadership Skills

In this book, leadership, or supervision, will be considered as communication skill. Why? Becasue effective supervision can only be practiced through effective communication. Indeed, just learning about important communication skills will go a long way toward making a supervisor effective. Sometimes supervisors have trouble expressing themselves to their subordinates. At other times their subordinates do not seem to listen. And at still other times, there seems to be a "bad climate" between the supervisor and the subordinate. Chapter six will consider many of the communication challenges facing the supervisor. The material presented in that chapter should clarify the relationship between good communication skills and good supervision.

So far, we have been discussing interpersonal communication skills. Two other communication skills are also important in the organization: public communication and written communication.

Public Communication

People in organizations are often called upon to make public presentations in front of groups. This public communication takes many forms. A manager will be called up to welcome new employees. A teacher will discuss a new curriculum proposal with a group of colleagues. A department head will have to defend the department's budget to a board of directors. All of these situations require the communicator to demonstrate good *presentational* skills.

Presentational skills are important in organizational communication. Normally, a member of an organization will communicate in dyads and small groups more often than in public situations. However, when the member is called upon to make that public presentation, it is usually in a formal setting with a large audience. Sometimes many attitudes will be formulated or changed as a result of the presentation. Thus it is important to develop and refine one's public communication skill.

Actually, this skill is really three subskills: planning, organizing, and presenting. These subskills are covered in part three.

Written Communication

Many books about communication consider only oral or only written interaction. This book considers both, though it emphasizes oral communication. The theory is virtually the same for both, and aspects of that theory are developed throughout the book. Good communicators in the organization need both oral and written communication skills.

Writing is a vital communication skill. Organizations typically develop volumes of written material every day to disseminate information both *internally* (within the organization) and *externally* (outside the organization). The memorandum, the production report, the newsletter, the brochure all play a role in the organization's communication program. Some writers[11] have suggested that one can spend too much time developing written materials, since other people in the organization do not always have the time to read them. This issue will be dealt with in part four.

FOR STUDY

1 Briefly, what constitutes an organization? What are its components? How does it operate?

2 What is an organization's environment? How does its environment influence an organization?

3 Organizations are at once similar to and different from each other. Why?

4 This chapter indicated that the organization has both human and natural resources. Which do you think are more important to the success of the organization? Why?

5 What role does communication play in the success (or failure) of an organization?

6 The approach that views an organization as a system is based upon certain assumptions. What are they?

case one
The New Product

The Jarman Manufacturing Company has been in business for 40 years. It employs about 1200 people in plants located in Eugene, Oregon, Glendale, Arizona, and Los Angeles, California. Jarman has always been noted for its major product, canvas deck shoes. For many years, Jarman held about 17 percent of the casual footwear market and competed fairly successfully with larger national organizations.

About five years ago, Jarman began to experience severe organizational problems. It had been able to exist fairly well on its 17 percent share of the market, which provided a good return on investment with enough left over for an attractive profit-sharing program for employees. But as the costs of labor and raw materials rose, Jarman began to fall on bad times. The Glendale plant was closed, and 250 employees were laid off. Jarman's share of the market dropped to just over 7 percent, as major companies entered the casual footwear field. At the annual meeting of employees that year, Sam Lyon, Jarman's president, told workers: "Things don't look too good for us, but we are not going to give up. What we need are new ideas, fresh approaches, and innovative plans. We are going to listen to people, and we are going to try to be flexible when people have good ideas."

Dave Murchison was Jarman's Los Angeles area sales representative. Recently, Dave's doctor had told him that he needed to take off 15 pounds. The doctor said that Dave should enter some kind of exercise program. The thought of going to the gym every day depressed Dave, so he decided to jog around his neighborhood each morning. Dave began his jogging program with a half-mile course. Soon he had worked up to one mile and was now running about five miles a day. He loved the activity. Each morning a feeling of escape and freedom came over him as he began to hit the pavement. Dave easily lost his fifteen pounds, but he enjoyed running so much that he kept up his program religiously. One thing that Dave noticed each morning as he ran was that lots of other people were out doing the same thing. It seemed as if everyone he knew either was running or was involved in some type of exercise program.

In the beginning, Dave had started running in the old pair of tennis shoes he wore when he was cutting his lawn. But the longer he ran, the less support the shoes gave him. He went to the sporting goods store to find himself a pair of shoes for running, but all the store carried was a light track shoe popular with high school and college runners, which sold for $45. Dave was both disappointed and excited: disappointed because he couldn't find what he wanted, but excited to share his experiences with his boss, Larry Tuller. Larry was Jarman's vice-president for marketing. It was his responsibility to handle customer research and make recommendations on new products.

25

The next day Dave and Larry met over lunch. "You wouldn't believe the number of people running, and yet you can't find a good pair of running shoes. We're already geared up to make these shoes. All we need is a little expert advice, some advertising, and a little public relations. We can produce a shoe runners will buy," Dave told Larry.

Larry began to get excited, too. Together he and Dave learned all they could about running. They talked with track coaches, podiatrists, orthopedic surgeons, world class runners, and local joggers. In their research, the two spend nearly $5000 of company money and were under much pressure to justify their expenses. Finally they had an idea solid enough to sell to Sam Lyon and the board of directors.

They developed a written proposal of their plan. It had four parts:

1. the development of an advisory committee of running experts to help with the design of a solid midpriced shoe for runners.

2. the conversion of the Arizona plant to the manufacture of the shoe,

3. the securing of a $300,000 loan to help finance the project, and

4. the mounting of a national sales campaign to promote the Jarman shoe.

After they had presented their written proposal to the board, Sam asked Dave and Larry to make a brief oral summary of the project. They were very persuasive in their appeals, and the board—almost as a last resort to save the company—decided to go along with the proposal.

It took about eight months of lead time to get the shoe designed and into production. Larry was given authority over the running shoe division and Dave was put in charge of marketing and distribution. For eight months both Larry and Dave worked 70 to 80-hour weeks, often commuting between company headquarters in Los Angeles and the production facilities in Glendale. Finally, the Jarman running shoe, under the trade name Street Pounder, was ready.

The advertising campaign consisted of displays in sporting goods stores and advertisements in running magazines. The focus of the campaign was "Now, runners, a shoe made just for you." Because this represented such a large investment for the company, Larry frequently had to act as a liaison between the project and the president and board of directors. He met weekly with Sam and twice a month with the board.

Dave used all of his sales and marketing expertise. He attended coaches' conventions, sporting goods dealers' meetings, and track meets. At a marathon in San Diego, a 26-mile race with many runners competing, he set up a booth with the Street Pounder on display. To get people to notice the shoe, he gave complimentary samples to some runners.

The advertising efforts began to pay off. *The Runner,* a magazine written by and for runners, did a story on the Street Pounder that said it was the best running shoe on the market. Sales began to take off. A local Los Angeles runner wore a pair of Street Pounders when he won the 1974 Boston Marathon. Requests for the shoe became so numerous that the Glendale plant could not keep up with the demand. The Eugene plant was converted from deck shoes to running shoes. Athletes formed the habit of wearing their running shoes even when they were not running. After just two years, sales topped $5 million nationally.

Larry and Dave knew they had a hit on their hands. But instead of resting on their success, since they knew their competitors would soon be entering the market, they started thinking up new products. Plans were begun for a Lady Street Pounder and a Little Street Pounder. They used the Street Pounder design to produce other models, such as a long-spiked shoe for outdoor track. They put small spikes on the Street Pounder for cross-country runners. They designed shoes for basketball, racquetball, volleyball, and tennis. Now the Jarman name is associated with high-quality athletic shoes. The athletic shoe division has far outdistanced the deck shoe division in sales and profits. Jarman is now on solid financial ground.

FOR STUDY

1 What communication principles were demonstrated in this case?
2 Think back over what Dave and Larry did. Use the terms contained in this chapter to describe their behavior.
3 What conditions within Jarman made this organization ripe for change? From what you know about organizations, would you say that they generally welcome change?
4 How do you measure the success of any organization? Speculate on some of the criteria that might be used.
5 Can you think of other cases where one or two people have had such a profound influence on an organization?

understanding communication in organizations

The rest of this book deals with the types of *communication behavior* that occur in organizations. Chapter two presents an overview of the nature of communication and the ways in which communication operates in organizations. Each of the remaining eight chapters will examine a specific aspect of communication, to enable you to improve your skills in that area.

This chapter begins by considering the nature of communication behavior in terms of its function and operation. Next, it examines communication in organizations from the macro, micro, and individual perspectives. Some representative communication situations are then discussed. Typical communication problems in the organization are examined. The chapter concludes with six perspectives on human interaction. These perspectives provide the theoretical foundation from which communication is analyzed in the remainder of the book.

communication: what is it?

People talk a lot about communication. But how many people really understand how the process works? To paraphrase Mark Twain, everybody talks about communication, but nobody does anything about it. Although it is one of the most basic of human processes, communication is also one of the most misunderstood.

Some people have suggested that as long as we can communicate, it is not really very important to understand how we do it. However, as most communication experts would agree, sooner or later communication breaks down. We then have a *communication gap* or *failure to*

chapter two

communicate. When this happens, we must examine the component parts of the process to learn why the failure occurred. After the diagnosis has been made, we can remedy the situation. An understanding of the basic communication process is a necessity for people who have trouble getting their point across. At one time or another, just about all of us will be in this category.

Definitions of Communication

Many scholars have defined the communication process. If we examine their definitions carefully, we begin to understand the variety of perspectives from which the communication act can be viewed. To Jurgen Ruesch and Gregory Bateson communication would include

> ... all [of] those processes by which people influence one another ... this definition is based on the premise that all actions and events have communicative aspects, as soon as they are perceived by a human being ... [and] that such perception changes the information which an individual possesses and therefore influences him.[1]

In this definition Ruesch and Bateson argue that there are elements of communication associated with almost every event or stimulus. The emphasis is on the individual's internal psychological condition. Lee Thayer simplifies this definition when he describes communication as occurring "whenever an individual assigns significance or meaning to an internal or external stimulus."[2] Martin Andersen, Wesley Lewis, and James Murray define communication as "the process by which one person, through the use of audible and visual symbols, engenders meaning in one or more listeners...."[3] This is a very important idea that pervades the literature about human communication. Simply put, *communication involves one person trying to create meaning in another.*

George Miller's definition focuses on another aspect of communication:

> Communication takes place when there is information at one place or person, and we want to get it to another place or another person.[4]

[1]J. Ruesch and G. Bateson, *Communication: The Social Matrix of Psychiatry* (New York: W. W. Norton & Co., Inc., 1951), p. 6.
[2]L. Thayer, "On Theory-Building in Communication: I. Some Conceptual Problems," *Journal of Communication*, 13, no. 3 (1963), 43.
[3]M. Andersen, W. Lewis, and J. Murray, *The Speaker and His Audience* (New York: Harper & Row, Publishers, Inc., 1964), p. 27.
[4]G. Miller, *Language and Communication* (New York: McGraw-Hill Book Company, 1951), p. 10.

Essentially communication does involve the transfer of information from one person to another. In organizational settings, this transfer is usually the purpose of communication behavior. Perhaps Raymond Ross has offered the best and simplest definition of communication:

> Communication is a process involving the sorting, selecting, and sending of symbols in such a way as to help a listener perceive and recreate in his own mind the meaning contained in the mind of the communicator.[5]

Each of the foregoing definitions provides insight into the process of human interaction. For the reader, it is important to keep the following three ideas in mind:

1 *Communication involves the creation of meaning in the listener.* Since meaning cannot be transferred, the sender attempts to create a meaning in the mind of the listener similar to the meaning in his own mind. It is never possible to create the exact same meaning, because no two humans are alike.

2 *Communication involves the transfer of information.* As communication takes place, one person is trying to pass along information to another. Information is transferred through the use of symbols, which can be verbal or nonverbal or both.

3 *Communication involves thousands of potential stimuli.* Any number of stimuli may be involved in the communication process. A stimulus becomes a message when the individual assigns it a meaning.

The Nature of Communication

Most introductory textbooks on communication note that human interaction is extremely complex. This book examines a wide variety of communication contexts and situations. In each, communication is likely to operate a bit differently. Let us consider two examples.

In the employment interview, which is covered extensively in chapter four, both of the participants pay close attention to each other, and each has an important stake in the outcome of the exchange. The interviewer wants to learn enough about the interviewee to make an intelligent decision about his or her qualifications. Obviously, the interviewee wants to get the job. The situation is relatively clear-cut and salient to both parties. Communication in the interview is usually two-way, and there is much exchange between the two parties. The climate is often supportive.

[5]R. Ross, *Speech Communication,* 4th ed. (Englewood Cliffs, N.J.: Prentice-Hall, Inc., 1977), p. 110.

However, the employment interview represents only one type of organizational communication. We can contrast it with another situation, in which the department manager is giving a speech about safety to a group of employees. Since there are many listeners, they are likely to be confused about objectives of the presentation. There is little opportunity for two-way interaction, and the climate may or may not be supportive, depending on the participants. In short, the public situation is very different from the interview.

In any organization there are thousands of potential communication contexts. Each may be unique, yet there are similarities among them. In most situations that require communication in organizations, at least one of the following four conditions is present.

SOMEONE NEEDS INFORMATION People need all kinds of information to survive in organizations. Members often find themselves in contexts that require them to give or ask for information. One rationale for creating the pyramidal organization, with a few people at the top of the organizational chart and a lot at the bottom, is that it can easily be used to disseminate information throughout the hierarchy. Information transfer is one important reason for communication in organizations.

SOMEONE NEEDS SOCIAL REINFORCEMENT Members of organizations have certain social and psychological needs that must be fulfilled. These include the needs for recognition, esteem, and growth. People communicate to fulfill these needs in others and to have others fulfill their own needs.

SOMEONE HAS DIRECTED SOMEONE ELSE TO COMMUNICATE In organizations people are ordered or directed to engage in communication. They are often told to give a speech, conduct an interview, or write a letter. People may also feel directed to communicate in a particular situation because they believe that doing so is part of their job.

SOMEONE COMMUNICATES TO ACHIEVE A GOAL Communication involves the psychological and physiological condition of the individual. Certain of our goals are met through communication, and sometimes our external style of interaction is influenced by what is going on inside us. People often communicate for important psychological reasons, and when we communicate with someone, we must feel some degree of reciprocity with that person. Otherwise serious problems may result.

Some Common Characteristics of Communication

Students of communication agree that the phenomenon has certain characteristics that may be generalized to most social situations.

COMMUNICATION IS DYNAMIC AND ONGOING A famous communication theorist once said, "You can never not communicate."[6] Although the statement might contain too many negatives to accommodate the English grammarian, it is indeed profound. The concept goes like this: Because we receive communication stimuli almost constantly from a wide variety of sources, the process of giving and receiving information is taking place constantly all around us.

Think back to the time when you attended your last football game. The pageantry, the weather, the person you were (or were not) attending the game with, the condition of the playing field, the quality of the hot dogs—all probably influenced you as much as the football played down on the field. Information from thousands of events and combinations of events, both past and present, is *processed* by our cognitive structure.

COMMUNICATION IS FUNCTIONAL AND PURPOSEFUL Communication helps people to get what they want. It may help them to reach goals or to obtain social reinforcement, as we have seen. But people also adjust to their environment and make sense out of their surroundings via communication. When we are cast into a new or different situation, we feel uncertain or confused at first. We begin to reduce this uncertainty through communication. We interact with others, we seek out information to provide us with input about our new environment, and we think through our own background and experience to retrieve information that may be helpful to us now. Eventually, when all this information starts coming in, we begin to adjust and feel more comfortable in our surroundings.

COMMUNICATION IS SOCIAL As we try to bring some certainty to our environment, we begin to develop skills that enable us to interact with others. It is through this interaction that we reach others and enable others to reach us. Communication becomes the vehicle through which we test out our perceptions and ideas with others. In so doing, we learn whether our view of the world is consistent with the views of others. The old adages "Man is a social animal" and "No man is an island" speak

[6]R. Birdwhistell, *Kinesics and Context* (Philadelphia: University of Pennsylvania Press, 1970), p. 16.

to this aspect of the human spirit. All of us need others, and this need is satisfied through communication.

COMMUNICATION IS COMPLEX We view the basics of survival—water, food, and shelter—as fairly simple. But communication is also basic to survival. Communication, however, is far from simple, primarily because it is *human beings* who do the communicating. People make communication complex because people themselves are complex and unpredictable. Their attitudes, orientations, perceptions, and ideas get involved in the process of sending and receiving information. As we shall see in the next chapter, people will hear not what was said, but what they think was said. Rarely will an individual transmit completely objective information without adding some element of the subjective. For these reasons communication cannot be considered an exact science. The study of communication must eventually lead to the study of other aspects of human behavior, such as personality, attitude, motivation, and learning. And, as the social psychologists tell us, there are few absolutes about any form of human behavior.

Models of Communication

A model is a schematic representation of a complex phenomenon. The model makes the phenomenon easier to understand. There are many models of communication. In fact, there are so many that it would be impossible to include them all in one chapter. The four models of communication presented are thus only representative examples. They are not necessarily the oldest or the best. They were chosen simply because they are representative.

DANCE MODEL Frank Dance developed the model depicted in figure 2–1 in an attempt to describe communication as a dynamic and ongoing process.[7] The Dance model is also referred to as the *helectical model*. Although at first the Dance model may seem simplistic, it projects an idea that is absolutely central to an understanding of the communication process. Process is difficult for many people to grasp. If we carried process thinking to extremes, we could never discuss communication, because by the time we did, it would have changed. Our discussion would then be out of date. In practical terms, the process nature of communication plays a role in our day-to-day interaction with others. The listener will be bombarded with stimuli—not only those we

[7]F. Dance, "Toward a Theory of Human Communication," in *Human Communication Theory*, ed. F. Dance (New York: Holt, Rinehart and Winston, 1967).

FIGURE 2-1   Dance model. Used by permission.

send, but many others as well. In any given exchange, thousands of stimuli with meaning will float into the listener's cognitive structure.

SCHRAMM MODEL   Wilbur Schramm pointed out that each of us has a finite frame of reference that we use to assign meaning to any individual stimulus we receive. This frame of reference is based on our environment, our learning, our native abilities, and the immediate situation we find ourselves in. We all have a frame of reference, but because we are all different, the components of our frames of reference are different, too.[8] In figure 2-2, Schramm was trying to suggest that person A and person B would communicate most easily in those areas where their frames of reference overlap.

[8]W. Schramm, "How Communication Works," in *The Process and Effects of Communication,* ed. W. Schramm (Urbana: University of Illinois Press, 1954), p. 172.

FIGURE 2-2   Schramm model. From W. Schramm, *The Process and Effects of Communication* (Urbana: The University of Illinois Press, © 1954).

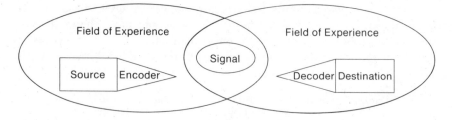

Suppose that two students are talking about snowstorms. One of the students is a lifelong resident of Chicago, where severe winter storms are routine. The other student is from Los Angeles, where it never snows. The Chicago student is trying to make his friend understand what it is like to live through a storm that drops 14 inches of snow in 24 hours. He will have great difficulty in communicating, because the Californian has never actually experienced snow. In this situation, their frames of reference do not overlap. However, through discussions, learning, and experience we can expand our frame of reference. If the Los Angeles student was interested in learning more about snowstorms, he might talk with people who have experienced snowstorms, read material on snowstorms, and look at pictures of snowstorms. Eventually, he might understand the Chicagoan's communications about snow.

SHANNON AND WEAVER MODEL The Claude Shannon and Warren Weaver model (figure 2–3) is one of the earliest attempts at diagraming communication[9] and the first to label the important parts of the communication process. Since the model was done originally to describe electronic, as opposed to human, communication, the reader will note that it is a linear model. That is, it seems to suggest that communication is a one-way phenomenon, going only from the sender to the receiver. According to this model, the listener would have no impact on the sender. In reality, of course, the receiver does provide *a response* to the

[9]C. Shannon and W. Weaver, *The Mathematical Theory of Communication* (Urbana: University of Illinois Press, 1949), p. 21.

FIGURE 2–3 Shannon and Weaver model. From C. Shannon and W. Weaver, *The Mathematical Theory of Communication* (Urbana: The University of Illinois Press, © 1949).

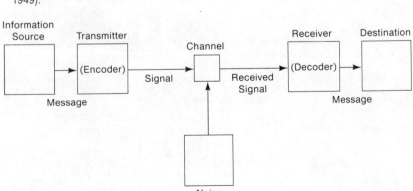

message heard. This response is referred to as *feedback*. Sometimes the sender adjusts his or her message based on feedback, and this ability to adjust is the basis of the concept of two-way communication. The significance of the Shannon and Weaver model is that it shows the essential parts of the communication process. Some of the terms developed in the model appear later in this chapter and throughout the book.

SANFORD, HUNT, AND BRACEY MODEL Aubrey Sanford, Gary Hunt, and Hyler Bracey proposed their model to demonstrate some of the situational characteristics that influence the communication exchange.[10] This model (figure 2–4) suggests five important situational variables that can influence the potential success of a communication exchange. They are (1) the climate, or attitudinal environment, in which the communication takes place; (2) the perceived communication purpose of the sender and receiver; (3) the communication skills demonstrated by the sender and the receiver; (4) whether the message has been intentionally or unintentionally transmitted; and (5) whether the message is verbal or nonverbal. The first three of these variables must be sufficiently positive to enable a transmission between the sender and receiver to take place. The last two must be sufficiently appropriate.

Elements in the Communication Process

As you can see, each model has a number of important components. Each part of the communication process provides a unique function in any exchange. Using all of the models presented, let us examine some of the important elements in the communication process.

[10]A. Sanford, G. Hunt, and H. Bracey, *Communication Behavior in Organizations* (Columbus, Ohio: Charles E. Merrill Publishing Company, 1976), p. 23.

FIGURE 2–4 Sanford, Hunt, and Bracey model. From *Communication Behavior in the Organization*, p. 16. Used by permission.

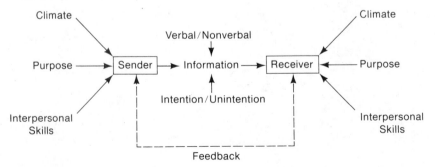

SENDER The sender is the person or thing that actually sends the information. In a social situation, the sender is probably the person doing the talking, but people can also receive communication stimuli from objects. As the Sanford, Hunt, and Bracey model suggests, the sender can transmit information either intentionally or unintentionally.

RECEIVER The person to whom the information is sent is the receiver. In some situations, such as a classroom setting or a large group meeting, there may be a number of receivers. Simply because a person in a specific communication situation has been labeled "receiver," it does not necessarily follow that this person has actually received the information sent. The ability to receive communication stimuli is one of the skills discussed in this book.

MESSAGE So far, we have called that which is being transmitted "stimulus," but this is imprecise. The information sent is a communication transaction and is most appropriately called "message." The terms "message" and "information" can be used interchangeably. The message transmitted can be sent through verbal channels using words; through nonverbal channels using actions, facial expressions, and gestures; or through both channels.

PURPOSE People communicate for a reason. Sometimes the sender's reason may be different from the receiver's. Conflict of purpose can create a barrier to communication. Our purpose in communicating at any given time is probably deeply rooted in our psychological state. Occasionally we may not even be consciously aware of our reason for wanting to communicate.

CLIMATE In social situations, we develop predispositions toward the situation and the people in it that cause us to form positive, neutral, or negative orientations. These orientations are called the "climate" of the situation. If we like someone a great deal, it will be easy for us to communicate with that person. If we are uncomfortable in a particular situation, we may find that communicating is difficult. A great deal of research suggests that climate strongly influences communication.[11]

FEEDBACK Feedback was briefly defined as the response a receiver gives to information transmitted. Feedback is important in both oral and written communication. It helps to keep communication open and free-flowing.

[11]L. James and A. Jones, "Organizational Climate: A Review of Theory and Research," *Psychological Bulletin*, 81, no. 12 (1974), 1096–1112; W. LaFollette and H. Sims, "Is Satisfaction Redundant with Climate?" *Organizational Behavior and Human Performance*, 13, no. 2 (1975), 252–78.

The theory of communication, the scientific body of literature that seeks to explain how people interact with one another, is discussed in the following chapters, as appropriate. These discussions of communication theory will assume that the student is familiar with the foregoing terminology.

What Does Communication Help Us To Do?

Communication enables us *to do* certain important things. It enables us to grow, to learn, to become aware of ourselves, and to adjust to our environment. When we can do these things, we are on the road to good mental health.

INDIVIDUAL GROWTH We develop and grow by communicating with others in our environment. And we occasionally change our environment, using communication to help us grow in new surroundings. We gain this information about things, places, and other people through communication. As we internalize more ideas, we grow as people.

LEARNING Closely related to individual growth is the process of learning. Learning, in this context, means the accumulation of information. Growth, on the other hand, involves the total personality of the individual. Almost all instructional strategies utilize some form of communication. As you listen to experts, attend classes, read books, view television, and perceive your environment, you learn.

SELF-AWARENESS We become aware of who we are primarily through communication. People tell us things about ourselves that we use to monitor our development as people. We gain input that tells us if we are successful in our behavior exchange with others. We develop a sense of our heritage and of our potential through communication. Who you are today is the product of thousands of communication exchanges that you have experienced throughout your life.

INTEGRATION WITH OUR ENVIRONMENT All of us exist within a world of people, ideas, places, and things. This world is our *perceptual environment*—a term that was mentioned earlier but was not defined. (This perceptual environment is similar to Schramm's *frame of reference*.) To live in our perceptual environment, we must continually alter our thinking and behavior, because some of our idiosyncrasies will not be tolerated by others. We learn what changes we need to make through communication.

A Review

The first part of this chapter has discussed the communication behavior that takes place within and between individuals. To some extent, the concept of the organization has been excluded from this discussion. So far, you should have a clear understanding of the organization and how it operates from chapter one and some understanding of communication behavior from the first part of this chapter. The rest of this chapter will demonstrate how communication operates in organizational settings.

communication in organizations

Communication in organizations takes many forms. The following discussion views it from three major perspectives. Each perspective represents one aspect of communication in the organization.

Macro Approaches

In a *macro* approach, organization is viewed as a global or total structure, interacting with other organizations in its environment.

All of the following tasks are macro activities. That is, they are jobs that must be done by the entire organization. For example, goal attainment is a macro activity for an organization. The macro activities that we are about to discuss are all related to the list of things that organizations must do that was presented in chapter one.

PROCESSING INFORMATION FROM ENVIRONMENT To exist, an organization must develop information from its environment. Some organizational theorists argue that organizations are *primarily* processors of information.[12] They take raw informational inputs from outside the organization and transmit these inputs inside the organization. Processing information means being attuned to what is happening in the environment, transferring the relevant information to decision points within the organization, and then formulating an appropriate response to the informational inputs. Later the information will be used in some of the tasks, e.g., goal setting, identification. Since organizations are always processing information, scholars interested in this approach have labeled this activity *organizing*.

[12]K. Weick, *The Social Psychology of Organizing* (Reading, Mass.: Addison-Wesley Publishing Co., Inc., 1969); B. Johnson, *Communication: The Process of Organizing* (Boston: Allyn & Bacon, Inc., 1977), p. 10.

Getting information from the environment is primarily a communication activity. People are the vehicle through which information is processed and transmitted within the organization. The individual assigns particular significance to what is going on outside and then sends messages about that significance to other individuals within the organization.

IDENTIFICATION An organization uses the information processed from the environment to reach some kind of negotiated agreement with its potential and existing customers. This process of accommodating customers is called *identification*. As an example of identification, consider the case of a typical rapid transit utility organization. This organization must somehow communicate to potential customer's that it offers safe, reliable transportation. To do this, the organization may advertise, provide free trial service, encourage its employees to be polite, maintain good public relations, and so forth. If the transit organization has a history of accidents or unreliability, it must probably overcome some negative information to reach the accommodation with customers. For the communication efforts to work, the potential customer must *identify* the organization as being able to provide safe transportation.

But here a problem arises. Each potential customer makes this identification in his or her own way. Therefore most organizations will attempt to identify with customers by using a variety of techniques. Most of these techniques involve some kind of intentional communication behavior. Organizations that have not reached an accommodation with potential customers run the risk of having no customers—a dire state for any organization.

You may be a bit confused here by the term *customers*. All organizations have institutions, other organizations, or people for whom they produce their goods and services. These are the organization's customers. A customer can be the federal government or Mrs. Adams of Brown Street.

Consider the case of a large aerospace organization that manufactures fighter planes. Its sole customer is the Department of Defense. It tries to reach an accommodation with this customer by using various communication techniques. These include the written proposal, which it develops to get the initial contract for the job; liaison with the government through its lobbyist in Washington, D.C.; periodic production reports on the production status of various jobs; and numerous face-to-face contacts between government and aerospace officials. If a satisfactory accommodation is not achieved, the organization runs the risk of losing the contract. This is exactly what happened in the case of North American Rockwell, which had the government contract to produce the prototype of the B-1 bomber. Under pressure from opponents of increased defense spending, President Jimmy Carter canceled plans for the expansion of the B-1 program. In Southern California, where much of the initial work was being done on the B-1, North American was forced to lay off thousands of workers. In this situation, North American failed to negotiate a workable accommodation with its customer, the government.

On a smaller scale, consider the case of the local electric company that supplies power to Mrs. Adams. Here the identification process is much simpler. When Mrs. Adams moves into the community, she asks her neighbors how to get her electricity turned on. They tell her to call up the company and talk with a customer service representative. The service representative takes her order. Assuming that the company then provides the necessary service, the identification process has worked. If there is a problem at Mrs. Adams's apartment, the electric company must once again make some kind of accommodation with the customer, to assure her that the problem can be solved. Whether the customer is large or small, identification almost always involves communication.

INTERACTION WITH OTHER ORGANIZATIONS   No organization operates in a vacuum. Every organization is influenced by the activities of other organizations in its field. Organizations must monitor these activities and those of the federal government to determine what influence the activities will have on them. If a competitor puts out a product that does the same job as yours, but does it better and cheaper, your operation is in trouble. Occasionally, organizations use highly sophisticated surveillance procedures to monitor each other. These include sensitive electronic devices and the services of paid industrial spies. Of course, most of this is illegal, and it is only practiced under extreme conditions. Most of the time organizations use simpler communication techniques —reading pamphlets, brochures, and trade magazines and talking with specialists in the field—to keep track of their competitors.

Sometimes interaction with competitors is highly institutionalized, as in the case of trade organizations. These are groups whose membership is open only to people in the field. They hold conventions and meetings and publish materials that provide relevant information to interested parties.

GOAL SETTING Of all the macro activities that require communication, goal setting is probably the most important. The organization should not begin to establish goals until it has processed relevant information from the environment, identified with potential customers, and done enough interaction with other organizations to clarify its purpose. The information generated through all this interaction can then be used in goal setting.

A goal is the place an organization wants to be after a given period of time. A goal for a college football team may be an 11–0 season and an invitation to the Cotton Bowl game on January 1. Goals for industrial organizations generally involve producing a product X for minimum cost and selling it for enough money to meet production cost with something left over for profit. The lower the production cost and the greater the profit, the more successful the organization. Often supplemental goals will involve reducing production costs or increasing the profit margin. To set goals, organizations must develop information about internal and external forces. Internal forces include the conditions of human resources and of the manufacturing process. External forces include customers' attitudes, availability of raw materials, status of governmental regulations, and behavior of competitors. This information is then used to formulate goals that the organization can realistically expect to achieve.

Service and voluntary organizations must formulate goals as well. The service organization must give the public a service it wants for a competitive price while keeping costs down. The voluntary organization must meet some kind of need while attracting enough people to fill its membership rolls.

Traditionally high-level managers have done most of the goal formulation in organizations.[13] Lower-level managers have then implemented policies for reaching those goals. Even under this relatively conservative view of management, goal-setting communication plays a significant role, because people at the top of a hierarchy depend on those at the bottom for information that must be plugged into the goal-setting formula. However, in some organizations, within certain constraints, people at the very level where the goal must be achieved are encouraged to contribute to its formulation.[14] We will label these *participatory* organizations. When goal formulation shifts down the hierarchy, communication is necessary, because the people who are

[13]H. Hicks, *The Management of Organizations: A Systems and Human Resources Approach,* 2nd ed. (New York: McGraw-Hill Book Company, 1972), p. 101.
[14]A. Lowin, "Participative Decision-Making: A Model, Literature Critique, and Prescriptions for Research," *Organizational Behavior and Human Performance,* 3, no. 1 (1968), p. 69.

setting the goal depend on each other for the free exchange of ideas and information. Chapter six deals at greater length with the manager's role in helping to establish goals.

Micro Approaches

Micro approaches focus heavily on the important units or subunits of the organization.

Communication is also required at this level.

GROUP MEMBERSHIP Within any organization, there are numerous social groups. In fact, organizations are really many *groups of groups.* Groups in organizations can have various purposes. The group's purpose may support the goals of the organization, as when a task group works above its production quota. It may undermine the organization's goals, as when a group intentionally destroys machinery. It may do both, as when a group works well when motivated and badly when unmotivated. Or it may be irrelevant to the organization's goals, as in the case of a company softball team. In any group, communication must be present if the group is to internalize its objectives. When the participants in a task group are informed about the overall objectives of the group, are comfortable with each other, see the immediate or long-term benefits to themselves of working hard, and can provide some degree of leadership, they will usually support the organization's goals.

ORIENTATION AND TRAINING Communication is the vehicle through which people are oriented to and trained for the specific jobs in the organization. People learn about the job from reading about it, having someone tell them how to do it, or having someone show them how to do it. All of these require communication. Orientation is a continuous process; it requires communication to bring someone else up to date about what is going on in the unit. This task can be accomplished by the leadership of the unit, as well as by the rest of the members.

MEMBER INVOLVEMENT In its most negative form, member involvement in the tasks of an organization is achieved by having the boss stand over a subordinate and yell, "Get to work, you X#Z*Y#&." This approach is frowned upon by contemporary experts on management. Gentle and sometimes quite subtle techniques are used today to encourage members to get involved in the operations of their work unit. Most of these techniques employ communication behavior.

Philosophically, there may be something wrong with the assumption that members must be persuaded or forced to work. There are those who say that we need to rethink the way we view people, especially subordinates.[15] But in the author's experience, many organizations still believe that they need to persuade members to contribute to the goals of the organization. Whether it is the pep talk at the beginning of the year by the corporation executive officer or the "worker-of-the-month" column in the employee newspaper, many techniques are still used to encourage the member to contribute. Much of the communication directed *downward* from upper management is intended to generate member involvement.

ESTABLISHMENT OF CLIMATE Climate was defined earlier as the attitudinal environment of a communication situation. Organizations, departments, units, subunits of all sorts, and work groups all have climates. These climates are sometimes perceived similarly by all of the members and sometimes not.

To illustrate this point, consider two typical work situations. In the first, all free and unnecessary talk is discouraged by the manager. Workers are made to toe the line and perform up to their work quota. Some workers may find that this situation improves their work performance. Most of us, however, would probably find it too rigid and stifling to our creativity. In the second situation, free talk among group members is encouraged and the leadership maintains a flexible approach. Many workers might find this freedom less than conducive to good work habits. Others might enjoy it.

Climates are established by the behavior of leaders, the behavior of peers, and the behavior of the organization. Sometimes certain physical conditions, such as an overcrowded work area or a very warm office, can contribute to climate. Organizations have been known to subscribe to such expensive techniques as piped-in music to create soothing physical conditions for workers. But by and large, climate is determined by the communication behavior of the leader toward the group.[16]

---

[15]This literature is voluminous. The three texts that will be referred to throughout this book are D. McGregor, *The Human Side of Enterprise* (New York: McGraw-Hill Book Company, 1960); R. Likert, *The Human Organization* (New York: McGraw-Hill Book Company, 1967); and R. Townsend, *Up the Organization* (New York: Alfred A. Knopf, Inc., 1970).

[16]G. Hunt and C. Lee, "Organizational Climate: A Laboratory Approach" (paper presented at the annual meeting of the International Communication Association, Portland, Oregon, 1976).

This has been a brief treatment of the role of climate in communication. Climate will be referred to throughout the rest of this text. For a much more extended discussion of climate, see Sanford, Hunt, and Bracey, *Communication Behavior*, pp. 209–31.

SUPERVISION AND DIRECTION Supervising and controlling others is the task of a few members of organizations. Organizations are designed to enable a few people who move to the top of the hierarchy to supervise the behavior of many people who fall below them in that hierarchy. A typical first-line supervisor in an organization may direct the behavior of anywhere from three to 70 subordinates. The supervisor is responsible for those under him, and his job is "people management." Supervision is activated through communication. In chapter six we shall see that effective supervision and effective communication go hand-in-hand. Establishing relationships among subordinates is one of the primary managerial tasks facing a supervisor. This is done through communication.

SATISFACTION When people are unhappy with some aspect of their work situation, they are said to experience *job dissatisfaction.* Two important causes of job dissatisfaction are related to communication. First, the worker may think that he or she does not have adequate information to do the job. Second, interpersonal relations among members of a unit may be poor.

Job satisfaction is a very complex area. People enjoy their jobs for many reasons. However, there is little evidence to suggest that good organizational communication will produce satisfied workers, or that satisfied workers will necessarily be productive workers. The two causes of job dissatisfaction identified above can be reduced by communication, however. When the structure of the organization—usually through our immediate supervisor—has provided us with enough information to enable us to do our job effectively, we feel satisfied. At the more visceral level, we feel satisfied when we like our co-workers and seem to have established good communication relationships with them.

Individual Approaches

Individual approaches focus on the communicative behavior of the individual in the organization. All of the tasks described in the preceding two sections are finally accomplished by individuals communicating with each other. Individual communication takes many forms.

TALKING TO WORK GROUPS Work groups are central to the effective operation of the organization. Therefore, one must develop the skills to interact with them. Talking to work groups can be done by a member, a supervisor, or outsider who is not a member.

ATTENDING AND INTERACTING AT MEETINGS Meetings are a way of life in most organizations, so one needs skill at interacting in meetings. This skill consists of being able to provide information when it is called for, to persuade others to accept a proposal, and to lead the meeting when necessary.

WRITING MANUALS Organizations produce reams of printed and written materials. Some of these are distributed inside the organization, some outside. Each piece of written copy is produced by someone who sits down at a typewriter and bangs out the necessary words.

DRAFTING A LETTER The task of developing a manual normally allows some latitude in terms of time. This means that the writing style can be polished and refined. Letters, on the other hand, are usually written under the pressure of a deadline, and the same luxury of refinement is not possible. Drafting good letters is an important communication task.

MAKING A SALES CONTACT Marketing the company's product is an important communication responsibility. Most sales contacts are one-on-one situations where the representative must be articulate and responsive to the needs of the potential customer.

ARGUING FOR A PROPOSAL In organizations, important decisions are made in small meetings where people argue out the opposing sides of a question before choosing a particular course of action. People in organizations must make a case for their proposal, be it a budget increase or a new program. To succeed, they need skill in persuasion.

Case Studies

This book is devoted to an examination of these and many other communication skills. This section considers a few of the practical organizational situations where communication is called for. To make the situations as realistic as possible, the case study approach is used.

CASE A

Michelle Harper, 22, has just graduated from Stevens State University with a combined major in communication and journalism. She has been hired to work for the Statler Scientific Instruments Corporation in its Oklahoma City headquarters. Her job title at Statler will be public information assistant, but her primary duty is to help put out the corporate monthly magazine. *The Instrument* is a glossy 6 X 9 publication, produced for and distributed to Statler's national work force of 5000 employees.

Larry Kirkston, the vice-president for public affairs, who supervises the production of the magazine, thinks that the quality of *The Instrument* has improved to such an extent that it should be distributed to a wider audience. One of the things Michelle was told when she was hired was that she and Gabriela Vinton, the editor, should try to develop such an audience. This wider audience might include potential customers of Statler and other organizations that produce instruments or supply the firms who do.

Most of Michelle's assignments require her to collect information on important events that might be of interest to the Statler Corporation and write up stories for *The Instrument*. She normally does this by reading current newspapers, magazines, government publications, and material from the Statler library. She also talks with people involved in the instrument field, asking them for their reactions to current events in the field. She is learning to use a camera, so that she will be able to take pictures for *The Instrument*.

CASE B

Bill Ryan is a manager in the paint finishing and adhesive department of the Steelware Office Furniture Company. Part of his job is to orient new college graduates into his department each year. In July of each year, Steelware hires about 50 college graduates who have majored in either chemistry or chemical engineering. Normally about seven or eight are assigned to Bill's department to help conduct research about materials related to finishing and adhesives. Before they actually begin work, Bill puts them through his own orientation program, which he calls his "baptism of fire."

There are really two parts to the program, which takes all of the new employees' time for four weeks, or a total of 160 hours. Bill knows that he must give his new researchers a great deal of information about Steelware and its current products, and in the first part of the orientation he passes along this information. He does so in a series of lectures about the company, its history, and its products. He expects his listeners to retain the material, so he has been known to give the group an objective test a week or so after a specific lecture has been presented.

The second part of the program is designed to show Bill how the young people perform under pressure. This part uses case problems related to management, chemistry, and interpersonal relations. The new workers read each case individually and then discuss it as a group. For some of the cases they are asked to recommend a solution. The group decides by consensus which of several potential courses of action would be most appropriate. Bill has developed a style that encourages the leadership to emerge entirely from the group.

Bill's orientation techniques have been criticized by other managers at Steelware, mostly because they do not think that Bill is getting any "work" out of his new subordinates. However, Bill is quick to disagree with the criticism. He has found that the orientation provides him with invaluable information. He has been able to assign the new chemists to particular projects with some confidence that they will be able to handle the workload. He has used the data to appoint project leaders for new tasks, and to recommend that certain people be considered for additional responsibility. But the overriding value of the program, as Bill sees it, is that it has enabled him to get to know the new members of the department, and enabled them to get to know each other. He says that since he initiated this program five years ago, he has been able to establish a close working relationship with each person who has gone through it.

CASE C

The board of trustees of the Woodlawn Unified School District oversees the operation of nine elementary schools, four junior high schools, three high schools, and a community college. It is composed of five citizens, elected for staggered four-year terms, who serve without pay. During the school year, the board meets on each first and third Tuesday evening for about four hours. The meetings normally draw about 20 to 30 people who are interested in some item on the board's agenda.

Board members have three responsibilities. They listen to presentations made to them by members of the public and school district employees. They hold private discussions about personnel matters; these are called executive sessions. And they vote in the public meetings on any proposal that requires a decision. Normally the results of the board meeting, including votes, are reported in the Woodlawn *Monitor,* the local newspaper, which assigns a reporter to cover each meeting.

Woodrow Gibson, a local attorney, is presently serving as president of the board. His duties include opening the meeting, moderating the discussion among board members, making and announcing the ground rules for members of the public who wish to speak to the board, and fielding any questions from the public or press attending the meeting. Each year the honor of being president of the board is rotated among members.

Sometimes a sticky issue comes before the board. Recently, for example, the instructors at the community college threatened to boycott classes over a salary dispute. When this happens, board members must develop statements on their respective positions on the matter. Each member presents his or her statement at the public meeting. Summaries of these statements appear in the next afternoon's *Monitor.*

Occasionally, board members will disagree among themselves as to a potential course of action for the school district. When this happens, they argue for their positions for a stated period of time before the official vote is taken on the matter.

CASE D

Matt Coopley is the superintendent of the Billings Plastic Coating Plant, a division of the Roslyn Corporation. Billings' biggest product is the hard plastic coating for metal parts that is used in the construction of automobiles. Nine department managers work under Matt's supervision, and each of them is responsible for a number of subunits. All of the manufacturing personnel fall under the supervision of the nine department managers. Within Billings, Matt is considered "upper management." He reports directly to the divisional vice-president, the top company executive housed at the plant.

Each year is divided into three four-month production periods. Company rules require that Matt meet with each of his department managers during each production period. At these meetings, Matt advises the managers about their progress and recommends areas for improvement. If the manager is doing a particularly good job, Matt compliments him. At least once a year, Matt is supposed to talk with the department managers about their own career development. He tells them how they might be able to advance within the organization, and how they might gain additional experience in their positions. A record is kept of each of these meetings, which eventually becomes part of the manager's permanent personnel file.

Normally, the meetings are held in an informal atmosphere. Matt and the subordinate sit on the couch or easy chairs that Matt keeps in his office. Matt always remembers to supply rolls and coffee for these sessions. He has found that the meetings seem to work best when both he and the manager can relax and discuss problems and successes in an open and honest way. Matt has been conducting these meetings for nearly four years now. Over the years he has discovered that if he emphasizes the manager's successes during the production period, and then ends the meeting with some very positive suggestions for improvement, the results seem to be beneficial. Matt has come to look forward to these required meetings as an opportunity to get to know his employees better.

CASE E

Anne Kern is a recruiter for the City of Channel Island, a community of about 80,000 near the ocean in a western state. When she came to work for Channel Island, she had just graduated from Western State University with a B.A. degree in sociology. She was hired to work in the testing section, developing written and oral tests for job applicants in the administrative and clerical areas. She was promoted out of that position to a job as a personnel assistant in the building inspecting department, where she handled most of the department's administrative and personnel matters. Recently, she was given her second promotion to the personnel department, where she is acting as a recruiter for the city.

Under pressure from the federal and state governments, Channel Island has been trying to recruit women for such nontraditional female jobs as fire fighter, building inspector, animal control officer, and police officer. However, before Anne came on the job, the city had been having little luck in encouraging women to apply for these positions. The mayor and the city council decided that recruiting women required a full-time person. That is where Anne fits in.

Anne goes to meetings that might attract young women and talks with them about career opportunities in the City of Channel Island. She travels up and down the state to attend conventions and conferences for such groups as the Junior League and the Junior Women's Club. Anne also regularly addresses high school, community college, and university classes. When she talks to these groups, she provides some details about the city, discusses the rather generous pay scale and fringe benefit package, and mentions the excitement associated with nontraditional positions. One of the questions she is often asked is "Why should I want to be an animal control officer?" To answer, Anne stresses that a woman is just as capable of doing the job as a man, that there are tremendous opportunities for advancement associated with the position, and that a beginning-level animal control officer will start at a salary nearly $12,000 higher than that of a newly hired clerk or secretary. Evidently Anne's approach works, for the number of applications from women for these positions has increased.

CASE F

The Hillsdale Community Church has a paid professional staff of six full-time clergy and a membership of approximately 3000. It is the largest church in Hillsdale and is known in the community for its conservative theology and its outreach mission of visitation to Hillsdale residents. Dr. Beth Carlson has been the senior minister at Hillsdale Community for six years. She does most of the preaching on Sunday and handles the major administrative details at the church. Her staff consists of the Reverend Ken Mitchell, associate minister in charge of the visitation program; Dr. Mary Guthrie, a licensed psychologist and an ordained minister, who is responsible for pastoral counseling; the Reverend Steve Grim, assistant minister, who works in adult education; the Reverend Larry Bailey, who has recently graduated from Gospel Theological Seminary and has been hired to work with the church youth; and the Reverend Sheila Harris, who directs the musical program and the church choir.

Since the staff takes Monday off, the week's schedule begins at 7:30 on Tuesday morning with a breakfast meeting in the church kitchen. Here Dr. Carlson conducts what she has come to call her "assignment meeting." For about two hours, the staff lays out the activities of the coming week. Each member presents his or her calendar for the approval of the rest of the group. Although it rarely happens, Dr. Carlson reserves the right to veto any decision made by the rest of the staff. She takes great pride in running a fairly tight ship and in seeing that all of the bases are covered.

These breakfast meetings feature a great deal of give-and-take. More than once when staff members presented their respective calendars, it was discovered that two or three of them had scheduled the same activity. Thanks to the meetings, needless duplication has been reduced and church efficiency has been improved. Dr. Carlson often moderates the meetings, but she will occasionally turn over the gavel to another staff member to give that person experience in conducting meetings. Because so many positive things are accomplished at these Tuesday morning meetings, staff members go to great extremes to protect the 7:30–9:30 time block.

CASE G

Larry Campbell has been employed as a college marketing representative for the United Publishing Company for the past four years. United publishes a wide range of college text materials in the humanities, social and hard sciences, and business. Larry calls upon college professors and teachers in the West Texas–New Mexico sales territory during the school year to tell them about new and existing books published by United.

Each summer, Larry spends two weeks being trained in New York at United's corporate headquarters. He and the other book reps are brought up-to-date on any changes in company benefits, pay procedures, profit sharing, and other aspects of their job. They also hear editors in the various fields discuss new publications and the state of the discipline in sociology, biology, marketing, and so forth. Since the college professor will expect the United rep to know what is happening in his field, it is important for Larry to remember this information when he starts visiting professors in September.

But the most important part of the training is the practice sales contact sessions that are held each afternoon. The four sales managers for the company play the role of college professors. Each book rep must conduct a hypothetical sales contact with a "professor," as the other reps watch. After the sales contact has been completed, everyone offers constructive advice. After the first practice, the book rep calls on another professor, and this time the contact is videotaped. The videotape is replayed for the rep, and he criticizes his own performance. Larry has found that these two-week training sessions help him to refine his marketing skill. They make him look forward to going back to work in the fall.

These seven cases demonstrate the wide variety of organizational contexts that require communication. Although the word "communication" was not used in any of the cases, extensive communication was required in almost all of the activities described. Conducting meetings, arguing for a position, participating in group discussions, making presentations, writing letters and reports, and listening to others are among the most vital things that members of an organization do.

problems in communication

In the seven cases, communication may have seemed easy and natural. This is not always the case. Often serious problems in communication develop. Although it would be beyond the scope of this chapter to cover all of these problems, we will discuss some of the most important ones.

Problems of the Hierarchy

The hierarchy gives some people power and authority over other people. It also prevents some people from gaining power. It is typical of humans that if they do not have power, they will sometimes go to great lengths to gain it. A person who is seeking power may engage in certain types of communication behavior and refuse to engage in other types. Consider the following example.

Bill is a highly ambitious college graduate who has been hired into the art department of a large advertising firm. Bill is highly ambitious. His department manager is John, an old-time learn-by-experience type, who believes that young people must remain in grade and pay their dues to their organizational elders. Because of John's attitude, Bill could feel that he must make his supervisor look bad in front of management. To do this, Bill may resort to spreading gossip about John, lying to him, reporting only good things to John about the job he is doing, and following only certain of John's orders. Assuming that he is devious enough, Bill may succeed in making himself look good while making John look bad.

At first you may think that this example is quite farfetched, and perhaps it is. But people do filter information, distort it, and sometimes even refuse to communicate when they are members of hierarchies. Because it is people who occupy individual positions within a hierarchy, the hierarchy is vulnerable to all the communication problems that are characteristically human. Let us look a bit closer at the three communication failures.

FILTERING Filtering occurs when people intentionally or unintentionally leave out some of the details of a message. We are sometimes reluctant to tell our supervisor anything that might reflect negatively on us.[17] When we intentionally leave out the negatives associated with our job performance, we are practicing filtering.

DISTORTION The structure of any hierarchy will tend, in itself, to distort information. When messages must travel up or down five or six different hierarchical levels, some of those messages will become garbled. This kind of distortion is, to some extent, unavoidable; it is a way of life in most organizations. However, people will sometimes distort information intentionally to serve their own purposes. When this occurs, the person is placing his or her own goals ahead of those of the organization.

REFUSAL TO COMMUNICATE Occasionally someone will simply fail to pass along a message. This means that someone else who is supposed to get a piece of vital information does not get it. This failure may be an oversight—the person simply forgets to pass the word along. Or it may be a deliberate refusal to communicate—as when one member of the organization decides that someone else should not have certain information.

[17]W. Read, "Upward Communication in Industrial Hierarchies," *Human Relations,* 15, no. 1 (1962), 3–15; K. Roberts and C. O'Reilly, "Failures in Upward Communication: Three Possible Culprits," *Academy of Management Journal,* 17, no. 3 (1974), 205–15.

Communication in organizations is not simple. It will probably break down at one time or another regardless of how conscientious the communicator tries to be. Often the breakdown will be the result of a conflict between the constraints of the hierarchy and the human desire to gain power within that hierarchy.

Problems with the Written Word

Because organizations keep extensive records and files, many people in positions of authority feel that it is easier to maintain historical documentation with written, as opposed to oral, communication. Therefore many organizations overrely on the written word. The memorandum becomes their primary means of communication. One large city issues memo pads inscribed, "Write it, don't say it."

But any form of written communication—whether it is a report, letter, note, or memo—is only effective when it has been read and understood. More and more, executives are reporting that they do not have the time to read all the things they are supposed to read. The busier the manager is, the likelier he is to take shortcuts in his reading. Important ideas committed to paper sometimes get lost in the daily shuffle.

There is nothing inherently wrong with written communication, as long as it is not overused. However, it cannot replace oral communication. Oral communication is immediate. Feedback is direct and apparent. With the written channel, everything gets delayed. It is difficult to check out the results of a written transmission. To insure more immediate face-to-face contact among members, some of today's more progressive organizations have redesigned their offices to conform to the open concept approach. In these organizations, the walls between offices have been removed. Desks that had been separated from one another are rearranged in close proximity. The purpose is to provide more direct oral contact. But redesigning offices, in and of itself, is not enough. An organization that limits itself to written communication is causing problems for itself all down the line. The cry of the executive "I sent you a memorandum on that!" has become the catchall excuse for no communication in many organizations.

Problems with Management Failures

It is hard for any individual to be a good manager all of the time. Almost any management expert will argue that one of the primary tasks of effective management is good decision making. But good decision making requires good communication. A manager who makes decisions or develops policy, but does not adequately communicate information about, or explain the reasons for, these decisions, is guilty of a failure in communication.

Managers who fail to communicate with employees usually do so for one of two reasons: (1) they do not think that communication is important, or (2) they do not know how to communicate. It is true that managers occasionally have good reasons for not communicating. They may need to maintain the security of special projects; they may wish to protect financial negotiations, and so forth. But these cases should be the exception, not the rule.

If employees are to feel committed to and concerned about the welfare of the organization, some kind of information sharing must go on. No one can feel loyal to something he knows nothing about. Yet this is just what many managers seem to expect. Apparently these supervisors feel that even though an employee has been kept totally in the dark about what has been going on in the organization, at a crisis period, such as a union vote or an economic crunch, this same employee should demonstrate maximum loyalty to the organization. It will not happen. Loyalty is created by establishing and maintaining a reciprocal relationship between the employee and the organization. This, in turn, requires that the employee understand the organization and his or her own role in it. Obviously this understanding depends on effective communication.

final perspectives

Some general perspectives on communication are related to all of the aspects of communication covered in this book. They are mentioned extensively in the remaining eight chapters. In their total, they represent the theoretical approach reflected in this book and provide the foundation for many of the concepts and guidelines contained herein.

1. *Communication needs to be receiver centered.* To achieve successful interpersonal communication, the sender must be extremely sensitive to the needs, expectations, and orientations of the listener. In communication, the message is being directed by the sender to the receiver. Therefore it is necessary for the receiver to determine the sender's level of treatment, style, and approach. In all forms of communication, then, the sender must be conscious of the listener's or reader's needs.

2. *Effective communication consists of making the most appropriate choice from a range of potential courses of action.* Communication is not an exact science. In any given interaction situation, a wide range

of behaviors may succeed in getting the message across to the listener. There is thus no single *correct* method. The successful communicator tries to make the most appropriate choice from among a number of workable alternatives. Before you make that choice, you should consider the receiver, the purpose of the exchange, the topic, and your own unique skills and abilities. In a given situation, you might use one approach while your classmate might use a completely different one, yet you might both be effective. Success in communication is relativistic; it depends on the relationships among many variables.

3. *The illusion of communication sometimes hinders real communication.* One of the greatest difficulties organizations face is the illusion of communication, *the assumption that communication has taken place when it has not.* If we think that our initial attempts at communication have succeeded, we will not try to communicate further. If our initial attempts at communication have actually failed, and we have stopped trying to communicate, the transfer of information will not take place. This principle is closely related to the first principle mentioned above. Only the receiver can determine whether or not communication has been achieved. If he or she has received and internalized the message, communication has succeeded. It is highly dangerous—and sometimes fatal, if important decisions are riding on the results—to *assume* that communication has taken place. Check it out first with the receiver, using dialogue and feedback.

4. *Communication problems are going to arise because people are imperfect communicators.* There is no way to prevent problems from arising in the process of transferring information. Instead of making gigantic efforts to prevent any problem from arising, it might be more realistic to adjust to a less-than-perfect situation. Simply *do your best to communicate; try to prevent major problems; but expect them to surface.* If major breakdowns do occur, try to keep them from devastating the operation of the organization. Communication failures are a way of life in most organizations, but somehow most organizations are able to succeed in spite of them. It is a matter of lowered expectations and adjustment.

5. *Effective communication is important in its own right and need not be justified by relating it to organizational effectiveness.* Some people believe that good communication produces effective organizations. Intuitively, this makes good sense, but there is insufficient empirical research to document the argument. However, the need for good communication in organizations need not be justified pragmatically. Good communication is important in its own right. That is why it should be encouraged and developed.

6. *Effective communication is learned through training and expe-*

rience. It is unrealistic to expect a new manager or employee to communicate effectively during the first few days on the job. One learns to communicate effectively by learning the appropriate techniques, having the opportunity to practice them, and having one's performance reviewed by experienced communicators in a nonthreatening environment. The organization must also encourage good communication; and the employee must be motivated to develop and improve good communication skills. If all of these things are present, effective communication should come.

FOR STUDY

1 What are the essential elements in the communication process? Identify them and describe the role of each.

2 This chapter has suggested that communication is highly functional. What does this mean?

3 Four models of the communication process were described in this chapter. Choose one model and defend it as best demonstrating the nature of communication.

4 Identify some of the things that communication does for organizations.

5 The hierarchy often structures the flow of communication in an organization. How does it do this? Might the hierarchy *restrict* communication? How?

case two

The Staff Breakdown

The Highland branch of the state Air Resources Board has been having many problems over the last three years. It has gone through five executive directors, and the turnover rate in the office is nearly 16 percent. Employees are electing to leave state service in spite of excellent job security and pension benefits.

It is the mission of the Air Resources Board (ARB) to study the quality of the air throughout the state to determine if it is meeting federal, state, and local standards. The branch employs an equal number of technicians, who handle sampling and reporting, and nontechnical support personnel, who handle clerical and administrative functions. The director of the branch has always been an environmental engineer, appointed in the state capital. The director is responsible for the day-to-day management of the branch. While all of the other workers at the branch have good job security guaranteed through the civil service system, the branch manager can be fired for cause.

The continuous upheaval at the Highland branch has made it difficult for the unit to meet its regular work quotas. The branch has two primary duties. First, it must issue a *permit to emit* to anyone in the geographical region who wants to emit smoke into the atmosphere. Before a permit is issued, the local branch must go out to the site of the smokestack to investigate its method of construction and take air quality readings on the ground and at the top of the smokestack. If the plant meets acceptable levels, the permit is issued. Second, the branch must conduct periodic inspections at sites where permits have been issued. These inspections are done to see if the plant is continuing to emit waste within the standards previously established. If the plant is emitting too much waste, or if the waste is potentially harmful to humans, the ARB has the power to issue a warning. If the warning is ignored, the agency has the power to close the plant. Inspections are conducted regularly and in response to complaints from citizens.

The following problems have arisen at the Highland branch. There is a large backlog of permit applications, and inspections have fallen off significantly. When a plant applies for a permit, it is supposed to take less than 60 days for the document to be issued. At Highland it is taking anywhere from six to eight months. Since a plant must be almost completed before it can be inspected, much money is tied up while the plant waits for the appropriate inspection. The plant cannot begin operation until the permit has been issued. Routine inspections for older plants are only made after a citizen complaint, and then only after the individual has written or contacted the branch two or three times. The situation has become so intolerable that many local residents have written the governor to complain about the quality of the air. The consensus seems to be that the air has become very dirty over the past few years. Industrial leaders have also complained to the governor that they can no longer afford to wait six months to receive their emission permits from Highland. They intend to take their new construction to a neighboring state, which has an economic climate favorable to business.

But some of the most severe problems at Highland are internal. Generally, the administrative staff has nothing to do with the technicians. The two groups seldom meet, and neither side seems to understand what the other is doing. The present branch manager is Bill Cramer. Like his predecessors, Mr. Cramer considers the major duty of the branch to be technical. As he sees it, the administrative staff functions to *support* the technical staff. Therefore, the technical people are salaried, do not have to keep track of their daily work schedules, and have offices on the top floor of the building, overlooking a river and park.

One of the tasks of the administrative unit is to take the data developed by the technical inspection teams and compile a report for the general public. The technician must sit down with a member of the administrative staff after each inspection and discuss the findings of the project. However, since the administrative personnel have no technical training to speak of, they have difficulty in understanding what they are told. Such terms as a "ozone reading," "oxide requirements," "sulfur levels," and "carbon counts" mean nothing to most of them. Yet, they must take these data and develop a report that will be intelligible to the average resident of the state.

The technical staff says that it is the administrators' responsibility to understand what is being said. "They need to go back to school to learn some elementary biology and chemistry," said one of the technicians recently over lunch. "They're in a highly technical field, and they should try and keep up." This seems to be the prevailing attitude among the technical staff. Several attempts have been made to solve the problem, but none has been successful. For example, the branch held a retreat in the mountains, at which all common problems were discussed. The retreat turned into a gripe session, and there were no positive results. A series of weekly all-staff meetings was also held, but they did not accomplish much, either.

Meanwhile, problems in the branch are mounting. Every couple of weeks some staff member leaves to accept employment elsewhere. Usually the person is leaving the administrative staff, although occasionally a technician will resign, saying that he or she is tired of "all of the hassles" of working for the state. It is taking longer to get the reports out and the permits issued. People in the office have stopped talking to each other. There is a rumor in the branch that Mr. Cramer's days as manager are numbered. One typist told another today that her sister, who works in the board office in the state capital, says the governor is fed up with the situation at Highland and is "going to send in someone who can clean up the mess."

FOR STUDY

1 In a few words, what do you see as the major problems at the Highland branch?

2 Obviously, communication at Highland is not good. What communication problems seem most severe?

3 What type of leadership is needed at Highland? What kind of person do you think the governor should appoint if Bill Cramer is fired?

4 This chapter has focused on the use of communication skills in the organization. Design a program that would enable the people working at Highland to develop and improve their communication skills.

5 Consider the relationship between good communication and organizational effectiveness. At the Highland branch, how could communication work to increase effectiveness?

interpersonal communication

PART TWO

good listening:
The Key to Communication Comprehension

Listening is the most important of all the communication skills. As early as 1926 it was estimated that 45 percent of our routine communication consists of listening, 30 percent of speaking, 16 percent of reading, and 9 percent of writing.[1] In contemporary organizations, probably even more of the typical member's time is devoted to listening. Yet few of us know very much about this communication skill.

A recent survey of California business leaders conducted by the placement office of a university asked what skills these managers looked for in recent college graduates seeking employment. Nearly 80 percent of those surveyed placed listening skills among their top five choices. A majority felt that listening was the *most important skill* for a potential employee.

This result is consistent with other research that deals with the importance of listening. An 18-month study of employee attitudes at Swift and Company reported that most of Swift's managers considered the ability to listen the most helpful in understanding employee attitudes and morale.[2] It also reported on the results of a study conducted by the Opinion Research Corporation. This study determined that the major complaint expressed by subordinates toward management was that management did not listen to them.

Chapter two emphasized the wide variety of potential communication situations that exist in organizations. In most of these situations, the ability to listen to and understand a message is crucial. Listening is basic to almost every form of effective oral interaction. Other related

[1]P. Rankin, "The Measurement of the Ability to Understand Spoken Language" (unpublished Ph.D. dissertation, University of Michigan, 1926), p. 43.
[2]C. Dover, "Listening—The Missing Link in Communication," *General Electric Review*, 61, no. 3 (May 1958), 7–10.

chapter three

cognitive and interpersonal skills also depend on listening ability. For example, you cannot hope to be effective in the interview unless you listen well. Good decision making depends on the ability to listen to information. Skilled problem analysts must be able to listen if they hope to develop good solutions to potential problems. These and other skills depend on the ability to listen to and comprehend a message.

This chapter begins by considering the definitions and models relevant to an understanding of the process of listening. After this, we will take a brief look at the treatment of listening in the research literature. Several researchers have suggested that listening really takes place at a number of cognitive and interpersonal levels. Some of these levels will be examined. The tasks that listening helps us to accomplish will be discussed next. Then we will examine some of the guidelines to effective listening that communication experts have developed over the years. The chapter concludes with final observations on listening.

listening: definitions and models

Think back to the discussion of the communication process in chapter two. The concept of listening may be thought of generally as the *receiving of a communication stimulus*. It is possible to define listening more scientifically. At the physiological level, listening occurs when the input of sound waves strikes the tympanic membrane in the ear and causes vibration to occur.[3] However, this definition ignores the fact that we receive much information without literally hearing it. Try to recall some of the conversations in which you participated this week. If you talked with a friend who seemed upset or out of sorts, you may have sensed how he was feeling from the way he looked or carried himself. If you talked with your supervisor and he seemed to be in a bad mood, you may have sensed this by comparing his interpersonal behavior today, when he was moody, to his behavior last week, when he seemed cheerful. If you went down to the grocery store to buy a box of cornflakes, and Mrs. Johnson, the owner, was feeling "up," you may have sensed this from the way she moved around the store. We receive information in social situations through many other channels besides our ears. For our purposes, we will consider Weaver's definition of listening as accounting only for the process of physical hearing. Later we will offer a more comprehensive definition of listening—one that

[3]C. Weaver, *Human Listening: Process and Behavior* (Indianapolis: The Bobbs-Merrill Co., Inc., 1972), p. 17.

includes the many other ways by means of which we receive information.

But first, let us clarify the nature of listening. The following examples illustrate two different types of listening behavior:

EXAMPLE 1

Supervisor: George, I've been giving a lot of thought to the new assistant foreman's position that should be coming up when Larry Stuart is reassigned to the trim department. Have you ever considered becoming part of management?

George: Yes, I've thought about it, but I'm not sure that I have the kind of smarts it takes to be a supervisor.

Supervisor: George, you're a bright guy. Besides, I'm not really sure that it takes that much intelligence to be a manager here. Anyway, if I made it anybody can. Heaven knows, I'm not very smart.

George (laughing): People expect a lot of the supervisor. They expect him to have all the answers and to know how to do every job. I'm just not sure that I can do all that.

Supervisor: I think that I'm picking up the fact that you're a little bit unsure of yourself. Also, maybe you're a bit afraid to test yourself in a new situation. Is that pretty close to it, George?

George: I don't know, Harv. I'm pretty happy where I am. I have a lot of friends and I enjoy my job. I just don't know whether I want all that additional responsibility.

EXAMPLE 2

Supervisor: Steve, we're having trouble with some of the headlines you're writing. They're being sent back from the composing room for being too long.

Steve: I know, Mrs. Shelton, but I'm having trouble with this headline guide. I guess I just can't use it.

Supervisor: Let me see if I can help you. You have to count one space for each letter, but I always leave two spaces to take care of any overage.

Steve: I haven't been doing that. Let's see if I can use your method with this head. First, I count one space for each letter and then I add two spaces ... yes, that seems to work fine. Thanks.

In the first example, the supervisor got much more information than George actually told him. Although George did not say so in words, he was sending out information about his indecisiveness. The supervisor, by being very observant and by thoroughly understanding George's behavior, picked up all the "vibes" George was sending. This example illustrates the idea that listening—as the term is used in this book—entails more than simply *hearing* what someone is telling you. Listening also includes the ability to grasp fully what someone is saying in words. This is the point of the second example. Mrs. Shelton, the supervisor, was directing straightforward information to Steve. It was not necessary for Steve to do much interpretation. The purpose of the exchange was to have Steve stop writing headlines that were too long and begin using a system the supervisor had worked out to help cut down on the practice.

These two examples illustrate two basic kinds of listening behaviors. The first is the ability to go beyond words and pick up all of the information being transmitted in a particular exchange. The second is the ability to listen solely to the words that are being transmitted in a particular exchange.

It is now possible to define *listening* as

> the total physical and psychological process of receiving informational inputs from others.

But this is only the first part of the listening activity. Suppose we have received information in an exchange with someone. Now what do we do with it? This is the second part of listening. This second part consists of two basic tasks. First, we search our frame of reference for additional information that we may be able to use to assign significance to the input we have just received. Second, after we have assigned significance to that information, we store it.

An illustration may be helpful. Suppose that you are interviewing an applicant for a position in your organization. You may ask, "Do you have any supervision experience?" The applicant may answer, "No, I don't seem to have the ability to lead." As this response is given, it enters your cognitive structure. Realizing that the position for which the applicant is interviewing requires a great deal of supervision (this is the information that you have retrieved from your memory bank), you then have two choices. You may formulate another question based on the association that you have just made. Or you may store the information for later recall.

Listening, then, consists of receiving information, recalling associated information from your experience, making certain relationships, and storing the information or using it to formulate a response. This process of receiving–processing–associating–retrieving will be considered again when we examine levels of listening.

Models of Listening Behavior:
Weaver's Model of Listening

The ideas in the previous section are based on the work of Carl Weaver, who developed one of the most basic, yet comprehensive, models of the listening process.[4] This model is reproduced in figure 3–1. As you examine it, you will note that a number of potential stimuli are available to the receiver. These stimuli, to return to the language of the previous chapter, are really potential messages. There is no possible way for any one individual to listen to all of the potential messages associated with a particular interaction situation. Instead, the receiver goes through the process of selecting which potential messages to listen to. In essence this is the concept of *selective perception* that was alluded to in chapter two. Because we are all different, the stimuli that you choose to listen to are likely to be different from the stimuli that I choose to listen to. Therefore, even though we may have "heard" the "same" communication, we will each assign it a different significance.

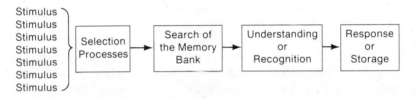

FIGURE 3–1   Weaver model of listening. From *Human Listening, Processes and Behavior* by Carl H. Weaver. Copyright © 1972 by The Bobbs-Merrill Co., Inc.

The Two-Person Model

Figure 3–2 diagrams the various aspects of a communication exchange between Person A and Person B. In the model, A has been arbitrarily assigned the role of the sender, while B acts as receiver. In a real communication situation, these roles would be reversing constantly. Seven basic factors influence the receiver's ability to listen in a particular communication exchange. These are (1) auditory and visual ability, (2) concentration ability, (3) situational constraints, (4) history of the communication relationship between A and B, (5) perceived purpose of the communication exchange, (6) perceived degree of difficulty of the message, and (7) perceived utility of the message. (Similar, but slightly different, factors influence the sender.)

[4]Weaver, *Human Listening*, p. 19.

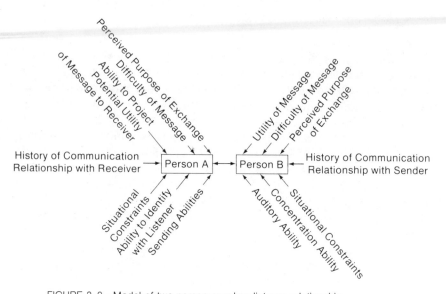

Person A ← → Person B

History of Communication
Relationship with Receiver → Person A

History of Communication
Relationship with Sender ← Person B

Perceived Purpose of Exchange
Difficulty of Message
Ability to Project
Potential Utility
of Message to Receiver

Utility of Message
Difficulty of Message
Perceived Purpose
of Exchange

Situational
Constraints
Ability to Identify
with Listener
Sending Abilities

Concentration Ability
Auditory Ability
Situational Constraints

FIGURE 3–2   Model of two-person speaker–listener relationship

AUDITORY AND VISUAL ABILITY   We must be able to hear sound waves and see behavior before we can listen to and get information from a communication exchange. Some people have more auditory and visual acuity than others. Other things being equal, these people should be the best listeners. However, it is possible, with training, to improve both our hearing and seeing ability.

CONCENTRATION ABILITY   To be able to obtain all of the important data being generated in a communication exchange, the receiver must concentrate on what is being said. This means that he or she must reduce any other outside influences that are likely to prevent full concentration. Since communication is so dynamic, it is not possible to reduce all these outside influences. Rather, the listener must limit their significance so that they do not interrupt the communication. To do this, the listener must (1) focus on the verbal components of a message (the words), and (2) observe the physical behavior of the sender to pick up the extraverbal information being sent.

SITUATIONAL CONSTRAINTS   In almost any communication exchange, what is going on "outside" will influence what is going on "inside." These "outside" influences are called *situational constraints*. A social conversation can be conducted in a quiet living room with a glowing fire in the fireplace much more effectively than in a busy airport waiting

68

lounge. When a business session that should take two hours has to be conducted in 15 minutes because the boss has to catch a plane, it probably will not produce the best kind of listening behavior. It is rarely possible to do much about situational constraints. However, the effective listener should be aware of them and attempt to reduce their impact.

HISTORY OF RELATIONSHIP BETWEEN SENDER AND LISTENER Establishing an interpersonal relationship is a time-consuming and difficult chore. Ground breaking, finding areas of common interest, developing norms, and so forth, all take time and effort. When all of these things are going on, it may be difficult for a receiver to be a good listener. Once a relationship has been established, its history—that is, how long it has lasted and how good it is—will also influence listening behavior. When we are angry with or mistrustful of someone, we will probably have trouble listening to that person. On the other hand, some people have suggested—with little scientific proof—that two people who have known another for a long time, such as a husband and wife, can "hear" each other's thoughts without any words being spoken. Most relationships fall somewhere between these two extremes. The point is, the history of the relationship between two people will influence their ability to listen.

PURPOSE Because of our frame of reference, we pay more attention to some messages than others. When we have a clear perception of the purpose of the communication exchange, we can easily decide whether or not we want to listen. If the purpose of the exchange is ambiguous and we have to work hard to fill in the details, we may quickly lose interest and choose not to listen.

DIFFICULTY OF MESSAGE When something is beyond our level of comprehension, we cannot listen to it for long. Messages, to be listened to, must be understood by the receiver. Hard, new, or complex messages that fall outside the receiver's intelligence level stand little chance of becoming informational input.

UTILITY We will devote much more attention to a communication exchange and try harder to listen when we feel that the message has some utility to us. When we have a stake in the outcome of the information being transmitted, we are highly motivated to get all the data. Although there is little systematic research to support the point, the author believes that this constitutes a direct, positive relationship. The more important the information is to us, the more energy we will devote to listening to that information. Good communicators try to capture their listeners' attention by providing reasons why this particular message should be important to them.

The Organizational Model

Before leaving this introductory section, let us consider a third model. Figure 3–3 represents the layers of influence on the listening ability of a member of an organization. Note that each layer becomes increasingly more personal to the communicator.

ENVIRONMENTAL CONSTRAINTS The organization's environment was considered extensively in chapters one and two. To recapitulate: *What takes place inside the organization is necessarily influenced by what takes place outside.* Two types of environmental constraints can work

FIGURE 3–3 Model of individual's ability to listen to a message in organizational context

to prevent good listening. One type is physical, and the other psychological.

Physical barriers to listening include atmospheric conditions, the location of the plant, and outside influences on the individual which make listening difficult. When the organization is in the middle of a battle with the federal goverment over whether or not it can dump waste into the local river, the individual's listening task is likely to be difficult. When the organization is faced with one of these crises, it leaves members little time or effort for anything else.

Psychological constraints are those factors operating on the individual which have nothing directly to do with his organizational behavior, but which may still influence that behavior. We are affected by our personal problems, our families, our love lives, and many other things. All of these can significantly influence our ability to receive work-related communications. If you are going through an emotional crisis, such as a death in the family or a divorce, you can expect your work output to be affected. The same holds for your listening behavior. If you are devoting most of your attention to a problem with your health, you are not likely to care what your supervisor has to say.

INTERORGANIZATIONAL CONSTRAINTS Interorganizational constraints operate like environmental constraints, except that they are normally generated from within the organization. Our ability to listen effectively to work-related messages is influenced by social conditions in the organization. It is quite usual for workers in large production and assembly line plants to go to work each day not knowing whether they will be working overtime that day. Normally, this information comes to the employee in the afternoon, after the managers have had a chance to assess the days's production. If employees are told that there will be a two-hour overtime period, they tend to continue to concentrate on their jobs and are receptive to job-related communication past the regular eight-hour shift. If, on the other hand, they are told that there will not be any overtime that day, some workers tend to concentrate less close to quitting time. A highly technical meeting of machinists should probably not be scheduled for 4:45 P.M., just before the 5:00 P.M. work whistle.

SOCIAL CLIMATE The early work by Fritz Roethlisberger and Edward Dickson undertaken at the Hawthorne Western Electric plant in Chicago produced many interesting findings. One of the most significant findings was that a highly sophisticated social climate existed among workers in the Hawthorne organization.[5] This social climate

[5]F. Roethlisberger and W. Dickson, *Management and the Worker* (Cambridge, Mass.: Harvard University Press, 1939), p. 129.

tended to influence worker productivity. But social climate will also influence listening ability. Let us assume that you greatly admire the man who works next to you at your station. This man is an expert in one phase of the operation of the department, and your boss has assigned you the task of learning this phase. If you like this man, have confidence that he is indeed an expert, and feel that he is being honest with you, you will probably devote some energy to listening to what he is saying. If you do not like him or have confidence in him, you will probably not listen to what he says.

Another far more subtle aspect of the social climate also influences listening. In some organizations (departments, units) the atmosphere encourages people to perform to the utmost of their abilities. In other organizations very little is expected of members. We can call the first kind of organization *task centered* and the second *nontask centered.* In the task-centered organization, the attitude of supervision and peers is "Let's get the job done effectively." The climate in these organizations is conducive to good message receiving. You are expected to listen well. In the nontask-centered organization, the prevailing attitude might be "We don't give a darn." You are expected not to listen to any job-related information unless it is absolutely necessary. In short, the social climate will influence the amount of energy the individual exerts to receive job-related information.

SENDER'S ABILITY TO SEND INFORMATION People vary in their native ability to transmit information. We would expect to be able to listen to a skilled sender more easily than to an unskilled one. Occasionally, we may find ourselves obliged to depend on very poor senders for vital information. When this happens, we are forced to work much harder at listening than we care to. Most of the time the listener is at the mercy of the sender. In the best of all possible worlds, both the listener and the sender would be perfect communicators. Of course, this seldom happens. Under daily pressures, even good communicators sometimes compromise by becoming sloppy. There is hope, however. As you work to improve your own communication skills, you will make it easier for others around you to receive the information you are trying to transfer. The more sensitive you are to your own communication responsibilities, the easier your listener's task becomes.

RECEIVER'S ABILITY TO LISTEN This may be the most important trait in the model. An especially skilled listener can overcome any barrier to effective listening. But most of us are not exceptional listeners. Such factors as native intelligence, perceptual skill, and personality will influence our ability to listen. Since there are so many potential negative influences that make effective listening difficult, the single most important characteristic of good listening is simply the ability to reduce all unnecessary distractions and to concentrate fully on the information being transferred.

RECEIVER'S MOTIVATION TO LISTEN To be effective listeners, we must *want* to listen. When we have no stake in the information being sent, when we distrust the source of the information, or when we have difficulty grasping the sender's intent, we may not be motivated to listen. Motivation is based on many interpersonal and organizational factors. People will devote energy to listen when they are motivated to do so. To be motivated, they must generally see an immediate payoff for themselves in the information being sent. As information takes on special meaning to me, I will try harder to grasp it.

A FINAL POINT The perceptive reader has already noticed that many of the layers on the organizational model are related to factors that are out of the control of the immediate sender and receiver. Examples are environmental conditions, behavior of supervisors, and the work climate. Therefore it is not always possible to remove all of the potential reasons for poor listening in an organization.

research in listening behavior

This section will examine some of the most interesting types of listening research. We will begin by considering a few studies that examine listening in the educational setting. Then we will look at the research on listening conducted in organizational settings.

Listening Research in Educational Settings

THE WORK OF HARVEY ARMSTRONG AND IVAN MOE Do children's listening and sight vocabularies differ? Is listening vocabulary a good predictor of general reading ability? To answer these questions, Armstrong studied school children between the ages of five and twelve. His research indicated that children had a much larger listening than sight (reading) vocabulary, and that the listening vocabulary tended to be an excellent predicator of the child's capacity to learn to read.[6] Moe followed up on the Armstrong study to determine if listening vocabulary or reading readiness tests were predictors of the child's reading poten-

[6]H. Armstrong, "The Relationship of Auditory and Visual Vocabularies of Children" (unpublished Ph.D. dissertation, Stanford University, 1953).

tial. He found that listening ability was a better predictor of reading performance than were measures of mental age, verbal intelligence, and nonverbal intelligence. Moe concluded that listening ability was a much better predictor of reading readiness for first graders than other forms of standardized tests.[7] In one of the earliest studies of listening behavior, Paul Rankin had previously determined that listening in children was as closely related to intelligence as were other basic school abilities, such as reading and arithmetic.[8]

IMPLICATIONS It is surprising that our schools have been so slow to teach students to listen. With the exception of a few "how to study" courses that emphasize note-taking and listening, and some courses on listening now being offered in university departments of speech communication and communication, little formalized listening training is available even today. Yet listening is a vital part of everyday communication.

Listening Research in Organizational Settings

THE WORK OF CHARLES KELLY One of the most sophisticated and comprehensive research projects on listening was conducted by Charles Kelly in 1962.[9] Kelly was interested in the actual on-the-job listening performances of members of an organization. He designed his study to deal with some of the questions proposed in the first part of this chapter: (1) Does motivation influence listening performance? (2) Is there a difference between listening ability and listening performance? (3) Is there a relationship between one's listening performance and one's overall supervisory effectiveness? Kelly found that subjects tended to do better on listening performance scales when they were motivated. When they were warned that they were going to be tested on their listening, and when awards were offered, the subjects tended to improve their listening performance more than when these inducements were not offered. This study showed no relationship between one's listening ability, as measured on a standardized listening scale, and one's supervisory effectiveness, as rated by subordinates.

From this study, two crucial ideas emerged. First, Kelly had originally approached the subject of listening as it were a unitary phenome-

---

[7] I. Moe, "Auding as a Predictive Measure of Reading Performance in Primary Grades" (unpublished Ph.D. dissertation, University of Florida, 1957).

[8] Rankin, "Spoken Language."

[9] C. Kelly, "Actual Listening Behavior of Industrial Supervisors as Related to 'Listening Ability,' General Mental Ability, Selected Personality Factors, and Supervising Effectiveness" (unpublished Ph.D. dissertation, Purdue University, 1962).

non. However, after working with industrial foremen, he concluded that there was no single identifiable phenomenon known as "listening ability." Instead, Kelly argued that listening skills appear to differ in different social contexts. For example, he noted that a supervisor will practice one type of listening when talking with a superior and another, entirely different type when talking with subordinates. A given individual may be very skilled at one type of listening and unskilled at another.

The second major finding to emerge from Kelly's research is the important distinction between what he called *empathic* and *deliberative* listening. In an article published 12 years after his original research, Kelly differentiates between the two types of listening:

> The difference between empathic listening and deliberative listening is primarily motivational. Both listeners seek the same objective: accurate understanding of communication from another.... The empathic listener lets his understanding of the speaker determine his modes of evaluation, which are automatic; the deliberative listener's understanding of the speaker is filtered through his predetermined modes of selective listening, and he actually spends less time as a communication receiver. The empathic listener is more apt to be a consistent listener, and is less prone to his own or other distractions.[10]

Let us put Kelly's idea in a practical context. Think back to a time when someone immediately jumped on what you were saying, either agreeing or disagreeing violently, without letting you finish what you intended to say. This might be called, to borrow Carl Rogers's term, "the tendency to evaluate."[11] Early evaluation is characteristic of deliberative listening. The empathic listener, on the other hand, tries to withhold evaluation of what the sender is saying. To go one step further, the empathic listener sincerely tries to identify with the ideas and attitudes that the communicator is expressing. Empathic listening is very difficult, as we shall see.

levels of listening

One of the best ways to understand the listening process is to look at its separate components. Seth Fessenden attempted to identify seven distinct levels of listening.[12] These levels were originally proposed as a methodology for studying listening behavior.

[10]C. Kelly, "Empathic Listening," in *Small Group Communication,* eds. R. Cathcart and L. Samovar (Dubuque William C. Brown Company, Publishers, 1974), p. 341.
[11]C. Rogers, *Client-Centered Therapy: Its Current Practice, Implications, and Theory* (Boston: Houghton Mifflin Company, 1951), p. 212.
[12]S. Fessenden, *Listening 75* (Indianapolis: The Bobbs-Merrill Co., Inc., 1955).

To Fessenden, the process of listening functions chronologically. Listening occurs when the ear performs a time-frequency-intensity analysis of speech sound and spreads them out in patterns. We can then recognize these patterns as they come in succession. The interpretation of the patterns follows pattern recognition. After this has been accomplished, the first of the seven levels of listening begins.

ISOLATION The first level of listening occurs when we begin to isolate particular sounds, ideas, facts, organizations, and other stimuli. Here the listener is only noting the individual aspects of the spoken word, and no evaluation is taking place. Isolation is really a cognitive process that depends on our field of experience.

IDENTIFICATION Once we have begun to identify particular stimuli, we give meaning, or identity, to the independent items. Isolation and identification are so closely related that it may be difficult to distinguish between the two.

INTEGRATION At this level our field of experience begins to play a significant role. We are really attempting to integrate what we are hearing with other information stored within our brain. For listening actually to take place, we must have background or understanding in the particular subject area of the message. The better our memory, the better able we are to listen. If we have no information to retrieve that can be used to integrate the new information, listening is difficult. As Fessenden points out, "One cannot integrate what one hears with what he already knows unless there are comparable data in his experience."[13]

INSPECTION After we have integrated what we hear with what we already know, we begin to compare and contrast the information. If what we hear simply reinforces what we already know, there is no problem. If the new information contradicts something we thought to be true, some type of resolution must take place.

INTERPRETATION Our cognitive processes now begin to appraise and evaluate *what* we hear as well as the *source*. At this level of the listening process, we are very much aware of what is going on. We are actively participating in the communication act. Such activities as ob-

[13]Fessenden, *Listening 75*, p. 290.

76

jecting, approving, recognizing, and weighing are all going on at this level of listening.

INTERPOLATION No message carries meaning in and of itself. Therefore, we must assign meaning to what we hear. This assignment occurs during the sixth level of listening. Since a single message may carry only a few of the possible ideas that could be expressed, we must provide supporting data and ideas from our own background and then use those data to fill in the details of the message we hear.

INTROSPECTION Finally, we must reflect on and examine what we have heard. This process enables us to assign particular significance to the information we have listened to. In this activity we are attempting to "personalize" what may have been very objective information. This seventh level of listening allows us to apply the information we have heard.

Fessenden's seven levels of listening are summarized in figure 3–4. Fessenden points out that they do not represent the entire activity. Rather, he says, they provide a methodology for studying listening behavior. Assuming that we accept the seven levels as proposed, they do suggest locations in which to search for problems that may arise in the listening process.

One of the most interesting aspects of the Fessenden paradigm of listening is the idea that listening is very much a participating activity. Before examining these seven levels, you may have been under the impression that listening was primarily *passive.* Normally we think of the sender as doing most of the work in the communication exchange. We see the sender as attempting to transmit information that the receiver can readily understand. Of course, this is a fairly accurate description of what the sender does. But the receiving of information is also an active cognitive process, as Fessenden demonstrates. If that information is to have special meaning, or *attitudinal saliency,* to the receiver, he or she must try as hard as possible to listen. The point here

FIGURE 3–4 Fessenden's levels of human listening

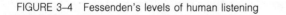

is simple, and it will be repeated throughout this book: *To succeed in both message sending and message receiving, we must work hard.*

Other Approaches

THE WORK OF ROGERS AND FARSON   Before we leave this discussion of levels of listening, let us return briefly to the ideas of Kelly. These ideas build on observations made originally by Rogers and Farson.[14] You will remember that according to Kelly, there are really two levels of listening. In empathic listening, the receiver is attempting to identify with the sender and to participate in the communication exchange. In deliberative listening, the receiver is predisposed to evaluate what he hears.

It was Rogers and Farson who originated the idea of these two levels of listening. They used the term *active listening* to describe what Kelly called empathic listening.

The authors develop the concept of active listening:

> To be effective, active listening must be firmly grounded in the basic attitudes of the user. We cannot employ it as a technique if our fundamental attitudes are in conflict with its basic concepts. If we try, our behavior will be empty and sterile, and our associates will be quick to recognize this. Until we can demonstrate a spirit which genuinely respects the potential worth of the individual, which considers his rights and trusts his capacity for self-direction, we cannot begin to be effective listeners.[15]

Above all, the active listener tries to avoid making early evaluations of what is being said. The problem with early evaluations is that once we make them, it becomes difficult for us to pick up the rest of the message. We become so preoccupied with finding data to reinforce the early evaluation that we may not hear subsequent information. Instead of bowing to this predisposition to evaluate, Rogers and Farson recommend listening for the total meaning of a message. They argue that every message has two parts, the content and the feeling or attitude underlying this content. Active listening means listening for both parts.

IMPLICATIONS   The works of Kelly and of Rogers and Farson demonstrate that listening occurs on several levels. In a typical communication exchange, we may be able to hear the content, or the purely objective information, that the other person is trying to transmit. This listening for content is an important skill, one that we can acquire through

---

[14]C. Rogers and R. Farson, *Active Listening* (Chicago: Industrial Relations Center, University of Chicago, 1955).
[15]Rogers and Farson, *Active Listening*, p. 17.

practice. But at the same time, in the same communication exchange, we must be sensitive to the other person's attitudes and predispositions. We must sometimes go beyond the sender's words to examine his or her underlying emotions. If we listen only to the words, we may get only part of the message. Consider the following four brief exchanges:

Question 1: Just whose responsibility is the tool room?

Response: Do you feel that someone is challenging your authority in there?

Question 2: Don't you think younger, able people should be promoted before senior, but less able ones?

Response: It seems to you they should, I take it.

Question 3: What does the super expect us to do about those broken down machines?

Response: You're pretty disgusted with those machines, aren't you?

Question 4: Don't you think I've improved over the last review period?

Response: Sounds as if you feel like you've really picked up over these last few months.[16]

In each of these examples, the listener has avoided the temptation to reply to the question with his own opinion, which might be an evaluation. Instead, the listener has offered a response that is intended to generate additional information from the sender in a nonthreatening way. The listener has avoided taking a black-or-white stand, which could eventually close communications. Active listening (Rogers and Farson) and empathic listening (Kelly) both require the receivers to do the same thing—postpone evaluation until they are sure that they understand both the content of and the attitude behind a message.

functions of listening
for members of organizations

Listening has many important functions. This section considers four of the most basic. These four functions apply directly to communication behavior in the organization and to other types of communication as well.

1. Listening enables us to gain work-related information. To accomplish a new or unfamiliar task, we must develop a certain level of information about that task. The primary sources of this information are

[16]Rogers and Farson, *Active Listening,* p. 17.

written materials about the task and people who can tell us how to do it. Good listeners can take the information that someone is transmitting to them orally and use it to accomplish the task.

Think back to your first job. As new tasks in that job kept appearing, someone probably tried to explain them to you. Assuming that this person knew enough about the task, and assuming that you were a good listener, you picked up enough information to enable you to do the new task adequately. As you practiced it, learned more about it, and built up a sensitivity to it, you may have become proficient at it. But to gain the adequate information at the beginning, you had to exercise some degree of listening skill. Sometimes this is difficult if the new task is technical and complex.

2. *Listening enables us to be more effective in interpersonal relationships.* It is through communication that we develop interpersonal relationships. We send and receive information, and as the interaction patterns become solidified, relationships are formed. The more proficient we are at forming these relationships, the more interpersonally effective we become.

Good interpersonal relationships are often developed by means of some type of exchange. That is, a relationship grows when there is some give and take between the participants.[17] We might think of a typical relationship as one in which Person A provides Person B with certain things he needs (e.g., ideas, emotions, rewards), and Person B provides Person A with certain things. The more critical these things are to the development of the person who receives them, the more important the relationship becomes. To learn what to provide, and whether or not it can be provided, each person listens to what the other person has to say.

Consider a typical superior–subordinate relationship. Some people believe that one of the superior's important tasks is to provide emotional and attitudinal support for the subordinate.[18] The superior must be willing to go to bat for the subordinate, should the need arise. The superior should also try—as much as possible within the constraints of the hierarchy—to make sure that the subordinate's needs are met. Only through good communication between the two can the superior hope to establish this type of the relationship. By the process of good listening, the superior finds out where the subordinate is "coming from." The superior seeks to draw the subordinate out and encourages

[17]T. Newcomb, *The Acquaintance Process* (New York: Holt, Rinehart and Winston, 1961), p. 21; F. Heider, *The Psychology of Interpersonal Relations* (New York: John Wiley & Sons, Inc., 1958), p. 19.

[18]D. McGregor, *The Human Side of Enterprise* (New York: McGraw-Hill Book Company, 1960); R. Likert, *The Human Organization* (New York: McGraw-Hill Book Company, 1967).

him or her to talk about problems and difficulties. The better the superior listens, the more data he or she generates to develop and maintain the superior–subordinate relationship. This is only one case where good listening contributes to interpersonal effectiveness. Other relationships —such as those of husband and wife, father and son, counselor and counselee, and salesman and customer—are also improved when both parties practice good listening.

3. Listening enables us to gather data to make sound decisions. We are constantly being forced to make decisions. Whether to take the bus or drive to work, whether to stay late and finish the report tonight or come in early and do it tomorrow, whether to submit this draft of the new manual for review or give it one more shot are decisions that we all make every day. To decide these matters, we must have sound and current information.

We get much of this information by listening to others. People often share their ideas, opinions, and experiences about these matters. We can either ignore what they have to say and do it our own way or listen to what they have to say and use their suggestions in our decision making. It is sound decision-making practice to obtain input from many different sources before making a decision. Thus, if it is a choice between driving the car or taking the bus to work, we may listen to traffic reports on the radio to see how congested the freeway is before we leave home. If it is a choice between going home now or staying late to finish a report, we may check with peers to see how important this report is and whether the deadline is flexible. If it is a choice between turning in or reworking the draft of the manual, we may first ask for comments from our co-workers. In each case, the extra effort of asking someone for advice and then listening to it provides us with additional information that we can use to make the best choice.

All of the examples cited are intentionally relatively simple and mundane. For crucial decisions—except possibly those which must be made under a tight deadline—most organizations will expect you to go out of your way to check out all of the *facts* on every alternative. Even so, this checking out will be useless unless you are able to listen to what others have to say.

4. Listening enables us to respond appropriately to the communication messages we hear. It is probably one of the most natural things that you do—when someone says something to you, you say something back. Your response is based on the information that you heard. Effective listening, then, enables you to generate the appropriate response.

This task is not as easy as it sounds, and some people have never developed the ability to do it. Consider these two dialogues between a father and his three-year-old son:

DIALOGUE 1

Father: Steve, how was nursery school today?

Son: I am television.

Father: Son, I asked you how was nursery school today?

Son: Television, on!

DIALOGUE 2

Father: Steve, how was nursery school today?

Son: Daddy, we learned to count.

Father: That's great. How far did you count to?

Son: Up to 10.

Giving appropriate responses is one step in learning effective interaction. In the first dialogue, little Steve was not demonstrating effective interaction, even though he was responding to his father's question. There was something going on between the time Steve heard the question and the time he formed a response, but it was not listening behavior. In the second dialogue, Steve was using listening skills to formulate an appropriate response to his father's inquiry.

In the organization the task of formulating responses is much more difficult because the range of possible contents is much wider. Instead of being asked about your day in nursery school, you might be asked, "What is your evaluation of the relative merits of a direct-mail advertising campaign over a mass media campaign in marketing the new line of men's clothing?" However, the same principle holds: *You will be successful in formulating an appropriate response only after you have demonstrated good listening behavior.*

steps in effective listening

Let us now turn our attention to some of the ways in which we can improve our own listening abilities. Many writers have compiled lists of ways to improve listening.[19] In this section, ten steps toward improved listening will be considered in some detail.

1. Listen for the sender's central idea. This is probably the most important step in good listening. If you can identify the sender's main

[19]The list presented in this section was based on guidelines originally offered by Dover, *Listening;* "Improved Listening," training tape developed by Kemper Institute for Insurance Training; R. Nicholas and L. Stevens, *Are You Listening?* (New York: McGraw-Hill Book Company, 1957); S. K. Okun, "How to Be a Better Listener," *Nation's Business* (August 1975), pp. 59–62; and Weaver, *Human Listening.*

idea for every communication exchange in which you find yourself, you must be practicing effective listening. To identify the sender's main idea, you must keep your own ideas in the background. If your own ideas begin to influence your listening, you may miss what the sender is trying to say. All this implies that every speaker does indeed have a central idea. This may be a lofty assumption to make about all communicators, but you should make it, if you want to be a good listener.

To focus on the central idea of the communication, you must distinguish it from the documentation and supporting material that the sender uses. This means that you must go through the cognitive exercise of organizing what is being said. Sometimes a communicator will make it easy for you by putting his ideas into some kind of logical order. Other times you must do all the work yourself.

2. Concentrate on what the sender is saying. This step follows logically from the first. No one can put forth maximum concentration all the time in every communication exchange. However, good listening does require you to work hard at listening. In the organizational setting, we often find ourselves doing three or four tasks at the same time. Sometimes we are forced to listen to important work-related instructions, when we are in the middle of other activities. Good listeners develop a style of listening that enables them to concentrate enough to get the information they need, even while they are doing other things. Take your listening very seriously. If you devote enthusiasm to your listening, you should develop good message-receiving habits.

3. Do not let emotions influence listening. Often we hear what we want to hear, not what the sender intended to transmit. We often assign our own values to stimuli coming in. If we accept a particular philosophy or dogma, we are likely to respond positively to all of the points contained in that dogma, as well as to those who represent it. In short, *our attitudes influence our listening behavior.*

It is difficult—if not impossible—to stop this from happening. However, you should recognize that it can happen. Earlier in this chapter, the concept of delayed evaluation was discussed. Those who recommend this approach to listening, feel that if we can simply delay our evaluation of a communicator's ideas until we can be sure that we have understood them, we will develop good listening habits. It may be human to want to agree or disagree immediately with what someone is saying. But skilled communicators control this tendency.

4. Do not reject what you hear as too familiar, unfamiliar, or trivial. It is very easy, when we hear something that is "old hat" to us, simply to turn off the communicator because we think we have heard it all before. We may do the same thing if we judge that what we are hearing is too unfamiliar or simply too trivial to listen to. If we do this often, we will miss a lot of important information.

Let us look at a typical industrial training situation. The supervisor is explaining a procedure to his subordinates. Joanne feels that she already knows the task, so she turns off the supervisor in the first few moments. Later, when new information is presented, Joanne misses it. Later still, when Joanne needs this new information, she cannot retrieve it. In listening, it is important to delay making judgments that cannot be reversed.

5. *Do not just listen for the facts.* In chapter two, we saw that in most communication situations, many things are happening at once. In our listening we should be sensitive to everything that is happening, not just to the facts the speaker is trying to transmit. The good listener will notice the surroundings, the reactions of the other listeners, the enthusiasm demonstrated by the sender, and so forth. All of these things are part of the message being transmitted. So is the information that the sender uses to document the facts. Being perceptive to the appropriateness, intelligibility, and relevance of the supporting materials is also an aspect of listening behavior. If the sender provides vivid and relevant supporting materials, it makes the listener's task easier.

6. *Avoid formulating arguments against the sender's ideas before you fully understand them.* It is very easy to develop counterarguments to what someone is saying while that person is talking. In doing so, however, you risk missing the sender's subsequent ideas. Thinking up opposition arguments takes time and energy away from your primary job as a listener—getting a good grasp on the ideas the sender is transmitting. When you fully understand these ideas, you may refute them, if necessary.

7. *Try to ignore uncomfortable surroundings.* Many physical surroundings are simply not conducive to good listening. They may be noisy, uncomfortable, or open to interruptions. Experts in listening behavior recommend that you try not to let these surroundings interfere with listening. Apart from soundproofed conference rooms, there is probably no place in any organization where you can give total concentration to a speaker. You will usually have to make some kind of compromise (e.g., this is the best room for a presentation; another room may be better for a group discussion). If conditions become so critical that they cannot be ignored, change the location or cancel the communication event.

8. *Try to personalize the sender's topic.* We are more interested in things that affect us than in things that do not. Good listeners capitalize on this and search each speaker's message for information that has special meaning for them. This is called *personalizing* the message. Occasionally a good communicator will personalize the message for you by providing reasons why you should be concerned with his or her

ideas. Usually you must do this work yourself. Plow through the message and select those aspects which are important to you. As you do this, you will become more interested in the ideas being discussed, and it will be easier for you to concentrate on the message. If the information is too abstract or irrelevant to be personalized, listening becomes a difficult chore.

9. Be perceptive to the sender's nonverbal communication. In chapter two we learned that a message has verbal and nonverbal components. The good listener will be perceptive to both. Often people will transmit one message verbally and another one nonverbally. Sometimes the two messages conflict. This forces the listener to choose between them. Most of us have learned how to make our verbal and nonverbal behavior consistent. When the two are generally consistent the listener can read the nonverbal cues to pick up the particular nuances and emphases of the message. In this context, nonverbal communication is used to fill out and embellish verbal communication.

10. Do not be afraid of difficult expository messages. Experts in listening point out that sometimes people will refuse to listen to information that they feel is too difficult or complicated. If you hesitate to listen to anything that seems too hard to understand, you will not learn much. To be a good listener, you should be willing to listen to what seems like difficult material. In organizations where each new job will entail receiving many difficult messages, you must be especially willing to devote your energies to grasping the material. Your career may depend on it.

final observations

Let us conclude this chapter by considering three ideas on message receiving. These are ideas that you should keep in mind as you attempt to improve your listening ability.

Neglect of Listening

Almost all listening experts agree that this skill has been woefully neglected in the literature about communication. We spend almost all of our time thinking about sending (talking, writing). Yet listening is an even more important communication skill. As you communicate, keep this in mind. We do much more message receiving than we do message sending. Do not neglect your own listening ability. Work on developing it to its fullest potential.

Listening as the Foundation
of Other Communication Skills

Early in this chapter a brief reference was made to the fact that most communication skills require good listening. This is why listening is considered at the beginning of the book. Once you have mastered the skills of good listening, you will have no trouble with the other skills. Listening is the foundation of effective communication.

Listening Is Hard Work

To be a good listener, you must work hard. You must make your brain struggle to understand what someone is saying. You must be objective and reflective in your communication behavior. It is not easy to do these things. But once you have learned to do them you are well on your way to becoming a good communicator.

FOR STUDY

1 In your own words, what does a person do when he or she listens? Label the cognitive processes involved.

2 What are some of the outside influences that may prevent one from listening effectively? Can they be overcome?

3 Identify four of the most important factors that make someone a good listener.

4 Distinguish between deliberative listening and empathic listening. What role does each play in effective communication in the organization?

5 Think of some potential questions regarding listening that could be studied through research. Why do you consider these to be important?

case three

The Training Program

At the Hollins Manufacturing Company, management trainees go through a special program. This training program teaches them how to talk with people. It also teaches them to be open and honest in dealing with subordinates. The Hollins training program was designed by Ted Cox.

Ted has been vice-president of administration at Hollins for six years. Before he took his present job, he was personnel manager at Hobart Fire and Tool. At Hobart, he developed several successful techniques for helping people to gain supervisory ability. He brought these techniques with him when he accepted his present position at Hollins.

When Ted came to work for Hollins, there were many problems with employee motivation and morale. About a year before, in fact, the entire maintenance department had walked out in a protest that centered on their supervisor's management techniques. They claimed that the supervisor had called them names, would not listen to suggestions, and had threatened to make them work harder. Apparently, these management techniques had backfired. The maintenance department had slowed down to a snail's pace, forcing the supervisor to crack down even harder. The situation in maintenance was not much different from that in other departments. Most of Hollins' supervisors felt that their duty was to make sure that all of the employees toed the line.

Perhaps this situation was understandable in the light of the pressures under which Hollins was operating. From the previous vice-president of the organization on down the chain of command, every manager seemed to stress production. Getting out as many units as possible became the organization's primary goal. However, the greater the effort at production, the more difficulty Hollins had in achieving a satisfactory rate.

It was into this environment that Ted Cox stepped six years ago. When he arrived, he noticed three important trends among the management staff. First, managers did not seem to take the time to talk with their subordinates individually. Second, when asked, many managers could not state what their subordinates' biggest problems were. Third, many managers indicated that they really did not care what, if anything, was bothering their subordinates. It seemed that an attitude of "we got our problems, they got theirs" prevailed among the management staff. This ran counter to everything Ted believed about employee–management relations. He began to take steps to change the situation at Hollins.

After consulting with the manager of training, Ted designed a two-day module for use in his new management development program. The module was called "Getting Along with Subordinates." It looked like this:

FIRST DAY

9:00–10:00	Trainees' assumptions about people
10:00–11:00	Exercise on building trust
11:00–12:00	Discussion of good listening principles
12:00–1:00	Lunch
1:00–2:00	Exercise on subordinates' assumptions about managers
2:00–4:00	Role playing on conducting employee interviews
4:00–5:00	Discussion of ways to understand subordinates

SECOND DAY

9:00–10:00	Discussion on motivating subordinates
10:00–12:00	Role playing on conducting appraisals
12:00–1:00	Lunch
1:00–2:00	Exercise on responding to subordinates' suggestions
2:00–4:00	Exercise on counseling subordinates
4:00–5:00	Debriefing and Evaluation

In addition to the management development program, Ted initiated a series of meetings with the management staff. In groups of four or five, Ted tried to meet with each manager at least three times a year. Most of them commented that this was the first time since they came to work at Hollins that they had ever sat down and talked with a vice-president. At these meetings Ted would inquire about the manager's job and his or her problems. As he got to know them better, his discussions turned to personal matters. He came to know about their families and their off-work activities. In time, some of the managers became his personal friends.

Ted really had two reasons for initiating these meetings. The first was the most obvious. He wanted to get to know the managers and their problems. But second, if he could demonstrate some interest in his subordinates, maybe they would begin to take an active interest in their people. After the meetings, Ted made it a point to follow up on the managers' written and oral suggestions, to show that he valued their contributions.

After Ted's first two years on the job, things gradually began to change. The new supervisors, who had been trained under the management development program, behaved differently toward subordinates than did the older supervisors. The new people made it a point to chat often with subordinates. They tried to get their input on issues facing the department. They encouraged suggestions. When the older supervisors began to notice this behavior, they paid close attention to the production figures. To their surprise, the top-producing units each month were those departments headed by newly trained supervisors. When the older supervisors realized this, they too began to change their style.

The change was helped by the regular management meetings that Ted held. The "veep's gripe sessions," as the meetings came to be called, became one of the favorite lunchtime topics of conversation. Almost all of the managers felt that they had someone at the top who was prepared to go to bat for them. The rapport between superiors and subordinates at each level of management improved.

Amazing things began to happen during Ted's third year at Hollins. Production increased markedly, and sales took off. Hollins was rapidly becoming a leader in its field.

FOR STUDY

1 What do you think happened at Hollins? Use your own words to describe the changes. Use the terminology of this chapter.

2 Why do people seem to prefer working at the "second" Hollins over the "first"? Can you think of some behavioral principles that might explain their preferences?

3 Why do people want to express themselves? What happens to this desire when people are stifled in their opportunities for self-expression?

4 Under what conditions do people refrain from talking? Were any of these conditions present at the "first" Hollins?

5 Had Ted been at the bottom of the hierarchy, e.g., a first-line foreman, would it have been possible for him to make the changes described in the case? Do all important organizational changes originate at the top?

the interview:
Achieving
Mutual Understanding

People generally spend about 60 percent of their day in conversation. This conversation takes many forms. The early morning discussion between husband and wife about the broken toaster qualifies as conversation. So does the discussion with the paperboy about the continually late arrival of the evening paper. Think back through a typical day. How many hours did you spend in conversation? The continual conversation that characterizes daily living is called *interpersonal communication* in this book.

In the organization, interpersonal communication is basic to standard operating procedures. As we saw in the first chapter, communication must be present for an organization to function effectively. The focus of this chapter is a special type of interpersonal communication: the *interview*.

In organizations it is common for two or three people to get together under *planned or prepared conditions.* Here the communication is not random, because an agreed-upon time and place have been arranged. Participants have a *reason* for meeting. Some kind of *expectation* exists about the result of this interchange. The communication is taken seriously. Occasionally, this planned interpersonal communication follows a structured format or guideline.

the interview: a definition

The last paragraph described an *interview.* The interview process can be defined as "an interpersonal communication exchange between two or more people that is planned and purposeful."[1]

---

[1]This definition is consistent with those in C. Stewart and W. Cash, *Interviewing Principles and Practice* (Dubuque: William C. Brown Company, Publishers, 1974); and

chapter four

This definition suggests that interpersonal communication becomes an interview when it moves from the realm of random communication to planned communication. For example, assume that you walk into the school cafeteria and you encounter your business management professor. In a random interpersonal communication, you might say, "Hello, Professor, how are you?" Now assume that you need to find out when the next exam will be given. You plan to go to the professor's office during office hours and ask questions related to this *purpose.* The second situation requires that you demonstrate interviewing behavior.

Interviewing behavior is characteristic of most of the important interpersonal communication that goes on in an organization. Because an organization has a purpose, most important communication in that organization should involve that purpose, at least in theory.

Under certain conditions, even random interpersonal communication turns into an interview. Suppose that when you run into your professor in the cafeteria you are able to ask about the upcoming examination right there on the spot. What begins as chit-chat under informal conditions becomes interviewing behavior. In the same way, important organizational decisions may well be made on the golf course or in the hallway.

This chapter is going to examine the communication situation of the interview for two purposes. First, it is important for you to understand the theoretical aspects of this form of interpersonal communication. Second, you need to acquire the skills that will enable you to become a competent interviewer and interviewee. The chapter discusses the uses of the interview, a number of important types of interviews, the components of the interviewing process, and the communication concerns of interviewers and interviewees. Finally, the chapter will suggest some steps toward good interviewing.

the uses of the interview

Because organizations must encourage the exchange of information, and because people often interact in twos and threes, the interview is an important communication technique in organizations.[2] Many organizations encourage their members to discuss job-related matters and to interact with each other about company problems. People who

---

A. Sanford, G. Hunt, and H. Bracey, *Communication Behavior in Organizations* (Columbus, Ohio: Charles E. Merrill Publishing Company, 1976.) The definition of interviewing as "systematic or purposeful communication" was first offered by Goyer, Redding, and Rickey in a project text developed for use in interviewing classes at Purdue University in 1963.

[2]Stewart and Cash, *Interviewing Principles,* p. 46.

are members of organizations have informational requirements that are associated with their tasks. If you worked as a letterer in a greeting card firm, you would need to have some idea about what the rest of the people in this organization were doing. If you were not a party to this information, the chances are that you would not be able to do the job as effectively as you should. Often one member of an organization will approach another for needed information, thus the interview.

Ready accessibility and often ready rapport make people go to their peers for information. Much two-person communication between peers is informal. An example would be two secretaries who talk about a new method for processing expense vouchers over lunch at the local hamburger stand. Two-person peer communication occurs between people of similar rank and status in the organization. The informality of the peer communication between two secretaries may be contrasted with the rather formal peer communication that might go on between two vice-presidents of an organization who are trying to reach a compromise on the budgets for their respective departments in the company's boardroom. People in organizations often use the interview to obtain information from peers about organizational matters.

Another important type of two-person communication occurs between a boss and a subordinate. Two-person peer communication is sometimes informal, since it happens outside the normal *chain of command* of an organization. Peer communication is not constrained by the hierarchy of the organization. The opposite is true of superior–subordinate communication. People who are casual and relaxed about approaching a peer may feel threatened and nervous about approaching their boss. Obviously, attitude change occurs because the boss has a good deal of power and influence over a subordinate. This point will be considered extensively in chapter six, when we investigate leadership and supervision.

Nonetheless, there are times when the employee must approach his or her superior about some matter of importance on the job. At other times, the exchange between a superior and subordinate will be formally initiated by the boss. At still other times, the subordinate will seek information from the superior on a very informal basis. Many variables—the level of trust between the two, the type of task, and the degree of interpersonal attraction—are likely to influence the effectiveness of superior–subordinate communication.

seven types of interview

In this section, we will examine seven of the most common types of interview that are used in organizations: informational, employment, counseling, appraisal, sales, public relations, and customer interviews.

Some of these types of interview occur only between a superior and a subordinate. Others occur between peers within the organization. Still others occur between a member of an organization and someone outside the organization.

Informational Interviews

Members of organizations need particular information associated with their jobs. The informational interview is a technique for gathering data. It might be defined as an *exchange between two people for the purpose of enabling one or both persons to gain information from each other.* The informational interview is often used by peers, between superiors and subordinates, and between members and nonmembers of an organization. Consider the following situations.

SITUATION 1 Sheryl is a sales representative for a pharmaceutical manufacturing firm. She has been having some trouble getting the final approval for a sale from a customer. She has heard that Joe, another sales representative from an adjoining territory, is an outstanding "closer." She calls Joe and makes an appointment to have lunch with him. Sheryl's purpose is to find out what makes Joe so good at closing sales.

SITUATION 2 Jim works as a supervisor on the loading dock of a grocery distribution center. In the lunchroom, he hears that a new policy concerning overtime is being discussed. Jim wants to get to the bottom of this. He walks into Mr. Sommers' office; Mr. Sommers is the manager of the warehouse and Jim's boss. Jim says, "Mr. Sommers, can I talk with you for a few minutes about something I just heard in the lunchroom?"

SITUATION 3 Bill owns an import–export business. His small firm imports speciality items for sale in the Middle West. Rapidly changing rules concerning tariffs and taxes have recently made Bill's job difficult. To find out exactly what is happening in Washington, Bill calls the office of Congressman Clinton Davidson. He arranges an appointment to talk to the congressman's field representative about the new rules.

USES OF THE INFORMATIONAL INTERVIEW In each of these situations, a member of an organization is seeking information. To obtain the information, each chooses to carry on formalized social conversation. This type of interview is used in a wide variety of organizations and professions. The lawyer who discusses a problem with a client is conducting an informational interview. So is the journalist who talks to the president of the local school board about the implications of the previous night's meeting. So is the pollster who seeks information on local residents' attitudes toward a proposed nuclear power plant.

In the typical large organization, people obtain information from a variety of sources. Sometimes the bulletin board or the memorandum is used to send information to members. Other times, organizations transmit information by means of production reports or message systems. However, there seems to be some evidence that members of organizations *prefer* to receive information by written *and* oral channels.[3] The interview is an important oral channel.

Often the interviewer and the interviewee will *both* be attempting *to transmit* information to one another. For example, imagine an interview between a superior who wants to find out how a subordinate is doing in his job and a subordinate who wants to find out what his boss thinks of his performance. Each has a preconceived purpose in mind.

You might correctly assume that the typical informational interview takes place in a highly formal atmosphere, as when a boss and subordinate sit down at a table to discuss a matter of mutual concern. But often just the opposite occurs. Two members of a department may stop on their way to lunch to exchange information. A reporter may stop a political figure in the hallway while both are going into a fund-raising banquet. Two managers may exchange information over a friendly drink in the local tavern. Informational interviewing takes many forms and can accomplish many purposes. It is an important method of communication in the organization. Later in this chapter we will examine some of the skills that will enable you to conduct good informational interviews.

Employment Interviews

The employment interview is conducted to determine if an individual is well suited for employment in a given organization. It is a special kind of informational interview. The goal of each participant in the employment interview is to gather information. The company interviewer wants to learn from the applicant whether he or she is suitable for employment in the organization. The applicant wants to learn about the organization in general, and specifically about the position for which he or she is applying. Occasionally applicants attempt to sell themselves for the position in addition to gathering data.

The employment interview is actually three separate interviews. It usually falls into three chronological phases, and a different interview is conducted in each phase. These phases are illustrated in figure 4–1.

[3]T. Dahle, "Transmitting Information to Employees: A Study of Five Methods," *Personnel*, 31, no. 2 (1954), 243–46.

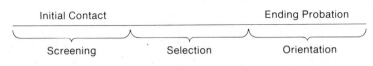

FIGURE 4-1   Phases of the employment interview

SCREENING PHASE   The screening phase occurs between the time when the initial contact is made between a potential employer and employees and the time when the serious candidates are finally chosen. Initial contact between an organization and a potential employee usually takes place by mail or telephone. An applicant may send a resume in response to a newspaper advertisement or make a telephone call after learning of a possible opening. After the contact has been made, the organization will have a contact person conduct a short interview with interested candidates. Sometimes the organization will decide to call in a few candidates for further interviews based on the resumes. The procedure varies greatly, depending on the organization and the nature of the position.

Screening interviews are often short. In less than a half hour a job applicant must be able to say rapidly and cogently what his or her unique qualifications are. Often in these screening interviews, the focus is on the "hard qualifications"—technical expertise, education, experience, and so forth. These interviews may be conducted by a member of the employment relations or personnel department. In smaller organizations, they are often conducted by the supervisor under whom the potential employee will work. After all the candidates have been screened, the employer chooses the three or four best ones. The process then moves to the selection phase.

SELECTION PHASE   The goal in the selection phase is to reduce the number of applicants from three or four to one or two. During the selection phase a typical organization is likely to use various techniques in addition to the face-to-face interview to help it make decisions. Consider the following illustration.

A student talked with a campus recruiter about a management training program for one of the nation's largest retailing organizations. On the basis of this initial screening interview and the woman's experience and college work, she was invited to a three-day session at the district headquarters of the organization. Her three-day visit to headquarters really constituted the selection phase.

During her visit the student was interviewed *individually* by a number of managers; she was interviewed by a *group* of different managers; and she was interviewed *in a group* of other applicants by

95

still other managers. She was given written tests, and she participated in various management cases and exercises. When she was not engaged in these activities, she was attending classes to learn about the organization. Throughout the entire three-day period, she was being evaluated on her performance. When it was all over, she returned to report that it was "the most grueling experience of my life." She was later offered a position with the organization.

This example is probably not typical of the lengths to which organizations will go to gain data about an applicant. The primary task of the organization, during this phase, is to get *adequate* information about the applicant in order to judge his or her potential as a member of the organization. The applicant, during this phase, would normally attempt to persuade the organization that he or she would be a valuable employee by calling attention to his or her background, experience, and talents and by demonstrating potential use to the organization.

ORIENTATION PHASE The orientation phase begins when the applicant has been selected for a position. In many organizations there is a trial period of a few weeks or months after the employee has come on the job during which he or she must perform satisfactorily. This is called a *probationary period.* During the probationary period, the applicant will probably be given a variety of jobs to determine where he or she will fit in best.

The interviewing during the orientation phase really has two functions. The first is educational. The applicant will probably be taught various aspects of one or several jobs. The second has to do with placement. During the orientation phase, the applicant will probably be interviewed several times by the personnel department or by his or her orientation supervisor to determine the type of permanent position for which he or she is best suited. Data collected from the applicant's various training positions will be used to determine the best permanent job.

All three phases of the employment interview have the same purpose: *to attempt to generate a complete exchange of information between the applicant and the organization, to enable the organization to decide whether to hire applicant.*

Counseling Interviews

People who work in organizations are often called upon to conduct counseling interviews. In a counseling interview, one participant attempts to *aid* and *advise* the other. The counseling interview may be initiated by either participant or by a third party. It is used in a wide variety of circumstances. A supervisor calls in a subordinate to determine why the subordinate's work has grown erratic. An employee who has outgrown her present job makes an appointment to talk with an employee representative in the personnel department. The high school principal suggests that all department chairpeople talk with their teachers about ways to improve their teaching methods. These are all examples of counseling interviews.

In many large industrial organizations and in most schools and universities, certain members sometimes act as professional counselors. It is not unusual to find trained therapists and counselors on the staff of an organization. However, professional counseling interviews are beyond the scope of this chapter. The focus here is on those types of counseling interviews between a superior and a subordinate that occur in the routine job situation. Other kinds of counseling interviews also occur in organizations, but most of the material on superior–subordinate counseling applies to other kinds of counseling as well.

Most managers eventually find themselves obliged to conduct a counseling interview. Often, the counseling situation will involve job-related matters (low productivity, inability to get along with others). Occasionally, the manager will have to counsel the subordinate about a personal problem (an upcoming divorce, alcholism.) Good counseling interviewers recognize those areas in which they are qualified to counsel and will refer the counselee to someone else when they are not qualified.

The counseling interview has two phases. The first is informational; the second is problem solving.

INFORMATIVE PHASE OF THE COUNSELING INTERVIEW   The first task of any counseling interviewer is to encourage the interviewee to describe the situation in some detail and in his or her own words. The term "situation" is used deliberately. The interviewee is often not convinced that he or she has a *problem*. In fact, one purpose of a counseling interview may be to determine whether a problem exists. Therefore, the interviewer needs to establish an interview climate that is objective and analytical. This can be done by making sure that all relevant information is brought out in the open. However, the typical interviewee is often hesitant to discuss the situation for several reasons.

First, the interviewee may be *reticent*. In an unfamiliar situation some people have difficulty opening up or talking with strangers. The more difficult, complex, or personal the problem, the more difficult it is for some of us to share our true feelings. For the counseling interview to succeed, however, it is necessary for the counselee to *level* with the counselor. To facilitate this process, a good counselor may (1) encourage the counselee by talking about some painless subject, such as the weather or a recent sporting event; (2) try to keep the content of the interview fairly light until an appropriate communication climate has been established; (3) gradually ease into the controversial content; (4) provide supportive feedback and empathetic listening; and (5) use non-threatening questions calling for the counselee's feeling at present. The interviewer who uses these techniques minimizes the risk of blocking communication before it gets started.

People are often slow to communicate their true feelings. Good counseling interviewers recognize this. They do whatever they can to ease the interviewee into the difficult content normally required by the counseling situation.

Second, the interviewee may feel *threatened.* This happens when the interviewee is not wholly convinced of the need for a counseling interview, or when he or she does not know how the information is being used. A large retail establishment occasionally conducts what it calls "correction interviews." The implication of this label is clear. It suggests that the employee needs correction—not counseling—when in fact this may not be the case.

Since the counseling interview usually involves one's job or profession, one may associate the threat of the counseling interview with a threat to one's job. Simply being called into the boss's office for a talk will probably make the employee feel threatened. When the interviewee feels threatened, good communication is rarely possible.

The likelihood of threat is reduced if the interview is initiated in response to a need expressed by the counselee. When this happens, it *should be* because the counselee wants very much to communicate. Occasionally students will schedule interviews with a professor "for special help" or "to talk about a problem." However, when the time for the appointment arrives, the student is unable to get anything out. Some degree of threat will exist in any counseling situation in which interpersonal or job-related problems are being discussed.

There are some things that a good communicator can do to reduce this type of threat: (1) The interviewer should be aware that the interviewee may feel threatened. (2) The interviewer should schedule the interview at a convenient time and in a comfortable atmosphere. (3) The interviewer should try to allay the interviewee's fears about the potential use of the interview data. (4) The interviewer should lay the proper groundwork regarding the purpose, scope, and initiation of the interview. (5) A relaxed environment, free of rigid rules and control, will help to reduce threat.

Third, the interviewee may not *trust* the counselor. Trust is the most important variable in the communication relationship between superiors and subordinates.[4] The counselee must believe that the counselor intends to use the data in the interview to help the counselee. The counselee should have confidence in the counselor's ability. If the counselee does not believe that the counselor can help, the counselor probably cannot. To apply the counselor's message, the counselee must believe that both the counselor and the message are worthwhile.

A good counselor can increase the likelihood of trust on the part of the counselee. The counselor should show sincere regard for the counselee. If the counselee perceives that the counselor is really looking out for his or her best interests, he or she should begin to trust the counselor. The counselor should take his or her own message seriously. The counselee will probably respond positively to a message that is communicated in a professional and serious manner. The counselor who treats his or her message in a lighthearted fashion is unlikely to win the counselee's trust. The counselor should be enthusiastic toward both the counselee and the counseling situation. Even though there is an emerging body of literature on the nondirective counseling interview,[5] it has been the author's experience that in the close superior–subordinate situation typical of most organizations, the counselee wants the counselor to express involvement and concern. Most supervisors have a big stake in their subordinates' development. Trust is built when the counselor demonstrates this personal interest. The counselor should demonstrate expertise, honesty, and consistency. The counselor's message must be believable. The manager who instructs a subordinate in a job he cannot do himself will probably run into trouble. The counselor who is relaxed with her counselees on Monday and formal on Friday will probably not win their trust. Trust is generated when the counselor is affable. Most people feel more free to talk with a counselor who is personable and open than with one who is distant and cold. An affable

---

[4]W. Read, "Upward Communication in Industrial Hierarchies," *Human Relations,* 15, no. 1 (1962), 3–15; K. Roberts and C. O'Reilly, "Failures in Upward Communication: Three Possible Culprits," *Academy of Management Journal,* 17, no. 3 (1974), 205–15.

[5]C. Rogers, *Client-Centered Therapy: Its Current Practice, Implications, and Theory* (Boston: Houghton Mifflin Company, 1951); F. Fiedler, "A Comparison of Therapeutic Relationships in Psychoanalytic, Non Directive, and Adlerian Therapy," *Journal of Consulting Psychology,* 14, no. 4 (1950), 436–45.
The nondirective counseling interview approach would suggest that the counselee is the only person who can initiate change. Thus, this type of interview allows the counselee to maintain control. The counselee, not the counselor, determines the length, topic, approach, and strategy of the interview.

counselor demonstrates a good sense of humor, empathetic listening skills, an even disposition, and sincerity toward the counselee.[6]

Fourth, there may be some *confusion of purpose.* For the counseling interview to be successful, the counselor and counselee must agree on its purpose. If an employee is called into the boss's office thinking that she is going to be rewarded by a raise and finds instead that she is going to be counseled for "faulty work habits," the results may be rather serious. Uniformity of perceived purpose is important in any interview, but it is vitally important in the counseling situation because complex and important data are often discussed there.

PROBLEM-SOLVING PHASE OF THE COUNSELING INTERVIEW After the purpose and nature of the counseling interview have been established, the counselor moves toward the problem-solving phase. This cannot be done, of course, until enough information about the problem has been generated. In this second phase, the counselor must help the counselee to state the problem. Assuming that the counselor has done an effective job in establishing the climate of the interview, the problem-solving phase should not be difficult.

As the counselee states the situation in his or her own words, the counselor tries to provide guidelines for identifying possible solutions. The more the counselee participates in developing original solutions, the likelier those solutions are to implemented. This point is crucial. After all, why hold a counseling interview unless there is some likelihood that the problem will be solved? Again, unless the *tone* of the counseling interview is one of improvement and self-help, it is unlikely to motivate the counselee to change. The following guidelines are based on the author's observation of and participation in counseling interviews. They should be useful to counselors who are trying to help their counselees solve problems.

Be deliberate. Problem solving is a very slow process. It cannot be rushed. Some counselors tend to want to help the counselee "see insights" in order to speed the process. However, if the goal is to change the counselee's behavior, the counselor must restrain the tendency to cut corners.

Be thorough. It is the counselor's responsibility to try to make the counselee aware of all of the ramifications of the problem. As the coun-

---

[6]These characteristics of trust are based on K. Giffin, "The Contribution of Studies of Source Credibility to a Theory of Interpersonal Trust in Communication," *Psychological Bulletin,* 68, no. 2 (1967), 104–20; and Griffin, "Interpersonal Trust in Small Group Communication," *Quarterly Journal of Speech,* 53, no. 3 (1967), 224–34. They are close to the concept of *ethos* as developed by Aristotle in *The Rhetoric.*

selee begins to articulate a potential solution, he or she should test it against every aspect of the problem. Each part of the problem, as identified by the counselee, should be resolved by the solution adopted.

Be realistic. A good counselor, especially in the work situation, will recognize his or her limitations. There are some problems that the counselor is just not equipped to deal with. When the counselor encounters such a problem, the counselee should be referred elsewhere.

Be persistent. The good counselor stays with a situation. The interview does not end when the counselee leaves the interview room for the last time. The counselor should follow up on the problem to determine whether it has been resolved. If it has not, steps should be taken to begin the counseling process again.

Appraisal Interviews

Members of organizations are periodically evaluated by means of interviews. These evaluation interviews are known by various names in various organizations. Here they will be referred to as *appraisals.* Employees of industrial organizations are normally called into their supervisor's office about once a year to be told how the organization perceives their work over that period of time. Sometimes appraisals are conducted by means of highly sophisticated formats and forms (see figure 4–2). Other times, the employee just chats across the table with a supervisor.

SUCCESS OF THE APPRAISAL For the appraisal interview to be successful, two things must occur. First, the goal of the interview must be *job improvement.* Second, a problem-solving climate must exist. Let us briefly consider each of these points.

Some organizations routinely appraise each managerial-level employee every six months whether they have anything to say. Soon the process becomes so sterile that neither the interviewer nor the interviewee takes it seriously. Sometimes a supervisor will disclose surprising or threatening information in the interview that he or she has never mentioned to the subordinate before. Other times, the superior is physically removed from the subordinate and so cannot evaluate the latter fairly. Again, the subordinate may not trust the superior to evaluate him or her fairly and completely. In each of these cases, job improvement is unlikely to occur. To summarize: The interviewee must respect the appraisal format and the appraiser if the goal of *job improvement* is to be attained.

FIGURE 4-2 Original Appraisal Form

Oslander Corporation
Review Form

Employee: _____   Department: _____
Evaluator: _____   Position: _____
Date of Review: _____   Period of Review: _____

General Work Performance

    1. Did the employee perform his/her job competently during the period of review?

    2. Does the employee give evidence of being a candidate for promotion and/or additional job responsibilities?

    3. Has the employee generally been responsive to supervision during the review period?

    4. Did the employee make a contribution to the productivity of his/her work unit? Cite examples of productivity.

    5. Has the employee contributed workable ideas and plans about his/her job and/or work unit during the period of review? Cite examples.

Group Relations

    1. Has the employee been looked to for leadership by his/her peers during the period of review?

    2. Normally, does the employee get along well with his/her peers?

FIGURE 4–2 Cont.

3. Does the employee demonstrate good work habits?

4. During the review period, has the employee appeared to have been a contributing member of the work team?

5. Can the employee be looked to for expertise by his/her peers in the work unit?

Overall Evaluation

1. What seem to be the greatest strengths demonstrated by the employee during the review period?

2. What seem to be the areas that need improvement (if any) during this and the next review period?

Employee's Response (if desired): _____
_____
_____
_____
_____
_____
_____

_____   _____
Evaluator   Date

_____   _____
Employee   Date

Let us consider briefly the relative merits of the organization that conducts appraisal interviews and the organization that does not. Research suggests that appraisal interviews are difficult to link to job improvement.[7] If this is so, we are left with two questions. Why conduct appraisal interviews if they do not necessarily lead to improved job performance? And why conduct appraisal interviews if they cause so many problems?

It is true that it is difficult to relate improved job performance to good appraisals. However, this need not prevent us from setting job improvement as the goal of the appraisal interview. The interviewer *should strive* to achieve the goal of improving the employee's job performance. At the same time, the interviewer should be aware that immediate and well-defined job improvement will not occur solely as a result of the appraisal. This goal is stated more for the interviewer's sake than for the interviewee's. If the interviewer maintains a focus on the *behavior* in the subordinate that needs improvement, the interview will not become unduly personal. Once the interviewee perceives that he or she personally is under attack, the chances are that the appraisal interview will degenerate into a shouting match or the interviewee will simply clam up. Setting improved job performance as a goal benefits everyone involved—the subordinate, the supervisor, and the organization. Note that when an employee has been doing a good job, this, too, should be pointed out in the interview.

Another major problem that can be avoided if the appraisal focuses on job performance is the failure on the part of the interviewer to communicate useful and relevant information to the interviewee. If the interview simply rehashes old or irrelevent information, the interview becomes an exercise in boredom. Current information about job performance and job evaluation should be stressed above all else. Note that this information should be consistent with what the employee has been told in the past. The boss who waits for the six-month review to lower the boom on the employee will certainly be providing new information. But the employee will never trust this particular boss again. If the review is to be a six-month appraisal, the evaluation should be based on work done during the previous six months. Perhaps the best kind of interview is the one that offers the appraisee no surprises.

Occasionally it is necessary for the interviewer to complete a form or evaluation on the interviewee. This form, or an abstraction of it, may become part of the employee's permanent personnel file. It often contains structured items like those in figure 4–3.

[7]R. Kahn and C. Cannell, "Interviewing," in *The Handbook of Social Psychology,* ed. G. Lindzey and E. Aronson (Reading, Mass.: Addison-Wesley Publishing Co. Inc., 1968), II, 526–95.

Employee Motivation

Very high; works hard with little direction									Very low; seems unmotivated; needs close supervision
10	9	8	7	6	5	4	3	2	1

FIGURE 4–3

During the evaluation, the interviewer will circle an appropriate number on the line for "motivation." Along with motivation, such other variables as attendance, ability to work with peers, leadership capability, and initiative might be included. The scores on these variables might be added and the employee given a composite rating (performance rating) for the appraisal.

As a rule, these highly structured appraisal forms are counterproductive. The appraiser tends to mark a particular score on the form without explaining why. Thus, an employee will receive a score of 8 for motivation and never know what the score means or how it was derived. If the appraisal interview is to be a truly useful channel of communication from the organization to the employee, the appraiser should take extreme care to provide complete details for every aspect of the appraisal that will become part of the official record. This cannot be done by means of shortcuts, such as numbers. It must be accomplished through extensive oral, supplemented by written, communication.

SOME COMMUNICATION PRINCIPLES TO REMEMBER IN THE APPRAISAL The following principles are important in the appraisal interview.

The appraisal interview should deal primarily with the assumptions, attitudes, and orientations of the interviewee. It is likely to have a tremendous impact on the interviewee's present and future self-image. Therefore it is important that the interviewee fully understand what is occurring in the interview.

The more preinterview communication and postinterview feedback, the less chance that the interviewee will be surprised. As much as possible, the appraisal should meet the interviewee's expectations.

As in any interviewing situation, the interviewer should attempt to establish a supportive climate. Because important job-related information is transferred in the interview, it is especially necessary for the interviewee and the interviewer to trust one another.

The interviewer should maintain a problem-solving (as opposed to an evaluative) style. The communication that takes place in the ap-

praisal should emphasize problem solving, not punishment or reprimand.

Sales, Public Relations, and Customer Interviews: Credibility

Organizations often use the interview in their "external" communication activities. A salesperson talks over a new product with a potential customer; a credit manager discusses an account with a buyer; a
public relations representative outlines the construction plans for a new
plant to the local newspaper editor. In each of these interviews, a
member is communicating the organization's message to a nonmem-
ber.

The interviewer represents the image of the organization. Since
the organization's image and the interviewer are both on trial, the
interviewer must be very careful about his or her communication behavior. It is normally necessary for the interviewer to seek some degree
of commitment or satisfaction from the interviewee. This requirement
makes this type of interview very different from those already considered.

The first step in this type of interview is to establish a satisfactory
level of credibility with the interviewee. To do this, the interviewer
must demonstrate consistency, dynamism, genuineness, and expertise.[8]

CONSISTENCY Before we believe an interviewer, we want to be
sure that he or she is a consistent and reliable person. The interviewer
who vacillates depending on the issue will have trouble establishing
credibility. Consider the following dialogue:

Steve (a salesman): Mr. Barker, this is absolutely the best automobile paint
that we have ever made.

Mr. Barker: That's funny, Steve. Two months ago, you told me your Autogard
paint was the best on the market and couldn't be beat.

Steve: Oh yeah! So I did.

Steve's inconsistency will probably cost him his credibility with Mr.
Barker and his firm. We tend to believe people who seem to be consistent, reliable, and dependable. If we have to buy a product from a
salesman during an interview, we will probably buy it from a salesman
we can depend on.

[8]This discussion of credibility is based on Giffin, "Contribution of Studies of Source
Credibility"; Giffin, "Interpersonal Trust"; and K. Andersen and T. Clevenger, "A Summary of Experimental Research of Ethos," *Speech Monographs,* 30 (1968), 59–78.

DYNAMISM   We tend to believe communicators who are enthusiastic about their message and their audience. It is hard to feel enthusiastic about a product that does not spark enthusiasm in the salesperson. Sales and public relations interviewers must work to achieve an involved, energetic style.

GENUINENESS   To establish credibility with the interviewee, the interviewer must project a genuine regard for the interviewee's best interest. The superslick interviewer who comes across as insincere is probably going to have trouble maintaining credibility. Rogers has suggested that receiver-oriented communicators are those who project a positive regard for their listeners.[9] This projection is probably best achieved through the use of questions that allow the interviewer to establish some degree of understanding and appreciation for the interviewee's position. This appreciation should govern the interviewer's future communication behavior.

EXPERTISE   Sales and public relations interviewers who want to establish and maintain credibility must project some degree of expertise about the topic being discussed. If it is obvious that the interviewer does not know what he or she is talking about, there is very little possibility that he or she will be believed. Knowledge of product is one of the salesperson's most important attributes.

Chronological Stages

The purpose of the sales or public relations interview is usually to obtain some type of commitment. This is done in four chronological stages. The interviewer must (1) explain the issue to the interviewee, (2) attempt to identify common ground with the interviewee, (3) attempt to gain the interviewee's support, and (4) attempt to provide closure.

EXPLAINING THE ISSUE   In most sales or public relations interviews, the interviewer initiates contact. This obliges him or her to do some preliminary groundbreaking. Often a potential customer is unaware of the exact purpose of the interview. The interviewer should explain this purpose openly and honestly. Failure to do so can lead to deceit and covert communication. You have probably opened your door to a salesperson who claimed to be taking a survey, only to receive a sales pitch a few moments later. For this type of interview to be successful,

[9]Rogers, *Client-Centered Therapy*, pp. 68–71.

the interviewer must be honest and thorough in explaining the issue to the interviewee. The interviewee must know exactly what to expect. Only then can the interview move on to the next stage.

IDENTIFYING COMMON GROUND After the issue has been explained, the interviewer must identify common ground between himself or herself and the interviewee. Most often, this can be done by indicating to the interviewee what *common needs* can be met if he or she participates fully. Consider the following example:

Bill: It's nice to be out in your neck of the woods again, Stan. How are things going with the new products we delivered last month?

Stan: They're okay. But we're having some problems with our stamping machine. It seems to be destroying as many units as it produces.

Bill: I've encountered that problem before. Mind if I take a look? You may not know it, but my firm maintains a complete line of machine parts. Maybe we have something that could be of service.

Stan: Fine, Bill. Thanks for your interest. Why don't we go out there and take a look at those machines?

Here Bill is attempting to develop some common ground between Stan and himself. He does this by demonstrating how his product could help Stan. By approaching Stan's problem in this way, he is attempting to develop a reciprocal relationship—one in which two people are mutually dependent. Bill might have handled this in other ways. He might talk with Stan about their mutual interests and background. He might talk about past acquaintances and common relationships. He might present Stan with new and important information. Or he might express their common commitment to the same end ("I know that we both want to make money"). Only when the common ground has been identified does the interviewer put the proposal on the table.

SEEKING SUPPORT At this point the interviewer must risk his or her ideas by making the interviewee a proposal. This is done by identifying his or her line of products, ideas, or concept to the interviewee. It is crucial that the interviewee thoroughly understand the proposal if he or she is to give an intelligent answer. Therefore the interviewer must be able to judge the interviewee's intellectual capacity. A proposal that is presented in a technical or abstract fashion may not succeed with a shirt-sleeve audience. A proposal that condescends to a sophisticated audience will probably miss the mark as well.

Occasionally an interviewer will not request support clearly and directly. The interviewee may not even be aware that his or her support is being sought. Hesitancy or vagueness in seeking approval for a proposal may be valuable in certain contexts, but the direct, straightforward request for support works best under most circumstances and with most interviewees. Also, when the interviewee knows that the interviewer expects a response, he or she is more likely to provide one —even though it is sometimes not the response the interviewer wanted.

PROVIDING CLOSURE   The last phase of the sales or public relations interview requires the interviewer to provide closure by gracefully concluding the interview. The interviewer makes a final request for support and lets the interviewee know that the interview is over. Realistically, what the interviewer wants to say is "These are my ideas. I hope you will consider them, and please let me know when you have decided." An interviewer who handles this aspect of the interview well makes a fine lasting impression on the interviewee.

the interview as a communication event

Earlier in this chapter you learned that the interview is used in many *different* contexts within the organization. We are now going to examine some of the ways in which all interviews are *alike*. Interviews are both similar and different. They are different because they serve different purposes. They are *similar* because they have common components. This part will briefly consider seven of these components: people, questions, organizational constraints, communication requirements, climate, preconditions, and postconditions.

People

All of the difficulties that people have in communicating successfully are intensified in the interview. People misunderstand, information becomes distorted, and feelings get hurt more often in the interview than in any other form of organizational communication. This entire book deals with ways to remedy some of the communication problems that people face in the organization, and much that has been mentioned elsewhere can also be applied to the interview. Here we will focus on *roles* and *expectations.*

In chapter one, it was suggested that one person may play many roles in an organization. A single individual may be a supervisor *and* a subordinate, a teacher *and* a student, a line worker *and* a staff worker.

Sometimes the roles that we see ourselves playing in an organization differ from the roles that others see us play.

With every role comes a set of expectations. The expectations are the requirements of that particular role. For example, if you are a supervisor, you will be *expected* to conduct appraisals. Conducting appraisals is an *expectation* placed upon the role. Normally, there are three kinds of expectations in an organization: (1) those held by our superior, which may be written down as part of our job description; (2) those we hold ourselves; and (3) those which are held by others, especially subordinates. The difficulty comes when these various expectations conflict. For example, a superior may have to negatively appraise a subordinate who is also a friend. The supervisor's job description requires a strong posture but because of the friendship he or she wants to be kind.

The good interviewer takes into account the potential problems caused by different (and, in some cases, conflicting) expectations. Sharing information before, during, and after the interview will reduce these problems, at least to some extent.

Questions

All interviews are really question-and-answer sessions. Five types of interview questions are presented in figure 4–4. Each type of question serves a particular purpose in a given interview. Normally the interviewer should plan out his or her questions in advance. Most of the time an interviewer will plan the exact wording of the question and the sequence of questions to be asked. It is not unusual for the organization

FIGURE 4–4   Types of interview questions

Type	Definition	Example
Open	A question that opens the range of response	Q: Why do you like living in California?
Closed	A question that closes the range of response	Q: Do you like living in California?
Mirror	A question that mirrors back a response, one asked for the purpose of clarification and elaboration	Q: Is your job here rewarding? A: Yes, I find it very rewarding. Q: You find it rewarding, huh?
Leading	A question that attempts to lead the respondent in a particilar direction	Q: You find your job here very challenging, don't you?
Loaded	A question that forces the respondent to choose among unattractive alternatives	Q: OK, which shall it be, transfer or termination?

to dictate the format of the interview by means of a structured appraisal form or employment questionnaire. Sometimes the interview is more fluid, allowing the interviewer to phrase specific questions from pre-planned topic areas.

The sequence in which the different types of questions are asked can also be important in the interview. An interviewer who begins with an open question, hoping to narrow down to a specific piece of information, is practicing the *funnel* approach. An example of the funnel approach is:

Q: How did you like your last job?

A: Fine; there was some problem though.

Q: Tell me, what aspects of your job did you like best?

A: Oh, probably the paperwork.

Q: How about managing people? Did you enjoy that very much?

A: It was O.K., but didn't give me my greatest satisfaction.

In the *inverted funnel* approach, the interviewer begins with a specific question, hoping to build up to a general idea. For example:

Q: Are you making enough money on this job?

A: Sometimes I wonder.

Q: Money—does it greatly motivate you?

A: Yes, but it's only one of several things.

Q: What do you see as the primary motivators on this job?

A: Perhaps the chance to grow with the company and get ahead.

Normally, one of these two approaches will help you to organize an interview.

Constraints

Because interviews take place within an organization, they are likely to be constrained by many rules, guidelines, and norms. These *constraints* sometimes block communication. Typical constraints would be wide status differences between the interviewer and the interviewee, the expectation that a supervisor and subordinate will never communicate about the job outside the superior's office, or a rule that all appraisal interviews are to last at least 60 minutes.

Each particular type of interview places its own specific constraints on the communication exchange. For example, in an employment interview, the applicant is trying to persuade the interviewer of his or her qualifications, while the interviewer is required to make a decision. In a sales interview, the interviewer is constrained by the fact that the organization *expects results.* Successful interviewers achieve their goal by overcoming these constraints.

Communication Requirements

Four requirements of good communication are particularly relevant to the interview. They are: (1) awareness of feedback, (2) sensitivity to nonverbal behavior, (3) display of dynamic involvement, and (4) empathetic listening.

AWARENESS OF FEEDBACK   Feedback was defined in chapter two as a *reaction to a message received.* Interviewers, both inside and outside the organization, need to be sensitive to the feedback that they give others and to the feedback that others give them. Feedback improves communication by allowing the sender to adapt his or her message to the needs of the receiver. It enables the sender to determine whether or not the message has been received. Good communicators try to read feedback, to adjust their messages accordingly, and to provide good feedback themselves. The most obvious type of feedback is facial expression and eye contact. A calm, attentive facial expression will indicate to the speaker that the listener has understood the message. A perplexed expression will have a different, probably opposite, effect.

SENSITIVITY TO NONVERBAL BEHAVIOR   Successful interviewers are sensitive to their own nonverbal behavior as well as to that of the receiver. Nonverbal behavior would include the facial expression, body movement, dress, voice quality, and posture of both participants. The supervisor who conducts an appraisal while acting as if she would rather be somewhere else or the employment interviewer who seems not to care about his firm are not likely to be very successful. One's nonverbal behavior should be consistent with one's verbal behavior. They should both say the same thing to the listener.

DYNAMIC INVOLVEMENT   Dynamic involvement is the appearance of being physically involved. The receiver should perceive that the sender is focused entirely on him or her. The interviewer should communicate this involvement by means of feedback and nonverbal behavior.

EMPATHIC LISTENING Kelly has defined "listening for understanding," or empathic listening, as occurring when the receiver is totally engrossed in what the speaker has said.[10] The empathic listener focuses on what the speaker says, not on the speaker's method of presentation. The empathic listener attempts to summarize and restate what has been said. The empathic listener also remains objective by withholding evaluation of what is being said.

All four of these communication requirements are important to a successful interview. Learn to practice them, if you want to be a good interviewer.

Climate

Climate is the attitudes that the participants in an interview manifest toward each other. Climate influences the pattern and nature of the communication that takes place. You can probably recall a time when you had to communicate with someone whom you did not like or trust. You probably found communication difficult. On the other hand, you probably find communication easy and straightforward when you interact with a friend. It's the same in an interview. Interviewers and intervieweees who like and trust one another are likely to have pleasant exchanges.

Climate consists of: (1) the *trust* demonstrated between participants; (2) the *honesty* of one participant, as perceived by the other; (3) the *enthusiasm* demonstrated *toward one participant* by the other, as perceived by the other; (4) the *enthusiasm* demonstrated by one participant *toward* the interview *content,* as perceived by the other; and (5) the interpersonal *attraction* between the two participants.[11] These elements are present in every interview. The climate of the interview will be positive to the *extent* that they are present.

Preconditions

Like other forms of communication, the interview is influenced by what takes place before and after the exchange—that is, by preconditions and postconditions. *Preconditions* are those tasks which must be done before the interview takes place. Some of these are rather obvious.

[10]C. Kelly, "Empathic Listening," in *Small Group Communication,* eds. R. Cathcart and L. Samovar (Dubuque: William C. Brown Company, Publishers, 1974), p. 341.
[11]These attributes of climate are the same as the attributes of trust presented earlier in this chapter.

The meeting place must be arranged for; materials must be procured; the agenda must be established, and so forth. However, there are other, less apparent preconditions that are equally important. These include allaying the interviewee's fears about the nature of the interview; providing for consultations with other people who may be involved in the interview; and arranging for record keeping and note-taking. Some of the preconditions involving the psychological and emotional state of the interviewee can be more important than the physical arrangements for the interview itself.

Postconditions

Postconditions are those things which must be done after the interview has taken place. Again, some are rather obvious. Appropriate reports and recommendations must be developed. Future contacts and meetings must be arranged for when appropriate. Files and materials based on the interview must be developed. And again there are postconditions that involve the psychological well-being of the interviewee. These include making sure that the interviewee has some feeling of closure in the interview, insuring that all the interviewee's questions have been answered, and letting the interviewee know what is coming next.

As you can see, the interviewer has communication functions to fulfill both before and after the interview. If these functions are not accomplished, the interview is likely to fail.

potential trouble areas
for interviewers

Certain problems keep cropping up in interviews. Some of them are considered in this section.

Lack of Ability to Control Time

One big problem most new interviewers face is the inability to control time. In most large organizations, people do not have much time to devote to an interview. An interview scheduled for 30 minutes that runs on for two hours creates a bad image for the interviewer and shows a lack of respect for the interviewee's time. Of course, *both* participants can deliberately decide to lengthen the interview. This sometimes happens when the content is highly relevant to both participants. However, this decision should be made by both, after considering the demands of the interviewee's schedule.

It should be fairly obvious why the interviewer should be concerned with time. An interviewee who has expected to be in an interview for 20 minutes has planned the rest of his or her schedule accordingly. After the first 30 minutes or so, the interviewee, instead of concentrating on what is taking place in the interview, begins to focus on the other appointments on the schedule that are being broken. Thus, the interviewee's attention is lost. When the participants are of different status, as when, for example, a first-line supervisor is being interviewed by the plant manager, the interviewee may not have the courage to remind the interviewer that time is running short. The control of time is primarily the responsibility of the interviewer.

Lack of Progress

Sometimes an interview, whether long or short, doesn't seem to be making any progress. *Progress* may be defined as steady movement toward the goals of the interview. Progress should be one of the interviewer's primary considerations. To maintain progress, it is sometimes necessary to exercise control by directing the flow of the communication back to the content.

Lack of Rapport

Rapport is *mutual regard, as perceived by each participant.* Where there is no rapport, there is little chance that the interview will succeed. Some of the characteristics of rapport are: (1) a mutual understanding and agreement as to the purpose of the interview, (2) similarities of background or interest, (3) physical attractiveness, (4) mutual dependency, (5) compatible personalities, (6) willingness to share ideas, (7) perceptual agreement, (8) sincerity on the part of one or both participants, and (9) good listening and speaking practices.

It is difficult to say exactly what creates rapport. But it is easy to tell when rapport is not present. Developing a sense of rapport involves learning to understand and empathize with the other participants in the interview.

Lack of Appropriate Data

The usual purpose of an interview is to get some kind of data from another person. In a legal interview, the lawyer gets data from the client. In the counseling interview, the counselor gets data from the counselee. In the employment interview, the potential employer gets data from the applicant. And so on.

Sometimes this task is difficult to achieve. The interviewer may be aware of his or her responsibility to get information and yet may forget it during the course of the interview. Sometimes an interviewer will close the interview, go home to record the data, and then suddenly realize that he or she failed to obtain the right information. Getting the accurate and complete story on which to base further dialogue is crucial to the success of any interview.

some steps toward good interviewing

This chapter will end by proposing six steps toward good organizational interviewing. As you read them, you will see that they are closely related to some of the points that were raised earlier in the chapter.

1. Know what you want out of the interview. Even experienced interviewers sometimes fail to achieve the purpose of the interview. Prepare for the interview adequately by determining exactly what information you expect. You will increase your chances of success. Some highly skilled interviewers are able to "wing it" in the interview—that is, are able to survive with little preparation. However, they are the exception rather than the rule. Most of us need to plan carefully to get what we want out of an interview.

2. Know when not to use the interview. A skilled interviewer knows when not to use the interview. There are many ways of gathering and disseminating information; the interview is only one of them. Like every other channel of communication, the interview has its strengths and weaknesses. It is better for accomplishing some purposes than others. The interview is good for gathering in-depth information or attitudes from someone. It is also good for obtaining information about one's own oral communication skills. But the interview is very costly in terms of hours expended, and it requires that the interviewer be highly trained. And interview data is a laborious and time-consuming task.

In short, the interview has certain inherent limitations. It should not be used because it would be "nice to interview everyone," or because "appraisals would make our employees feel like part of the organization." The interview should be used only when the specific situation calls for it.

3. Treat the interview primarily as a communication event. To conduct good interviews, you must be skilled at interpersonal communication. You must understand the principles of good communication, such as practicing good listening, giving and receiving feedback, and using receiver-oriented approaches. Communication requires the sender to focus on the behavior and attitudes of the receiver. All of the problems you are likely to experience in the typical communication situation are present in the organizational interview.

4. Follow up each response. Many otherwise good interviewers will miss the chance to gather extra information because they neglect to *probe,* or follow up, a response. To probe successfully, the interviewer must listen carefully to what has been said and then ask the speaker to follow it up or expand on it. In doing this, the interviewer should keep the progress of the interview in mind. Good probing makes for good interviews.

5. Be flexible, but stick to the subject. The successful interviewer is flexible. The respondent must feel comfortable enough to open up and free enough to explore related areas. However, too much flexibility will send the interview off the track. Sometimes an interesting digression will help to build rapport and improve the climate of the interview, but this is unusual. The interviewer who maintains a moderate level of both control and flexibility remains free to communicate naturally while still achieving his or her purpose (see figure 4–5).

6. Be aware of your responsibility in the interview. The burden of success in the interview rests with the interviewer. It is his or her responsibility to carry the ball. Normally, when the interview fails, it will be because the interviewer has failed. The responsibilities of the interviewer are: (1) to open and close the interview, (2) to maintain adequate progress, (3) to provide adequate follow-up, (4) to ask appro-

FIGURE 4–5 Achieving flexibility

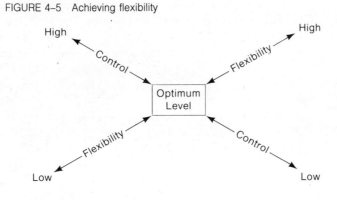

priate questions, (5) to make appropriate reports, and (6) to develop fuller success of the interview usually depends on how well the interviewer accomplishes these tasks.

FOR STUDY

1 Identify at least five specific uses of the interview in the typical organization.

2 The interview is an effective means of transferring information from superiors to subordinates. But it has a significant weakness. What is that weakness?

3 What conditions must be present for the counseling interview to be successful? Why is the rapport between the counselor and counselee so important in this form of interviewing?

4 Name some important communication principles that apply to the interview.

5 List some of the communication skills that make one a good interviewer.

6 Why do interviews fail? List some of the potential problem areas that might block the progress of an interview.

case four

The Sales Staff

David Murtaugh is the western regional sales manager for the W. C. Baker Publishing Company, located in St. Paul, Minnesota. David supervises 36 sales representatives stationed in the 11 western states. He maintains his office and home in Scottsdale, Arizona, but is often on the road supervising his staff. Their task is to market college textbooks to professors. The sales rep will visit five or six professors each day to discuss the latest Baker textbooks in each professor's area of specialization.

Since sales representatives are stationed all over the West, they have a great deal of autonomy. David makes it a point to visit each rep at least three times a year, and there are two national sales meetings, one during Christmas vacation and the other during the summer, so David gets to see each rep at least five times a year. However, it takes a great deal of individual initiative for a sales rep to function independently. David has recognized this and has planned his schedule in such a way as to meet his reps' basic needs.

Normally, David will visit each rep for two days. The first day he observes the rep's marketing technique. David will follow the rep on his or her rounds at the university, watching how the rep handles the professors and schedules the day. The two will eat meals together, and the discussions are about routine business or family matters. Usually, the two will take in a movie or ball game during the evening of the first day.

The second day of the meeting is more structured. It usually begins with rolls and coffee at 8:00 A.M. David begins by giving the rep feedback on his impressions of the rep's sales performance the previous day. He spends about an hour talking about both the strengths and weaknesses he observed. Normally, David follows up with a letter summarizing his evaluation. He mails this letter to the rep and places a copy in the rep's personnel file. After this, the two negotiate a schedule for the rest of the day. A typical schedule for one of these meetings might look like this:

10:00–10:30	Changes in incentive rates
10:30–11:00	New policies on company cars
11:00–11:45	Personnel changes at headquarters
11:45–12:00	Discussion of rep's personal problems
12:00–1:30	Informal lunch (no business discussed)
1:30–2:30	New books by Baker
2:30–3:00	New books by competitors
3:00–4:00	Relationship between sales rep and sales manager

119

| 4:00–4:30 | Sales rep's needs and expectations |
| 4:30–5:00 | Sales manager's needs and expectations |

Both David and the rep contribute to the agenda, but neither has the right to veto a particular item. The session is fairly flexible. If neither party has anything to place on the agenda, either they play tennis or golf, or David takes an earlier plane to his next meeting. However, David never schedules a meeting for the very next day. That way, he can stay an extra day with a particular rep if necessary. Normally, the session is over around 5:00 P.M., and the two end their day with a cocktail in the hotel lounge before the local rep drops David off at the airport. Sales reps have often commented among themselves that the climate of these meetings is such that they feel free to discuss anything with David.

Some interesting things have begun to happen since David instigated this program nearly four years ago. Because he has chosen to include a lot of play activities (tennis, movies), as well as work, he has built up a good interpersonal rapport with his subordinates. David has noticed that he receives many more telephone calls from reps now than he did before the program got started. They call to tell him of their successes and to ask his advice about their failures. This frequent communication has enabled David to keep in much closer contact with each subordinate. It also keeps the reps in contact with each other. One rep will tell David about techniques that have worked to sell a professor on a given book. In turn, David will pass this information on to other reps. During national sales conventions, the western group acts like a cohesive team, and it has been the most successful region in sales for the last four years. Each year, David and the three top sales reps have won a company-paid vacation to Europe or Hawaii, as the top producers in marketing. The last two times that David won the vacation, he gave it up to the youngest rep under his supervision, thus boosting morale for all of his subordinates.

The situation in the western region has been so positive over the last four years that everyone seems to like and trust everyone else. There is one cloud on the horizon, however. The national sales manager's job has just opened up in the head office. On the basis of his track record, David is the natural choice to fill it. He may leave his present position and move to St. Paul. Many of the western sales representatives have told David that although he is highly qualified for the national position, they hope he will not take it. They do not want to lose him as a manager.

FOR STUDY

1 Describe David's two-person communication style. It is obviously successful. Why?

2 What do you see as the relationship between social and professional two-person communication? When one is able to be friends with the boss, is a good working relationship probable?

3 What are some ways to build rapport in an interview? What techniques does David use?

4 What communication abilities does David demonstrate? List five words that describe David's interactions.

5 Why is David so concerned about having a written record of meetings and discussions? Based on your experience in organizations, is this necessary?

the small group:
Developing
Effective Participation

An old adage says, "Two heads are better than one." Many organizations believe in this adage. They use a process called "participative" or "democratic" decision making.[1] Participative decision making relies heavily on the small group.

the small group defined

It is common for several people who are working on similar problems in an organization to meet to analyze and solve a particular problem. The idea is that two or three people are better able to analyze the problem than one person. The next logical step would be to assume that, in general, *group* analysis is superior to individual analysis. This chapter will explore the relative merits of individual and group decision making.

The term *small group* may seem nebulous to you. In this book, a small group means a group of people in an organization—generally more than three and fewer than ten people—who choose, are delegated, or get elected to meet, to discuss, and if possible to solve, common problems. This definition has the following five implications.

1. *Groups are composed of people.* People who are members of the organization form the groups that do the work of the organization. Therefore, these groups are subject to the same failures, difficulties, and problems that all people experience in interpersonal communication. This *humanness* of groups must be recognized. It is not realistic to

[1]D. Ewing, "Who Wants Corporate Democracy?" *Harvard Business Review*, 49, no. 6 (1971), pp. 12–28.

chapter five

assume that groups, just because they are groups, will be able to accomplish significantly larger tasks than single individuals, yet many organizations make this assumption. A group is only as good as the talents, abilities, and intelligence of its members.

2. *Group members bring different degrees of commitment to group activities.* Members are often either delegated or assigned to take part in the discussions of a particular group ("Bill, I want you to represent the department on that committee"). If we are assigned to a task, especially if we do not think that the task is worthwhile, we will probably bring less motivation to the job than we would if we sincerely believed in the task and had volunteered to participate. Even in those group tasks for which *everyone* has volunteered, the levels of commitment expressed by members often vary. Generally, our level of commitment (desire to participate) is determined by our own skills and by the extent to which we identify our own individual goals with those of the group ("What will I get out of this?").

3. *Groups within the organization must operate within the existing hierarchy.* When a particular group is assigned a task in an organization, that group will take on the characteristics of and be influenced by that organization. The group that is highly valued by high-level administrators in the organization will have greater influence than one that is not highly valued. Groups that have been created to serve unimportant purposes ("Oh, there may be a problem here—let's form a committee to study it") will have little status in the hierarchy. Groups are both influencers of and influenced by the organization in which they operate.

4. *Group members share a common purpose.* One thing that sets a group apart from a simple collection of individuals is that group members share a *common purpose.* Groups have some task or mission. True, not all members will share a lively enthusiasm for the task, but the common purpose—at least in theory—binds group members together.

5. *Groups require communication.* No group can hope to accomplish its purpose unless its members can communicate. Members who refuse to share information and exchange ideas will not participate sufficiently to keep the group functioning. As communication breaks down, the group is doomed to failure.

The rest of this chapter will explore these five points. We will begin by examining the *nature* of groups in organizations. Next, we will investigate some *important group variables.* Then we will study the communication process in groups. The chapter closes with a brief philosophy about groups.

the nature of groups
in organizations

During the late 1960s and early 1970s, blue-ribbon groups were often formed to investigate grave sociological problems in the United States. Thus the Walker Commission was formed to examine civil disorder.[2] The Scranton Commission was formed to examine growing campus unrest.[3] These and many other groups like them were delegated to study a particular problem for a short period of time. The group was expected to come together to establish ground rules, study the problem, make recommendations about it, and then disband. In some cases, the federal bureaucracy implemented the recommendations of these groups. In other cases, their recommendations were ignored. These groups were called *task forces.* The task force is one of many models that are currently being used in organizations. Sometimes the task force is called the "ad hoc committee" or the "special committee" or the "emergency committee." But whatever the title, the task and the procedures are much the same.

Organizations also contain more established groups. For example, the vice-president of personnel who meets regularly with the director of equal opportunity, the director of industrial relations, the director of wage and benefits, and the director of training and development can be said to be holding a *hierarchical group meeting.* These hierarchical groups are normally specified by the organizational chart and are said to be *formal.*[4]

Formal Groups

The typical organization has many formal groups. Each boss who meets with his or her subordinates is creating a formal group. When the president of the organization calls in the vice-presidents, this is a formal group. When the first-line supervisor meets with his or her workers, this is also a formal group. Not all formal groups are hierarchical. Occasionally, people of similar rank in an organization (all the vice-presidents, all the sales staff) will meet to consider common problems. These would also be formal groups, because in these meetings, an individual participates as a representative of his or her own position in the organization.

[2]D. Walker, *Rights in Conflict* (Chicago: National Commission on the Causes and Prevention of Violence, 1968).

[3]W. Scranton, *U.S. President's Commission on Campus Unrest* (Washington, D.C.: U.S. Government Printing Office, 1970).

[4]A. Sanford, *Human Relations Theory and Practice,* 2nd ed. (Columbus, Ohio: Charles E. Merrill Publishing Company, 1977), p. 146.

Formal groups do the work of the organization. Such titles as "executive committees," "cabinet," or "directors" are often used to describe formal groups.

Within formal groups, communication is often prescribed by the nature of the session. For example, if a group of first-line foremen are meeting with the plant supervisor to consider a recent downswing in production, the tone of the meeting is likely to be somber. If a group of first-grade teachers at Wilson Elementary meet regularly to discuss their mutual interests over coffee, the meeting will probably be a cheerful one.

To create a climate that will encourage upward communication, organizations sometimes have administrators meet with people from various levels on the organizational chart. These meetings are called *diagonal.* The president of a major midwestern university has breakfast with a group of five freshmen every Wednesday morning. The purpose of this breakfast is to encourage the freshmen to tell the president what is on their minds. The chief of police in a big western city meets twice a month with three or four patrolmen, bypassing all departmental sergeants, lieutenants, and deputy chiefs. Diagonal meetings can be an effective means of passing information quickly from the bottom of the hierarchy to the top. However, they pose some special problems. Quite naturally, the person who is bypassed may think that the session has been held to keep information from him or her. In such cases, feelings, and even productivity, may be damaged.

To summarize: formal groups are important to the organization because they carry out many of its tasks. These formal groups are specified by the organizational chart. They are the official meeting groups of the organization. Formal groups depend on good communication, as we shall see. First, however, let us learn something about informal groups.

Informal Groups

The *informal group* consists of members of an organization who meet together by choice.[5] These groups have most of the qualities that make groups pleasant. People join informal groups in the organization for three reasons:

1. To facilitate social interaction.
2. To gain additional information about the organization, and
3. Because their own goals are linked to those of the informal group.

[5]See Sanford, *Human Relations,* pp. 231–47, for a complete discussion of the role of informal groups in organizations.

The following section considers these reasons in detail. It also offers examples of important types of informal groups.

SOCIAL INTERACTION Mary, Dale, and Jon are urban planners for a large city. Usually, they eat lunch together in the courtyard of their building. Since they are also avid tennis players, they often join Della, a file clerk in the purchasing department, to play mixed doubles after work. Sometimes, after the tennis match, the four go out for dinner.

This is a typical example of an informal group. The members of the group work together, but they also like to spend time with each other socially. Because most people spend at least 30 percent of their time at their jobs, they often develop highly personal relationships with their co-workers.

Social interaction is informal, often highly spontaneous, communication among people.[6] Social interaction is fun. It makes the day go faster and gives one's job an added appeal that is not provided by the task or formal groups to which one belongs.

Since the purpose of many informal groups is to facilitate social interaction generally *unrelated* to the job, there tend to be wide status differences among members. For example, in one organization an informal group meets regularly on Friday evening for poker. It consists of two vice-presidents, a middle-level manager, and two longtime hourly plant employees. In the daily routine of the organization, it would be highly unlikely for the vice-presidents to be in a formal group with an hourly worker. Yet they meet together informally each Friday night without giving the status difference a second thought. It is almost inconceivable that work-related matters are not discussed in these poker sessions. This communication gives each of the poker players access to information that he normally would not have. When the poker players go back to work, this information will probably be transmitted to their peers. This transmission will take the form of rumors. Many rumors begin when people repeat things in the organization that they have heard in informal groups.

People join informal groups for a wide variety of reasons. One important reason is that people like to chat with their friends.

ADDITIONAL INFORMATION Susan Chandler works as a computer programmer for a large data processing firm. Her job requires her to be familiar with many new and unique programs. However, Susan's immediate superior has been doing so much travelling lately that he has not

[6]W. Brooks, *Speech Communication,* 3rd ed. (Dubuque: William C. Brown Company, Publishers, 1978), p. 24.

had time to train Susan in the new uses of the computer. Susan, feeling herself falling behind, has begun to go on break with some of the senior programmers. Over coffee, she often asks her senior colleagues about new computer approaches and techniques.

Susan has been forced to join a particular informal group to gain job-related information that should have been transmitted to her through the routine channels. People will often join informal groups for this purpose when the official channels of communication are inadequate. The communication generated in the informal groups will supplement (or even supplant) the information that comes through official channels. When the "word" is not forthcoming, sometimes the "word" is manufactured by informal groups. This is normal and generally harmless.[7] It is sometimes called learning things through the grapevine. The grapevine is a *communication network among members of informal groups.* There is one in every organization.

The content of the grapevine is often an indicator of the level of satisfaction among employees. It also measures the adequacy of the formal network of communication. For example, an employee keeps hearing rumors that workers are going to be laid off because the organization has not shown a profit lately. Actually, however, the firm is doing well. The persistence of these rumors suggests that the organization has not done a good job of keeping its employees informed about its financial status. When this kind of misinformation is transmitted via the grapevine, it usually indicates some kind of morale or other human problem.

Sometimes the grapevine transmits personal or highly interesting information that is entirely unrelated to the job. For example, we may hear via the grapevine that our boss has just separated from his wife. This kind of rumor is fairly typical. If we hear *only* this kind of personal or personality-centered information on the grapevine, we can assume that the formal channels of task-related communication are functioning adequately. We cannot tell whether the grapevine is doing what the formal channels should be doing until we have examined the *content* of the grapevine.

OVERLAPPING GOALS   Sylvia Thompson works for Organization X. Sylvia likes athletics very much. She enjoys feeling that she is in good physical shape. About eight months ago, Organization X built a gymnasium for its employees. Unfortunately, the administrators decided to allow female employees to use the gym only two hours a day—one hour

---

[7]K. Davis, *Human Behavior at Work,* 4th ed. (New York: McGraw-Hill Book Company, 1972), pp. 171–73.

before and one hour after work periods. Male employees were free to use the gym any time they liked, as long as they were not taking time away from pressing work. Sylvia has joined with some other female employees in an informal group to protest this discriminatory policy.

This example illustrates the third reason why people join informal groups—because their own personal goals coincide with those of the group. Bowlers join company bowling leagues. Would-be athletes play on the softball team. The ambitious join the management club. The religious meet for Bible study. In each case, people decide to congregate together because they share common goals.

Informal groups can be functional, dysfunctional or irrelevant to the success of the organization. Their contribution will depend on their members' attitudes. When the group is organized to accomplish universally accepted goals (e.g., collecting money for the United Way, determining the role of women and minorities in the organization, planning a Christmas party), it contributes a great deal to the organization. Often informal groups can create a sense of esprit de corps for the organization that cannot be obtained in any other way. Informal groups that are created to oppose the organization on some issue (e.g., to protest the firing of a popular worker, to "get" a domineering supervisor) obviously can cause a lot of damage.

characteristics of important groups

Whether the group is formal or informal, it is characterized by certain variables. Each variable operates in both formal and informal groups.

Objectives

All groups have objectives. *Objectives* might be defined as *the goals of the group.* In the formal group, the goals may be highly specific. Often they are written down. A member can go to a rule book or manual to read what is expected of such a group. The duties of the individual members of the group may also be specified. In some groups, this statement of goals is referred to as the *charge.* The elements of the charge that are normally developed for formal groups include:

- *Expectations:* what the organization or the sponsoring agency expects of the group.
- *Areas of Responsibility:* the duties of the group—both what it should and what it should not do.

- *Criteria for Membership:* who may be part of the group and who may not.
- *Interrelations with Other Groups:* mandated relationships with other groups.
- *Reporting of Relationships:* groups, like individuals in the organization, are supervised. Normally, the line of this supervision is part of the charge of the group.

In organizations, the objectives of highly formal groups are precise. This precision enables members to learn and adapt to the group's requirements rapidly, without disrupting the life of the organization.

The objectives of informal groups are usually much more difficult to define. In some informal groups, they are hidden. The following example shows how objectives change as a formal group becomes less formal.

At one university, a group of faculty members were assigned by the dean to meet together each month to draw up standards for awarding scholarships. At the end of the committee's deliberations, the objective of the group was met. The committee presented the dean with the list of recommendations. During the process, some of the members of the committee discovered that they had a lot in common. Now each Friday afternoon they meet at the faculty club to discuss the latest book or film. The objectives of the informal group are not precise. Its composition changes from one Friday to the next. No minutes are kept. Yet the members continue to meet. If asked to define the objectives of their group, they would have to say something like: "to meet together and share ideas."

As this example demonstrates, formal groups can change into informal ones. When this happens, the two groups' objectives may also change. The objectives of the formal group are met during informal time. One leading organizational theorist has suggested that this benefits the organization and should be encouraged.[8]

In any group, not all of the members will accept the statement of the group's objectives—or more importantly, work for them—with equal enthusiasm. Of course, to spend time working toward a group's objectives, we must see their relevance to our own development. If we join a group that advocates a cause we believe in deeply, we will probably work hard in the group as long as we continue to believe in the cause. In an organization, however, people are often asked to join committees, task forces, or groups without knowing or necessarily agreeing with their purpose. When we are *forced* to join a work group, we feel differently about its objectives than when we choose to join. Ideally, all

[8]R. Likert, *The Human Organization* (New York: McGraw-Hill Book Company, 1967), p. 252.

members should feel highly committed to the group's objectives. But in practice, certain *adjustments* must be made. We usually cooperate with the group as long as we see cooperation as part of our job.

Commitment to the objectives of informal groups will vary with the situation in which members find themselves. If you play on the company softball team, your commitment to its objectives will probably depend on how the team is doing, how much you want to stay in shape, how badly you need a night out on the town after the game, or how pressured you feel in your regular job.

The following five steps may be used to resolve the problems associated with conflicting perceptions of group objectives among members:

1. *Make sure that all members can articulate the group's purpose satisfactorily in their own words.* Many members simply go along with the group without ever really understanding its objectives. Early in the creation of a new group, or when new members come into an existing group, members should state the group's objectives. To insure that this activity remains nonthreatening, it should be approached as a learning experience for everyone.

2. *The group should continually strive to attain and modify its objectives.* The group that has already achieved its original objectives and has not modified them has no reason to exist. Discussions based on the questions "Where are we?" "Are we making progress?" "How can we get to where we want to go?" should be part of every group's deliberations. The glossing over of serious failures to achieve the group's objectives can only lead to more serious problems. The process of taking stock is vital to a group's success.

3. *If people are having trouble with some of the group's objectives, the difficulty should be expressed openly.* The most appropriate time to face a lack of commitment to objectives is when it first presents itself. When one member cannot go along, he or she should not be criticized but encouraged to explain why. Then the rest of the group should discuss the member's reasons.

4. *Conflict over objectives is to be expected; it should be perceived as positive.* Conflict over objectives is inevitable. It should be viewed as a way to clarify and deal with aspects of group communication, not as a source of discord. Successful groups deal openly with this kind of conflict. Members who hide their frustration and ambiguity about the group's objectives seldom contribute much to the group anyway. Thus, frank discussion of disagreements can do little to impair the effectiveness of the group and may be used to unify it. Of course, this requires a climate that encourages the frank discussion of disagreement. A member who is willing to take a risk and share his uneasiness with the group,

only to be attacked by the other members, will probably never take that risk again. In fact, he may very well never contribute anything further.

5. *It is unrealistic to expect every member to contribute equally to the progress of the group.* In any group there are going to be people who cannot devote themselves totally to the group's progress. As long as everyone is willing to accept this inequality, there is no serious problem. If other members will not accept the inequality, they must counsel the noncontributing member. If this does not work, the group must make some hard choices. It can (1) use more stringent measures to involve the member, (2) reassess its ability to carry on in spite of the member, or (3) find a diplomatic way to remove the member. Spotty participation should not be viewed as a failure on the part of the group, but rather as a challenge.

Norms

All groups routinely establish codes and rules that enable them to operate effectively. These codes and rules are called *group norms.* Groups in organizations usually determine their own ways of rewarding and reinforcing adherence to norms. They also have ways of punishing failure to respect norms. The following example shows how group norms operate.

The elementary teachers at Walnut Street School have met for the last month to revise the social studies curriculum. Normally the group meets for two hours after school on Tuesday. The first three meetings were successful, and most group members reported a good deal of progress. But in the fourth meeting a problem arose: Les and Donna left the meeting early, without saying anything to anyone. In last night's meeting, Les and Donna again started to leave. This time, Seth, the building lead teacher, asked them in front of the group to explain their behavior.

By calling attention to their leaving, Seth was attempting to embarrass, or punish, Les and Donna. He felt they were violating the norms of the group. In the brief history of the social studies group at Walnut Street School, probably no one had ever written down the *official* meeting schedule and norms. However, each teacher was well aware of both. When group norms are violated, members will often react directly.

Norms are equally important to informal groups. Informal groups have rules, usually loose, rarely written down, but rules nonetheless. Consider a group of police sergeants who meet regularly after work for a friendly game of tennis. The norms of the group are such that rarely will a player try to slam the ball, because the group likes games that feature long rallies. When a player occasionally forgets and comes to the net to slam an opponent's soft volley, his kill shot is immediately met with jeers. If the catcalls and jeers do not work, the group may soon be looking for a less aggressive player to take the slammer's place.

Communication problems involving norms often arise in groups. If a group member is unaware of the norms or does not know how they are applied, he or she may violate them inadvertently. While it is not uncommon for a group to train a new member in the most obvious rules that govern the group, rarely will the same group orient a new member in its subtle customs and techniques. The new member may learn about these subtleties only through trial and error.

Structure

Structures are hierarchical relationships and working arrangements that have been imposed on the group, either by the group itself or by others. They enable the group to coordinate the activities of its members. The most obvious structure is the unique status hierarchy that operates in the group. This hierarchy defines the tasks that each member must accomplish in order for the group to achieve its goal. Certain tasks, such as exerting leadership or contributing to the progress of the group by proposing useful ideas, are normally associated with high status. Other tasks, such as recording or listening, are not associated with high status.

Other structures also operate within the group. For example, the way in which the group uses time or assigns responsibility may be structures. Rigid structures sometimes limit flexibility. Some research suggests that groups with loose structures—those which offer members a good deal of flexibility and freedom—will develop spontaneous and fulfilling interpersonal relationships.[9]

Many organizational groups have two structures—one imposed by the organization and one that the group has developed for itself. This kind of group is really trying to serve two masters—itself and the organization. Probably it will generate some kind of operating philosophy that will enable it to function within both structures.

Consider the example of the task force formed by Organization X. The task force's goal is to develop a new method of appraising employees. The organization mandates that the highest ranking manager will chair all interdepartmental committees and groups. This is an orga-

[9]N. Frederiksen, "Administrative Performance in Relation to Organizational Climate" (paper presented at annual meeting of the American Psychological Association, 1966, San Francisco).

nizational structural requirement. However, in the task force on appraisal, the highest ranking manager is the supervisor of the research and development department. This supervisor knows absolutely nothing about leading meetings or conducting appraisals. In order to get the job done, the task force must generate its own leadership structure. As it does so, while maintaining its titular head, the group begins to merge the various structure requirements.

Structure has three important implications for communication. First, a group should be aware of its own structures and know how they were established. Groups often get so wrapped up in the task under consideration that they lose sight of the rules under which they operate. Second, the group must learn to recognize which structures it can change and which it cannot. Often groups in organizations must play with the hand they have been dealt. Certain structures are mandated and must be followed, like it or not. The group that continually and intentionally violates mandated structures is simply digging its own grave. But occasionally a group will continue to operate within an unworkable structure that could be changed. A group that can change an unworkable structure should do so, rather than accept it passively. Third, to change an unworkable structure, the group must be flexible. This usually becomes necessary when the group task moves from one stage to the next. Early in the deliberations of most task groups, the participation structure must be such as to encourage many ideas, because at this stage the group must generate as much material as possible for consideration. But as the group moves on to make choices based on this material, the loose and free-flowing participation structure may become unworkable. If the group continues to allow anyone to express any random idea, it will never get anywhere. It must develop new, workable structures.

Performance Standards

Every organizational group has certain productivity requirements. These productivity requirements can be used to judge whether or not the group is successful. *The group's attempts to achieve its productivity requirements constitute its performance.*

Performance is measured in different ways, depending on the situation and the particular group and also on who is doing the measuring. Some groups, especially informal ones, will tend to measure their own performance, using their own standards. The performance of formal groups is usually measured by the organization or sponsoring unit. Occasionally, the standards of a group will be different from the standards of the organization. This difference can create conflicts.

WAYS OF MEASURING PERFORMANCE The most obvious measure of performance is *objective*. Success is determined by the existence of a particular object. (The group was successful because it produced the desired report). The existence of the object is an outward manifestation of the group's success. It does not say anything about the quality of the deliberations that went on inside the group. Often an organization that commissions a group to perform a task will judge the group's success solely on the basis of whether it has accomplished that task. This type of performance standard is easy to apply. Either they have done it or they have not.

Another, more subtle measure of performance is *subjective*. This measure is often applied by the group to itself. The characteristics judged by subjective standards are not always easily quantifiable. They include such variables as the extent to which the members develop through discussions, the extent to which their sensitivity increases, their respect for each other, and the extent to which their communication skills increase as a result of group deliberations. The measurement of these characteristics is usually left up to the group members themselves.

Outside pressures, such as organizational requirements, have little to do with the achievement of subjective success. A group may be judged successful by some objective criterion ("They finished the report on time") and yet may judge itself a failure using its own subjective criteria ("We wound up with nobody speaking to anybody else"). Group productivity is usually the result of some combination of objective and subjective factors—of task accomplishment combined with member satisfaction.

Some groups, often informal ones, measure their own productivity simply by whether they stay in existence. Examples are the "Friday afternoon at the local pub" group or "the fun for lunch bunch." The measure of productivity in these instances is rarely little more than whether the members continue to attend group meetings. As the members stop attending, obviously the group will cease to exist.

COMMUNICATION AND PERFORMANCE Communication helps the group to meet its performance standards. First, of course, members must be aware of these standards. Awareness in itself will not produce high performance, but members will be more likely to work hard for a goal if they know what both the organization's and their fellow members' standards are. In the best of all possible worlds (which rarely exists), the group members' own standards of success are exactly the same as the standards imposed on the group by the organization. When group members are working toward targets they consider important and when the organization also considers these targets to be the standards for the group, performance should be high.

Consider the following example. The executive committee of a large organization is responsible for the supervision of a national sales staff. The standards of the organization require contact between the executive committee and each salesperson at least once a week. Through discussion and consultation, members of the executive committee have also agreed that this is a fair standard and one they would establish for themselves, given the opportunity. In this example, performance is high when the weekly contact is made. The group's standards and the organization's standards are the same. Performance should be high, all other things being equal.

Member Satisfaction

Member satisfaction occurs when the activities and interactions of the group fulfill the expectations of the individual members. Member satisfaction is valuable in and of itself—it is better to have a happy group than an unhappy one. Some groups, especially informal and self-help groups (e.g., sensitivity and T-groups) seek member satisfaction as an end in itself.

Member satisfaction does not necessarily make for a productive group. Some researchers have suggested that it is, rather, productivity that creates member satisfaction.[10] It may well be that certain satisfaction variables, such as cohesiveness and communication satisfaction, are related to certain productivity dimensions, while others, such as leadership satisfaction, are not.[11] The relationship between productivity and member satisfaction is complex. Figure 5–1 illustrates some of the important variables and the ways in which they are related.

Six variables contribute to member satisfaction. The individual member will be either satisfied or dissatisfied with each of these variables. The member's goals and the group's goals must also correspond. The member must achieve something that he or she wants when the

---

[10]V. Vroom, *Work and Motivation* (New York: John Wiley & Sons, Inc., 1964), p. 13; Vroom, "Industrial Social Psychology," in *The Handbook of Social Psychology*, eds. G. Lindzey and E. Aronson (Reading, Mass.: Addison-Wesley Publishing Co., 1968), IV, 196–268; E. Lawler and L. Porter, "Antecedent Job Attitudes of Effective Managerial Performance," *Organizational Behavior and Human Performance*, 2, no. 2 (1967), 139–55.

[11]C. Lee, "An Experimental Study of Organizational Climate" (unpublished Master's thesis, Ohio State University, 1975); G. Hunt and C. Lee, "Organizational Climate: A Laboratory Approach" (paper presented at annual meeting of the International Communication Association, 1976, in Portland); G. Hunt and C. Lee, "The Effects of Leadership Style on Group Performance and Member Satisfaction" (paper presented at annual meeting of the Western Speech Communication Association, 1976, in San Francisco).

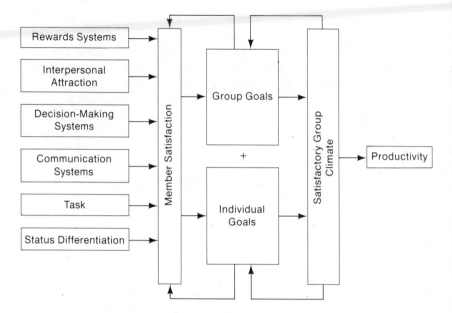

FIGURE 5–1   Model of group productivity and member satisfaction

group achieves something that it wants. Finally, the group climate must be conducive to free and mutually satisfying interaction. When all of these conditions are met, (1) there is general satisfaction with each of the six variables, (2) there is a high level of member satisfaction, (3) there is a matching of individual and group goals, (4) the climate of the group is conducive to free communication, and (5) as a result, there is a high level of group productivity.

The following sections examine each of the variables that contribute to member satisfaction.

REWARD SYSTEM   The reward system deals with the ways in which behavior is rewarded and punished by the group. Does the group reward its members fairly? Are punishments handed out equitably? Do all members participate equally in establishing and implementing the reward system? If the answer in each case is "yes," members will probably be satisfied with the reward system.

INTERPERSONAL ATTRACTION   Group members who report that they *like* each other are manifesting a high degree of *interpersonal attraction*. It is natural to prefer to work with people whom we like. Group members will tend to be satisfied when they like each other.

136

DECISION-MAKING SYSTEMS Most people prefer to belong to groups that allow them to participate in group decisions.[12] If all group decisions are made without consulting a particular member, we would expect that member to become disenchanted. A disenchanted group member may withdraw from the activities of the group.

COMMUNICATION SYSTEMS Most people prefer to belong to groups that tend to diffuse the pattern of participation throughout the group.[13] Patterns that allow many face-to-face interactions encourage members to express opinions in a low-threat environment.[14] Each member should have an opportunity to take part in the flow of communication.

TASK The appropriateness of a particular task depends on the preferences of the individual members of the group. Most of us feel comfortable when we think that we can accomplish a particular job. Certain people will prefer highly regimented tasks, while others will prefer loosely structured ones. Fred Fiedler has suggested that particular types of tasks are related to particular leadership styles.[15] His research indicates that in a highly structured group, tasks that call for a little individual initiative are best led by people who practice autocratic leadership styles. Tasks that require a great deal of initiative are best led by those who practice democratic leadership styles.

STATUS DIFFERENTIATION In most groups, the important roles—giving ideas, providing direction, encouraging participation—should be widely diffused among members.[16] These are high-status roles. Some researchers have found that the more often an individual plays a high-status role, the more satisfied he or she becomes.[17] Generally, in better groups many members play high-status roles.

Patterns of Communication

Earlier in was suggested that there must be a pattern of communication in the small group that encourages face-to-face interactions among members. In the best groups, members will be willing to share

[12]Vroom, "Industrial Social Psychology," p. 201.
[13]A. Lowin, "Participative Decision-Making: A Model, Literature Critique, and Prescriptions for Research," *Organizational Behavior and Human Performance*, 3, no. 1 (1968), 68–106.
[14]J. Gibb, "Defensive Communication," *Journal of Communication*, 11, no. 2 (1961), 141–48.
[15]F. Fiedler, *A Theory of Leadership Effectiveness* (New York: McGraw-Hill Book Company, 1967), p. 116.
[16]K. Benne and P. Sheats, "Functional Roles of Group Members," *Journal of Social Issues*, 4, no. 1 (1948), 41–49.
[17]H. Leavitt, *Managerial Psychology*, 3rd ed. (Chicago: University of Chicago Press, 1972), p. 67.

information and ideas with each other. This sharing often contributes to coordination among members, and to the development of common bonds that enable groups to generate a strong working relationship. Communication becomes the framework that holds the group together.

Harold Leavitt and Harold Guetzkow have done classic studies on the flow of information within organizations.[18] A review some of their major findings may help you to understand group interaction. This research assumes that certain members of a group fall into patterns of interaction called *communication networks.* We may think of a communication network as a schematic diagram that charts the interaction among members. Not all of the members are equally "plugged into" a particular network. The network theorists believe that a subunit may develop to carry on the most important decision making and influence the group's activities to the exclusion of the rest of the members.

Let us examine some of the standard networks that have been developed through laboratory research.

CHAIN NETWORK   In the chain network, each member depends on the person next to him or her for task-related communication (see figure 5–2). Since there is limited coordination or perception of interrelationship among members, it is sometimes very difficult for them to get the job done, because they lack a sense of mutual dependency. Since group members have only a partial idea of the overall structure of the group and a personal communication relationship with only one or two other members, member satisfaction tends to be low.

FIGURE 5–2   Chain communication network

Y NETWORK   Some of the problems posed by the chain appear to be solved with the Y communication network (see figure 5–3). In the Y network, two people in the middle help to coordinate and pass along information to those on the outside. The Y is better suited to the accomplishment of tasks, because information can flow in a number of directions. What normally happens in the Y is that the members who begin to assume central or coordinating functions immediately feel more

[18]H. Guetzkow, "Communication in Organizations," in *Handbook of Organizations,* ed. J. March (Chicago: Rand McNally & Co., 1965); Leavitt, *Managerial Psychology,* pp. 269–331.

satisfaction. The rest of the members, however, remain less satisfied. The Y is very common in groups where one or two members are willing to step in and assume responsibility for the task.

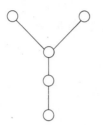

FIGURE 5–3   Y communication network

CIRCLE NETWORK   The circle (see figure 5–4) reduces some of the satisfaction problems posed by the Y network, but it poses some other problems of its own. In the circle, most of the status differences present in the other networks are eradicated. People seem to have relatively equal status. However, some task responsibilities are not met, because no one can assume strong, central coordination and facilitation functions.

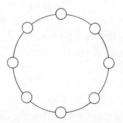

FIGURE 5–4   Circle communication network

ALL-CHANNEL NETWORK   The networks already considered have certain advantages and disadvantages in terms of productivity and member satisfaction. Most experts in small groups recommend a communication network that looks like figure 5–5.[19] This is called the

[19]J. Brilhart, *Effective Group Discussion*, 2nd ed. (Dubuque: William C. Brown Company, Publishers, 1974), pp. 46–47; A. Fisher, *Small Group Decision-Making: Communications and the Group Process* (New York: McGraw-Hill Book Company, 1974), pp. 119–20.

all-channel network, because all members have equal access to the information being transferred.

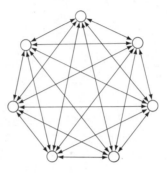

FIGURE 5–5   All-channel communication network

In theory, under the all-channel network, all members have a face-to-face communication relationship with each other. Since the all-channel network assumes that all members have equal status, there should be a systematic movement on the part of the group members to assume the responsibilities for task accomplishment and maintenance of the group. Coordination and integration are possible because each member has a face-to-face relationship with every other member. Hurt feelings and negative attitudes are reduced, because each member is able to see and be motivated by the group task.

The reader should approach the all-channel network with reservations. *It is not as good as it sounds.* Under ideal conditions, the all-channel network will do most of the things suggested above. But the all-channel network will operate effectively only if all the members like and trust each other, if none of them aspires strongly to leadership, and if they are all enthusiastic about the task. This set of conditions occurs seldom.

Members should be aware of the patterns of communication in a group. However, they should not assume that they can preestablish a communication network. The network results from routine interaction among members. Often it is outside their control. Group members can, however, become sensitive to the emergence of the network, as they see themselves interacting and reacting. Once rigidly established, these networks are difficult to change.

Leadership Styles

Every group has an influence pattern that provides the structure of the leadership.[20] This is called the *leadership style.* The leadership style is a product of the ways in which members influence each other toward the common goal. Since leadership will be considered extensively in the next chapter, it will be examined here only briefly as an important determinant of group success.

Group leadership styles may be classified on a continuum running from highly authoritarian to highly participatory. In a highly authoritarian leadership style, one or two members do all of the influencing and are rarely influenced by others. The group is dominated, often with the permission and the support of the other members, by one or two people. For certain types of tasks, such as those which are highly structured and must be accomplished rapidly, the authoritarian style may work very well. People who study and write about small groups argue that participatory styles are *always* preferable to authoritarian styles. This is, at best, an oversimplification. The best style is probably a product of the individual members' attitudes and the requirements of the task.

In the participatory styles, the group members themselves act as leaders. Each member, or at least a majority of members, participates in influencing the group. As members exert influence, they are also influenced by other members. Influence, then, becomes a give-and-take process that is negotiated among members. The underlying assumption of the participatory styles is that all of the members have an equal stake in the activities and purposes of the group. Since all members have helped to determine these activities and purposes, they should be willing to work hard to implement the decisions they have just made.[21]

Interaction with Other Groups

Any group in an organization must necessarily maintain close working relationships with other groups in the same organization. Since most organizations are composed of *groups of groups,*[22] intergroup interaction is one of the most important forms of organizational communication. Normally groups charged with a particular mission in an organization will have as part of their mission the responsibility of

[20]A. Sanford, G. Hunt, and H. Bracey, *Communication Behavior in Organizations* (Columbus, Ohio: Charles E. Merrill Publishing Company, 1976), p. 130.
[21]Vroom, "Industrial Social Psychology," p. 211.
[22]Leavitt, *Managerial Psychology,* p. 69.

keeping other groups informed of their activities and decisions. This is necessary because each group in the organization will be, at least to some extent, influenced by the decisions made by every other group. To paraphrase John Donne, "No group in an organization is an island." Good groups will consider the consequences of their actions to others before they make decisions.

Sometimes petty jealousies and conflicts will enter the deliberations of the group. These conflicts must be faced.[23] Sometimes there are fights over status. Other times, there are fights over the "turf" involving a particular issue. One group may believe that it is responsible for a given area, while another group feels that the area falls within its jurisdiction. Consider the following example, which occurred in a large manufacturing organization.

One morning, the foreman of the day shift discovered a breakdown in the production line. Apparently one of the men on the night shift had deliberately destroyed a crucial part in an important machine after an argument with his foreman. The director of manufacturing and the plant superintendent stepped in immediately. They saw the breakdown as a manufacturing problem, and they both believed that they should handle the investigation of the incident. However, the personnel manager saw the breakdown as a personnel problem. He notified the union president, and they both came back into the shop to take charge of the investigation. When the director of security was told what had happened, he, too, charged into the shop. He saw the breakdown as a security problem.

In fact, all of the managers were right. Each had a stake in the outcome of the problem. In a highly charged, emotional meeting, after two hours of heated discussion, the personnel manager was selected to head the investigation, but he was instructed to make regular reports to the others involved. This conflict among the various groups was solved through compromise. Compromise is not always so easily achieved, however, when reputations and tempers are on the line.

The important thing to remember about intergroup conflict is that every group has duties and obligations, and sometimes these duties begin to constrain the duties of other groups. Perceptive groups establish and maintain strong communication links with each other. In this way, they make sure that jurisdictional disputes are recognized and resolved before they go too far.

[23]A. Filley, *Interpersonal Conflict Resolution* (Glenview, Ill.: Scott, Foresman & Company, 1975), p. 46.

common causes of failure
in small groups

All groups experience failures in communication. These normally fall into three categories: participation failures, task failures, and motivational failures.

Participation Failures

Unless members are willing to participate, it is difficult for the group to accomplish its task. Six kinds of participation failures plague groups.[24]

1. *Feeling that my contribution is not needed.* People who must often work in groups are quick to agree that everyone's contribution is important. This is a token acceptance of the concept of democratic decision making. But occasionally the idea of widespread participation gets lost. People who do not see themselves as integral to the group may hesitate to contribute. "The group can manage just fine without me—there's no reason for me to participate," they say. One of the early ideas that emerged from small group research is that encouraging members to contribute is everyone's responsiblity.[25] We can say things like, "Bill, what do you think of this?" or "Sally, looks in deep thought. Let's hear her comments about the proposal." Orientation of new members, perceptive observation, and an open, trusting communication climate will enable groups to overcome this participation failure.

2. *Feeling that my status is too low to enable me to participate.* Occasionally, groups are made up of people on different hierarchical levels. A vice-president may find himself or herself seated next to a first-line supervisor. It would take a very self-assured first-line supervisor to participate freely under these conditions. The problem of status is intensified when we are forced to participate in a group with our boss and our boss's boss. Since our boss has direct power over our very existence, we may feel unwilling to open up. The problem is only solved when people of high status choose to reduce status differences, verbally or nonverbally. Such techniques as having group members call each

[24]This list is modified from the one originally developed in D. Barnlund and F. Haiman, *The Dynamics of Discussion* (Boston: Houghton Mifflin Company, 1960). Other books on small group communication have presented others that have the same basic theme.
[25]Benne and Sheats, "Functional Roles," p. 42; R. Bales and R. Strodtbeck, *Interaction Process Analysis: A Method for the Study of Small Groups* (Reading, Mass.: Addison-Wesley Publishing Co., Inc., 1950), p. 12.

other by their first names and arranging the seating to encourage equality may be cosmetic approaches, but sometimes they help.

3. *Feeling that my communication skills are inadequate.* Sometimes people do not participate in group discussions because they have no faith in their communication skills. They say things like, "I'll make a fool of myself," "I stammer when I talk in a group," "I have a girlish voice and the other people will laugh if I speak up." This problem is intensified when one or two members are particularly articulate. It can be solved if the group will devalue message-sending skills (the way someone sounds) and emphasize the understanding of ideas and concepts. Sometimes the important factor is not the initiation of an idea, but the skills used to refine and apply the idea. Members should be made aware of the skills involved in analysis and integration as well in initiation. When one group member is particularly quiet, it may be necessary to reinforce that member's participation when he or she does choose to participate.

4. *Feeling that it is not appropriate to participate.* People who do not feel that they are legitimate members of a group may be uncomfortable about participating. Groups sometimes send delegates to monitor the meetings of other groups. These people will remain outsiders unless efforts are made to assure them that their comments are valued. Group membership requirements, be they explicit or implied, should be such that they do not exclude good ideas generated by nonmembers. But we should be willing to risk participation if we have a worthwhile contribution to make. This participation problem often manifests itself in groups where a boss is meeting with subordinates. Under these conditions, a member may never be sure if it is appropriate to participate. Some research suggests that the wider the participation is in a group, the more productive the group will be.[26] This is a strong argument for widespread participation.

5. *Feeling uncomfortable with the climate in the group.* The climate of an organization is created by the members' attitudes about that organization.[27] As organizations have climates, so do groups. The climate of a group might be defined as the predispositions and assumptions members have toward one another and toward the task. This climate becomes the attitudinal environment in which all of the group's discussions take place. It will influence everything that happens in the group. Group climates range from defensive, when members do not feel free to contribute ideas or suggestions, to *supportive,* when mem-

[26]D. Potter and M. Andersen, *Discussion: A Guide to Effective Practice* (Belmont, Calif.: Wadsworth Publishing Co., Inc., 1970).

[27]L. James and A. Jones, "Organizational Climate: A Review of Theory and Research," *Psychological Bulletin,* 81, no. 12 (1974), 1096–1112.

bers are able to communicate openly about their ideas and contributions. After analyzing many counseling groups, Gibb developed the following paradigm:[28]

DEFENSIVE CLIMATES	SUPPORTIVE CLIMATES
1 Evaluation	1 Description
2 Control	2 Problem Orientation
3 Strategy	3 Spontaneity
4 Neutrality	4 Empathy
5 Superiority	5 Equality
6 Certainty	6 Provisionalism

Members of supportive groups interact more often and with better results than do members of defensive groups. A supportive climate will sometimes mediate the flow of communication.[29] The best climate for any group is one in which most of the members feel fairly comfortable with each other and fairly relaxed about contributing.

6. *Feeling that my contribution will not be appreciated.* Everyone wants to be approved of. In groups that reward good member participation, members are likely to participate actively. In groups that do not encourage or reward participation, the participation rate will be lower. We will participate when we feel that our input is important to the group's progress—and that the group recognizes its importance.

Task Failures

Earlier in this chapter, it was suggested that each group has an objective—a particular task that it must do. When the group does not accomplish its objective, it suffers a *task failure.* Sometimes task failures are caused by outside problems (e.g., problems in leadership, motivation, or participation). Other times, they are caused by problems associated with the task itself. This section will investigate two areas that contribute to many task failures—task ambiguity and limited resources.

TASK AMBIGUITY Often groups fail to achieve their task because members do not know what is expected of them. In the typical organization, groups often receive such nebulous assignments as "investigate a problem," "develop a plan," or "make a recommendation." When these rather loosely structured task requirements are placed upon the group, it must be able to agree on a working definition of the

[28]Gibb, "Defensive Communication," pp. 142–43.
[29]Hunt and Lee, "Organizational Climate," p. 12.

task and set some preliminary ground rules. Otherwise it is almost certain to fail.

Almost all tasks may be classified according to the criteria shown in figure 5–6. Most of us prefer tasks that are highly interesting yet moderately ambiguous. If a task is interesting, we can spend time on it and feel that the time was well spent. If the task is relatively ambiguous, we can feel challenged without feeling frustrated. Unfortunately, not all tasks are structured in this way. Some tasks are so routine and monotonous that we get little sense of accomplishment from completing them. Other tasks—especially group tasks—are so ambiguous that the group is never able to complete them. When the group is forced to spend time determining *exactly* what is expected of it, it has that much less time to spend on interaction and analysis. We might define *task ambiguity* as the relative clear-cutness of the task.

Groups can remove the ambiguity associated with a particular task by communicating about it, among themselves and with others. The more information the group has, the better able it is to remove the ambiguity.[30] Removing ambiguity and clarifying task expectations is an important aspect of small group communication.

LIMITED RESOURCES   Groups often fail because they lack the human or physical resources necessary to accomplish the task. The human resources of any group are its members' combined intellectual abilities and physical energies. There is very little a group can do about the inherent intellectual abilities of its members. However, the group can generate these abilities by encouraging its members to develop them. It can do this by asking them to meet new challenges and obligations. The group that does not grow begins to *stagnate.*

Physical resources are those physical requirements which a group

[30]K. Weick, *The Social Psychology of Organizing* (Reading, Mass.: Addison-Wesley Publishing Co., Inc., 1969), p. 101.

FIGURE 5–6   Task clarification

	Interesting	Uninteresting
Unambiguous	Moderately involving, moderately challenging, leads to task specialization	Boring, repetitious, stifling, unchallenging
Ambiguous	Highly involving, challenging, some confusion over purpose possible, highly rewarding when completed	Challenging, moderately involving, confusing, conflict-producing

needs to accomplish its task. They include statistics, evidence, data, and so forth, which the group can use to generate possible solutions. Members decide which physical resources the group needs. One essential physical resource is sufficient time. The group that has only one day to accomplish a four-day task will be forced to take potentially dangerous shortcuts. Even superhuman effort will not always insure success under these circumstances.

Motivational Failures

Groups sometimes fail simply because members do not want to get the job done. It is naive to think that just because a group in an organization has been given a job, it necessarily wants to do the job. There are many conflicting motivational issues at work. Groups will work hard when they are able to see the potential reward for their effort. The next section considers an important influence on group motivation—individual goals. This discussion is based on the material on group objectives and norms presented earlier in this chapter.

INDIVIDUAL GOALS   Group motivation is also influenced by the goals of the individual members. These goals will encourage or discourage the individual to achieve group goals. The individual will be highly motivated when the goals of the group are highly important to him or her. For example, we want to take part in group discussions when we think we will get something out of the group's deliberations. The "getting something out" may be related to career development (e.g., salary increases, promotion) or personal development (e.g., the opportunity to grow).

A Review

There are three major causes of communication failure in small groups. By focusing on participation, task, and member motivation, we should be able to identify and deal with group communication breakdowns.

important group communication skills

You will succeed as a group member if you have the skills you need to interact. Let us consider six of the most important of these group communication skills.

Organizing

Organizing skills deal with planning, arrangement, timing, and detail. Group members need a framework in which to operate. The framework should reflect the task to be accomplished. Arranging for a meeting place and setting an agenda can be even more important than contributing a critical idea. Organizing skills allow the member to become a specialist about those matters, often mundane, which must be done regardless of the topic under discussion. It is common for groups to develop experts in certain communication tasks. Organizing experts would be those who remind the members of their responsibilities and suggest ways of fulfilling them.

Analyzing

Groups must have members who are able to dissect, focus, and direct an issue under consideration. These are *analyzing skills.* Analysis involves taking the ideas that others have contributed and refining them for use by the entire group. It entails making specific applications of general information. Perhaps the following dialogue will help you to understand the importance of analyzing skills:

Jon: I heard that the sales staff has been having trouble explaining rejected parts to customers.

Bonnie: I've heard the same thing. Bill Lester, who works in marketing, told me that our customers have been rejecting from 10 to 15 percent of our new products.

Karl: I don't know how long we can stay in business this way.

Kevin: Well, it may be a serious problem, but at this point we have to accept it as hearsay. May I suggest that, as a group, we try to get to the bottom of this? Let's see if these are just rumors or if we have a real problem to deal with.

Kevin is taking the information contributed by others and refining it into a course of action by the group. His plan is based on sound analysis and an understanding of the current work situation. Analyzing skills are very important to any group. They should be encouraged and rewarded.

Presenting

Group members are often called upon to report on their deliberations to appropriate bodies and agencies. A member must also be able to articulate his or her position to other members. Both tasks require *presenting skills.* These skills are discussed at length in part four.

148

Harmonizing

Certain members must be able to *harmonize* the group. They must be able to promote compromise. The communication posture of the group should be mutually supportive. Interpersonal problems can destroy the group. Helping to resolve them is one of the most important skills a group member can have. An intervention to solve a problem should be based on what is *best* for the *group.*

Coaching

Group members must sometimes coach or help other members. This might involve: (1) orienting another member to what is happening in the group, (2) encouraging participation, (3) teaching another member to solve a problem, (4) developing and improving the climate of the group, or (5) helping to train group leaders. Ideally, several group members will assume responsibility for coaching. This skill, like the others detailed in this section, is really the responsibility of the entire group. It involves assessing where the group is and helping it to get where it needs to be. It involves projecting a helping relationship wherever possible. Sometimes it involves working behind the scenes in the group to help another member. The coach does not necessarily have to be the star of the group.

Sometimes coaching involves helping other members to develop their true potential as group communicators. All groups need people who will work to keep the group on the right path through honest criticism, gentle prodding, helpful advice, and thoughtful training and orientation. These are some of the things that coaches do.

Summarizing

Whatever the group does, someone must succinctly summarize and recap group deliberations. There are two types of summaries.

INTERNAL SUMMARIES As the group completes a major section of discussion, it is necessary to restate, conclude, and recapitulate what the group has decided. This is called making an *internal summary.* Often the internal summary sparks the group to move on to the next point in the analysis. Internal summaries enable the group to reorient members and to encourage nonparticipants to become involved in the ongoing discussion.

FINAL SUMMARIES The final summary is the last major recap of the group's discussions. It includes the major points covered, an elaboration of what the group is going to do next, and the group's important findings and recommendations.

ways of thinking about groups

This chapter concludes with a brief philosophy related to groups in organizations. The major premises of this philosophy are based on many of the ideas already presented. The section thus provides a review of the chapter.

1. *A group may be better than the combined skills of its members.* Some writers hold that a group is a greater source of input and intellectual insight than any collection of separate individuals could be.[31] It follows from this assumption that group decision making is superior to individual decision making. There are inherent difficulties in this position. The effectiveness of group decision making will depend on: (1) the intellectual abilities of the members, (2) the requirement of the task, (3) the extent to which the problem requires creativity, (4) the time constraints under which the decision must be made, and (5) the motivation of the individual members.[32]

A group can often do things that a collection of separate individuals cannot do. A group brings a wide perspective to the analysis of most problems; it is often able to generate better decisions than an individual could; its decisions are likelier to be implemented; and it offers certain satisfactions to its members. It is fair to conclude that groups are strong decision-making tools. But groups are *not* always better than individuals at making decisions. Some decisions must be made by individuals. Individual decision making is generally better when the situation requires a quick and direct form of action.

2. *The way members feel about each other is important.* This chapter has considered the attitudes that group members hold about one another. These attitudes influence the group's ability to accomplish the task. Members have particular biases, limitations, and frailties. When one member is "down," he or she may influence the group negatively. Highly cohesive groups are usually productive, but cohesion is not easy to develop. Because feelings and attitudes dictate an individual's response to appeals for productivity, the requirements of the task will interact with the feelings of the members. Good groups will recognize this interaction and deal with members' feelings promptly, so that they never block the progress of the task.

3. *The goals of the group will be influenced by many things, but especially by the goals of the organization.* Group goals are determined

[31]Vroom, "Industrial Social Psychology," p. 240.
[32]Lowin, "Participative Decision-Making," p. 73.

150

and refined by members, through an elaborate combination of discussion and analysis. We would expect the goals of a group, charted by the organization, to be heavily influenced by that organization—and so they are. But a group will apply the organization's goals in its own unique way.[33] Thus it would be unproductive for an organization to place rigid standards on its groups. Asking for strict adherence to specific policies and procedures stifles creativity. The group needs room to operate. Certainly all formal groups mandated by the organization should clearly perceive the organization's goals. However, the group will also be influenced by the collective goals of the individual members and by its own emerging goals. Occasionally the three sets of goals will conflict. One group task may be to resolve this conflict.

4. *Groups will reflect the personalities of their members.* Groups will reflect the idiosyncrasies, quirks, foibles, and limitations of their members. Like their members, they may be uptight, stodgy, or ambitious. In an organization, a group may take on the personality of its home department, its leader, or its members' occupational class.

5. *Groups have communication requirements and obligations that must be fulfilled.* Like the individual who must operate within an organization, the group must meet certain communication requirements. These requirements include its obligation to communicate with other relevant groups inside and outside the organization. There are also communication requirements *within* the group. These requirements include the exchange of information, the members' willingness to participate, the coordination of efforts, and satisfactory analysis of the task. Meeting its communication requirements is one of a group's most important tasks.

6. *Groups are not panaceas; they cannot solve all of an organization's problems.* Organizations sometimes appoint a committee to investigate a problem after all else has failed. The words "Let's form a committee on that" have sounded the death knell of many a creative idea. A humorous game reproduced here as figure 5–7 was developed by Professor Halas Jackim to poke fun at this tendency to solve all problems by committee. In reality, committees are well suited to some tasks and ill suited to others. The questions that need to be asked are "What is the task?" and "Is a committee the best vehicle for accomplishing the task?"

[33]A. Turner, "A Conceptual Scheme for Describing Work Group Behavior," in *Organizational Behavior and Administration,* ed. P. Lawrence (Homewood, Ill.: Richard D. Irwin, Inc., 1961), pp. 162–64.

FIGURE 5-7

SCORING THE COMMITTEE GAME*

By Halas L. Jackim

There are three kinds of people in the world—those who make things happen, those who simply watch things happen, and those who play the Committee Game.

The game is not simple, it requires skill and subtle strategies, not unlike poker. It has taken the author 23 years of infiltration in committees to enable him to distill and reveal the real nature of the game.

Most committee-game devotees become compulsive, insisting that their committees meet no less than once a week, while real connoisseurs of the art are often found holding breakfast meetings and evening meetings in order to squeeze in that extra game or two each week.

Before describing the rules, etiquette, and scoring system for the game, allow me to state the overall objectives: a) To prevent the development of significant decisions; b) To delay or diffuse an issue by making it unrecognizable.

Etiquette

• It is proper to show disgust for any act aimed at achieving a speedy discharge of a committee's mission. Use of the words "dirty," "mechanistic," "structured," and "the cult of efficiency" is in good taste when describing such acts.

• Resist all attempts at delegation of personal responsibility; insist on committee action.

Rules

• Any number may play, although a group which numbers five to 15 members provides the greatest satisfaction.

• Players start playing as individuals, but may team up with compatible counterparts as the game progresses.

Scoring

The true pleasure in serving on committees comes from scoring and watching others score. The following should help the novice keep up with the more experienced player and the experienced player to better assess his game:

5 points for converting the obvious meaning of a statement into something different by approaching it from a creative-oblique angle.

5 points for "forgetting" an earlier decision and bringing it up for renewed discussion (additional 5 points if player gets away with it).

5 points for citing a study, book, or other authority and quickly changing the subject before being questioned about it.

Source: Halas L. Jackim, "Scoring the Committee Game," *The Chronicle of Higher Education,* 10, no. 18 (July 21, 1975), p. 10. Used by permission. Appeared originally in *The Chronicle of Higher Education.* Copyright 1975 by Editorial Projects for Education, Inc.

FIGURE 5–7 Cont.

5 points for criticizing the administration of the institution.

5 points for canonizing the need for student participation.

5 points for gesticulating with glasses, pipe, or pen to dramatize a point.

5 points for telling the group that it has a communication problem.

5 points for delaying a decision by using ploy of need to consult with constituency.

5 points for taking twice as long as needed to say something.

10 points for injecting an irrelevant issue (5 extra points if it manages to sidetrack the committee's deliberations).

10 points for getting committee to reconsider its procedures.

10 points for throwing in a new term, preferably from a foreign language.

15 points for phrasing a statement in such a way that a player opposed to it fails to recognize it and votes for it.

25 points for wearing down the opposition to the point where it will vote for anything simply to adjourn the meeting.

A final warning is in order. Players can be disqualified for:

- Persisting in their desire to clarify committee's goals.
- Insisting on identifying obstacles to committee's progress.
- Expecting to see implementation of committee's recommendations.

FOR STUDY

1 Name some of the potential uses of the small group in the organization. Why are groups widely used?

2 Distinguish between formal and informal groups. What role does each play in the success of the organization?

3 What are group goals? How might potential conflict between group goals and individual goals be resolved?

4 In determining the success of a group, what are some possible measures of group performance?

5 Communication networks may determine how information flows in groups. Describe some possible network shapes. Tell how each is established.

The Team

Recently the Hoover Manufacturing Company has initiated a team-building approach to management. The organization has been restructured into about 300 production teams of five to seven members each. Each team is responsible for a particular phase of production.

The major products at Hoover are electronic components for calculators, radios, televisions, and so forth. There is no assembly line at Hoover; rather, each assembler works at a station to turn out his or her quota of components. Before the reorganization, employees complained that they did not really feel like part of the organization. People who worked on machines said they had no idea how their job fit into the overall structure of the organization. Absenteeism and turnover were high. Often when people were asked to work overtime so that a particular project could be finished, they refused, causing late deliveries on important projects. Over the last 12 months before the reorganization was initiated, Hoover's share of the market had dropped 2 percent, and the company had lost $300,000. More and more rejected parts and complaints about shoddy workmanship were filtering back from Hoover's customers.

Tom McCormick has been president of Hoover since 1975. Last April he attended a management seminar held in Puerto Rico. Its title was "Job Enrichment: A Way To Restructure Jobs for Greater Motivation." The seminar made a profound impression on Tom. It started him thinking about how he might implement a job enrichment program at Hoover.

His executive committee was enthusiastic when Tom outlined the following five-step proposal:

1. All work would stop for 48 hours while every employee was assigned to a team. This assignment would be based on a careful study made by a team of consultants. Each team member was trained briefly on his or her responsibilities.

2. Each team would be responsible for setting its own schedule, quotas, and standards. It would also be responsible for everything that happened in the unit. A team leader would be elected. He or she would report to a coordinator, whose job closely resembled that of the old first-line foreman.

3. Teams would keep each other informed about their activities through a team member called a linker. A linker's responsibility, in addition to his or her own job, would be to keep the unit posted on what was happening in the rest of the organization. The linker's position would be important, because each team needed to share its successes with the others.

4. As a part of its work shift, each team would meet once a day, even if only briefly, to discuss important matters. The team leaders would conduct the meetings after checking with the coordinator to determine what should be talked about that day. The team would be given the authority to do whatever was necessary to insure that everyone attended these meetings.

5. In addition to the regular salary system, an incentive bonus system would set aside a percentage of Hoover's monthly profits (when the month was profitable) to reward teams that had performed unusually well. The incentive system would be designed so that each team could decide how to split up the bonus money among its members. Since every member of the organization would be a member of a team, each employee could qualify for a bonus each month—assuming that his or her team performed outstandingly.

The executive committee adopted this program on the spot. At first, however, it did not work out well at all. Many of the team leaders elected did not know how to lead. What was supposed to be a short, well-organized team meeting often turned into a gripe session that dragged on and on. Then a few teams began to realize that the more time they spent on meetings, the less time they had to devote to production. Finally, most teams learned to conduct efficient meetings and began to learn to motivate their members to be production minded. A problem developed when highly competitive teams began to sabotage each other's work. This stopped when they were told that the incentive system depended upon the success of the entire organization.

The team-building approach at Hoover was monitored by a close evaluation unit. Carefully drawn comparisons were made before and after the inception of the program. Turnover and absenteeism were closely watched. Gradually, the statistics began to demonstrate the success of the program. Absenteeism dropped about 2 percent per month. Later, more substantial changes were documented. These included an increase in the percentage of teams meeting quota and a drop in the number of rejected parts. The Hoover share of the market began to grow. Most important, people reported that they enjoyed coming to work at Hoover. It seemed to be a better place to work.

FOR STUDY

1 Why do you suppose this team-building program worked at Hoover?

2 Using what you learned in this chapter, design a brief training program that could be used with newly elected team leaders to teach them the principles of small group communication.

3 What type of group communication system would be necessary for a production team to function effectively at Hoover? How might this system be started?

4 Some group theorists have suggested that a person who has a stake in the making of a decision will be more likely to implement it than a person who does not. Do you think that this principle worked at Hoover?

5 Does the team approach work on all kinds of jobs? What conditions must be present for the team approach to be effective?

supervision:
Achieving Dynamic Leadership Through Communication

In the previous chapter, the role of small groups in organizations was examined. That discussion deliberately excluded perhaps the most important aspect of group success. Leadership is so crucial to both the small group and the organization that it deserves a chapter of its own. This chapter will focus on those communication skills which enable managers to exercise good leadership.

leadership: a definition

The concept *leadership* has been defined as "the sum total of the behavior of an executive in his direct relations with subordinates."[1] Hall has argued that leadership does *not* involve the *activities required by* one's position. Rather, "leadership involves what a person does above and beyond the basic requirements of his position."[2] In this book, leadership will be defined as:

> The process of influence that a person exhibits toward another person within an organization.

First, we will examine some of the typical tasks that leadership must accomplish. Second, we will study some historical approaches to leadership. Third, we will examine some of the techniques of leadership and discuss the communication skills vital to good leadership. Finally,

[1]D. Hampton, C. Summer, and R. Webber, *Organizational Behavior and the Practice of Management* (Glenview, Ill.: Scott, Foresman & Company, 1973), p. 601.
[2]R. Hall, *Organizations: Structure and Process* (Englewood Cliffs, N.J.: Prentice-Hall, Inc., 1972), p. 246.

chapter six

we will consider what happens when there is no leadership in an organization.

the tasks of leadership
in the organization

The work of the organization is done by people. But some people assume the responsibility for developing standards and influencing other people to meet them. This *developing* and *influencing* is the task of managerial leadership.[3] We will describe six of the manager's most important leadership tasks.

Creating

The first job of any leader is to invent or discover new things. The new program, the new policy, the new routine are often created by a leader.[4]

Suppose that the research and development department has recently created a new product that has great commercial appeal. The leader of the marketing unit must create a new marketing plan for this product. To do so, innovation will be required. While past experience may provide the necessary background information, the individual manager and his subordinates must use their own brain power to develop the marketing strategy. Hicks has suggested that there are four approaches to this creative process.[5]

LOGIC The creator approaches a problem with a hypothesis, a supposition about how the problem should be solved. The hypothesis is tested by the creator as he or she discovers additional facts. Through experimentation, a variety of approaches are tried. Eventually, the best approach to solving the problem will be discovered.

IDEAL LINKING The creator pieces together many bits of information to draw relationships and generalizations. Education and life experience provide much of this information. This work resembles that of a police detective who pieces together the various clues in conducting a criminal investigation.

[3]See H. G. Hicks, *The Management of Organizations: A Systems and Human Resources Approach*, 2nd ed. (New York: McGraw-Hill Book Company, 1972), for a thorough treatment of the tasks of leadership.
[4]In this context, the terms *leader* and *manager*, are used interchangeably to mean someone delegated by the organization to *manage other people*.
[5]Hicks, *Management of Organizations*, p. 121.

PROBLEM SOLVING   The creator first defines the problem. After the problem has been defined, it is necessary to: (1) obtain the facts, (2) identify the ramifications of the problem, (3) formulate alternative solutions, (4) select the best solution, and (5) put the best solution into practice. This typology was first suggested by Dewey in 1910, but it is still a very useful way to structure the process of creativity.

FREE ASSOCIATION   The creator attempts to unite the rational/conscious and irrational/unconscious parts of the mind to develop a solution to the problem.[6] Purportedly, ideas flow freely when discussions and brainstorming sessions are loosely structured and freewheeling. These sessions give people the chance to propose ideas in a nonevaluative environment where they will not be criticized for making unconventional suggestions.

The creation of new ideas is one of the leader's daily tasks. However, his or her crucial decisions involve the question of delegation. When it is necessary to solve a problem, does the leader attempt to do it himself? Or does he have subordinates do it for him? The answer to that will depend upon the abilities of the subordinate, the abilities of the leader, and the requirements of the situation. The "do it yourself or delegate it" dichotomy is a nagging proposition that is always facing leaders.

Planning

Organizations must plan for the future. Planning involves: (1) accurately perceiving conditions in the organization's environment, (2) developing useful ideas that will enable the organization to formulate its objectives, and (3) determining how to reach these objectives. Planning enables the organization to coordinate what otherwise might be very random behavior toward a single purpose.

The leader must be able to develop and exercise good planning skills.[7] Communication skills help the leader to plan. Through reading, writing, talking, listening, and thinking, the leader gathers the data necessary for planning. There are two types of planning: short-range planning and long-range planning.

SHORT-RANGE PLANNING   Short-range planning allows the leader to account for the day-to-day operations of the organization. Depending on the organization or department, the time span for short-term plan-

[6]Hicks, *Management of Organizations,* p. 123.
[7]Hicks, *Management of Organizations,* p. 125.

ning could range anywhere from a few minutes to several years. In the research and development lab of a large organization, the time frame for a particular project may run for weeks or months. Short-range plans may cover an entire year. In the accounting office, short-range plans may cover only a week, since this office has such high-pressure tasks as issuing invoice checks and payrolls.

Short-range planning involves formulating guidelines to meet the immediate demands of the task. The process is detailed in the diagram presented in figure 6–1. Short-range planning may be done in one of two ways. If a prearranged policy or guideline already exists to meet the demand issue, short-range planning consists of identifying the policy and attempting to implement it. If the policy has been correctly formulated, it should not be difficult to achieve the goal, which in most cases is simply to meet demands placed on the organization by the problem in question.

When no prearranged guideline exists, short-range planning consists of developing a workable policy, analyzing and evaluating that policy, and then implementing it. This type of short-range planning is sometimes difficult and time consuming. However, it is not possible to have a policy or guideline for every contingency, so the leader must sometimes be prepared to develop one.

Short-range planning often is a group effort. The leader helps the group to generate discussion in order to achieve the desired goal. As with any type of decision making, *the plan must be consistent with the objectives of the organization.* Planners must consider the implications of the plan for other units of the organization. In most cases, it will have a significant impact.

LONG-RANGE PLANNING   For an organization to continue to exist, the possible events that could influence that organization over time must be discussed. Long-range planning spells out techniques and programs that the organization intends to use to meet its stated or implied objec-

FIGURE 6–1   Planning model

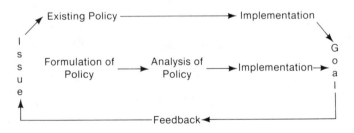

tives. In other words, *long-range planning spells out how the organization intends to manage its future.* Long-range plans must necessarily be more general and flexible than short-range plans, since no organization can predict the future with total accuracy. Long-range plans can be specific or general enough to be used over and over again. A yearly budget and a general rule, respectively, would be examples.

In organizations, the high-level managers usually engage in long-range planning, while the lower-level managers engage in short-range planning.[8] Such issues as the changing nature of governmental regulations, trends in the marketplace, availability of investment capital, and meeting improvements in the competition receive the attention of long-range planners.

The extent to which an organization practices participative decision making may be indicated by the degree to which it involves its lower-level managers in long-range planning. The rationale most frequently given for involving only high-level managers in long-range planning is that they have a broader perspective than lower-level managers. They are able to take many points of view into consideration, and they are better informed than the lower-level manager. For these reasons, their input is usually more highly valued.

It is necessary to coordinate long-range and short-range planning. Obviously, it is by integrating a series of short-range plans that the organization is able to achieve long-range results. This integration is achieved primarily by means of communication among long- and short-range planners.

Organizing

Part of any leader's job is to organize the various aspects of the task to be accomplished. Perhaps the best working definition of organizing might be the expression "getting things in gear." Organizing involves four separate duties.

ASSESSING THE TASK To organize a task, the leader must first understand that task. The leader must also communicate that understanding to the other people involved. The leader must be able to assess what is required to accomplish the task. Leadership also involves understanding the interrelationship between the immediate task and the other activities of the organization. Finally, the leader must be able to account for contingencies.

[8]Hicks, *Management of Organizations*, p. 130.

ASSESSING PEOPLE Organizing involves assessing people. Assessing people in this context means determining the strengths and weaknesses of the people who are going to do the task. The leader must make sure that adequate talent is available to accomplish the task. If not, he or she must take steps to acquire it. To assess people, the leader must know the abilities of the work group. This is only possible if the leader has maintained a frank and open communication environment—one that encourages trust and rapport. Hidden talents and the less obvious contributions of group members become apparent in such an environment. Assessing people means honestly evaluating one's subordinates' contributions to the organization.

ASSESSING TIME Organizing involves knowing how much time is required to accomplish a particular task. Occasionally, the organization will place a time requirement on the work group, or the task itself will determine the time perimeters. Sometimes the group will place its own time limits on a task. To assess time, the leader must understand the task and must also be able to explain time requirements to the group.

MATCHING TASK, PEOPLE, AND TIME To organize a task, it is crucial for the leader to be able to match the task, the people, and the time requirements—to choose given people to do the job in a given time. The leader must first establish the procedures for reaching this match. Then he or she must persuade group members that his or her choices are sound. This is a very delicate process. First, the leader must gather information about task, people, and time while remaining accountable to his or her superiors. Second, whenever people are chosen for particular jobs, personality clashes and hurt feelings can develop among those not selected. These can damage the climate and cohesion of the work group. A good leader must be able to restore confidence if it breaks down. When a leader makes a bad choice, time, attitudes, and rapport are all affected. The leader must reassess his or her original thinking before the bad mix does irreparable damage. Decision making at this level is not just a matter of facts and figures. Many human elements are involved. Matching task, people, and time requires strong analytical skills and excellent interpersonal relationships. It is a difficult challenge.

Reporting

We have suggested that a leader must be accountable to his or her superiors. At the same time, the leader must be accountable to his or her subordinates. The accountability is routinely achieved through reporting. *Reporting* is the process of keeping both superiors and subordinates informed about existing conditions in the work unit. It is an integral part of leadership. There are two types of reporting, formal and informal.

FORMAL REPORTING   Formal reporting occurs in regularly scheduled meetings and conferences. It resembles presentational speaking and will be considered extensively in chapters seven and eight. Formal reporting enables a leader to maintain important contacts up and down the hierarchy of the organization.

INFORMAL REPORTING   Informal reporting can be defined in terms of managerial attitude. It requires a commitment on the part of the leader to keep group members informed about the organization's policies and procedures. Although this type of briefing may also be accomplished through formal meetings, it is done most effectively through informal discussions and interactions with subordinates. Since the leader, because of his or her position in the organization, has access to more information than subordinates, he or she is responsible for passing on relevant information to subordinates. This is an important task of leadership.

Controlling

Control systems deal with both human and nonhuman resources. Financial costs, for example, are tightly controlled in most organizations. Since human resources constitute an aspect of cost in an organization, it is necessary to exercise control in this area as well.

All organizations have systems that are used to control the behavior of their members.[9] Actually, control systems are simply ways of aligning existing job performance with the level of performance desired by the organization. The range of control techniques varies greatly. One leader stands over the subordinate with a whip and chair; another applies very gentle persuasion. Most established guidelines, procedures, and rules in the organization provide some degree of control. However, the major responsibility for control falls to the leader.

Since the control system is to be implemented by the manager, the manager should have the authority to implement the system completely. There must be a way for the manager to punish those who do not adhere to the system. Punishment may range from suspension to

[9]In this context the term *control system* does not necessarily have rigidly bureaucratic or authoritarian connotations. Control systems range from a highly participative situation in which each person has control over his or her own behavior to a situation in which the organization controls every aspect of a member's behavior.

reprimand to a gentle whisper in the ear. However, the manager who does not have the authority to punish offenders cannot successfully exercise control.

Communicating

Since this entire book deals with communication, only limited space will be devoted to this topic here. To restate the position stated throughout: *Communicating with superiors and subordinates is the MOST important job that a leader in an organization must do.*

Communication in this context involves an attempt on the part of the leader to establish open relationships with subordinates. This obliges the leader to receive as well as transmit information. The other leadership skills mentioned are oriented toward the objective dimensions of life in the organization. Effective managerial communication is often subjective.

A Review

The leader in an organization has a number of specific tasks. These include creating, planning, organizing, reporting, controlling, and communicating. All of these tasks require communication skills. Each task helps the organization and the leader's immediate work group to operate effectively.

historical approaches to leadership

The tasks of leadership remain fairly consistent from one organization to the next. However, there are numerous historical approaches to leadership. In this part, we shall examine four of the most representative.

The Autocratic Approach

The first studies on leadership appeared in the early years of the twentieth century.[10] These studies attempted to bring the analytical methods of the natural sciences to the study of humans at work. Thus, this school of leadership has been called *scientific management.*

---

[10]L. Gilbreth, *The Psychology of Management* (New York: Macmillan Publishing Co., Inc., 1914); R. Hoxie, *Scientific Management and Labor* (New York: Appleton-Century-Crofts, 1915); H. Gantt, *Work, Wages, and Profits* (New York: The Engineering Magazine Co., 1916); F. Taylor, *Scientific Management* (New York: Harper & Row, Publishers, Inc., 1947).

The autocratic approach to leadership is based on the assumption that people have to be prodded and cajoled into working. It was common during this period for workers to be paid by piece rate—that is, paid by the unit for each unit they produced. It was assumed that the worker would exert maximum effort only for maximum pay—or in other words, that *people were only concerned about money.*

The scientific management school was primarily interested in redesigning the job. Employers would study how best to squeeze the maximum effort out of each worker. Very little attention was paid to the workers' attitudes or values. In fact, many of the writers in this school assumed that workers were totally devoid of feelings. They saw workers as people who could be forced to work hard simply because they valued money above all else. The role of the worker was finally reduced to little more than a cog in the larger machine of effective production.[11] The role of the leader was simply to get the maximum effort out of the worker by the use of economic incentives and punishments.

We still occasionally encounter a leader who practices the autocratic approach. This type of leader often assumes that money is the only thing the worker values and will use it as a whip to bring recalcitrant workers into line. Such punishment techniques as docking an employee's pay for arriving late to work or handing down a suspension without pay are examples of negative reinforcers that are based on the autocratic approach to leadership.

The Democratic Approach

In response to the work of the scientific management theorists, a group of social scientists from the Harvard Business School began in the 1920s to conduct experiments at the Hawthorne Plant of the Western Electric Company, just outside Chicago. These experiments have come to be known as the *Hawthorne Studies.* The variables studied included lighting, room ventilation, supervision, and work group competition.

The findings of the Hawthorne Studies are far too extensive to be covered here.[12] Some of them gave birth to the human relations school, here called the democratic approach to leadership. For our purposes, the major finding to come out of this research was the recognition that a strong social system exists within an organization. Contrary to the assumptions of the scientific management school, the Hawthorne Studies suggested that employees do have attitudes, values, and ideas. This

[11]Hicks, *Management of Organizations,* p. 132.
[12]These findings are summarized in F. Roethlisberger and W. Dickson, *Management and the Worker* (Cambridge, Mass.: Harvard University Press, 1939).

was the origin of the idea that employees might well participate in making decisions.

Some other results emerged from this research. Perhaps the most famous was the discovery that the productivity of the employees being studied seemed to increase regardless of the variable examined. If the lighting in the work room was changed, productivity increased. If supervision changed, productivity increased. This held true whether or not the change constituted an improvement. It finally became apparent that the increased productivity was more closely related to the *attention* than to the manipulations performed by the experimenters.

The implications of the human relations school spread rapidly throughout American industry. Before the Hawthorne Studies, the worker had been largely ignored. Now the worker's values and attitudes became important. The basic premise of the school was that a happy worker was a productive worker. Therefore, much effort was expended to make the worker happy. Later, more sophisticated scientific research suggests that this early view was oversimplified.[13] Yet many leaders in organizations still adhere to it today.

The Trait Approach

The trait approach holds that leadership is based not on what someone does, but on what someone is. Based on the work of Ralph Stodgill and Arthur Coons, this approach proposes that people who have certain attributes or *traits* will become leaders.[14] Some of these traits are intelligence, participation, sociability, capacity, and communication skills.

INTELLIGENCE People who are perceived to be intelligent are looked to for leadership. In this context, the term *intelligence* means the ability to sound intelligent in group interaction. It does not necessarily mean analytical ability. Good common sense, good judgment, the ability to think a problem through, and the ability to adjust quickly are aspects of this concept of intelligence.

Intelligence is sometimes related to the topic under discussion. In a work group considering plans for a new advertising campaign, the director of marketing will be perceived as intelligent. He may not be

[13]V. Vroom, *Work and Motivation* (New York: John Wiley & Sons, Inc., 1964); E. Lawler and L. Porter, "Antecedent Job Attitudes of Effective Managerial Performance," *Organizational Behavior and Human Performance*, 2, no. 2 (1967), 139–55.
[14]R. Stogdill and A. Coons, *Leader Behavior: Its Description and Measurement*, Monograph 88 (Columbus: Ohio State University, Bureau of Educational Research, 1957).

perceived as intelligent if the topic under discussion is a new manufacturing process.

PARTICIPATION Participation deals with the extent to which the group member is involved in, and is percieved as indispensible to, the affairs of the group. Highly energetic people usually become leaders. The leader who is routinely involved in the daily operation of his or her unit might well be perceived as possessing this trait. In group discussion, the person who speaks up first is often the one who demonstrates leadership. Willingness is a very important attribute for leaders. The nonparticipant is rarely looked to for leadership.

SOCIABILITY Sociability is very closely related to personality and likeability. Popular people are routinely elected as leaders. Good work group relations are almost always important. The leader can help to achieve good work group relations by displaying such characteristics as cheerfulness, honesty, concern, and empathy. Of course, leaders cannot be expected always to be sociable. However, the trait approach assumes that the person who is perceived as a leader will generally also be perceived as sociable.

CAPACITY The person who seems *to be able* to serve as leader is said to have the *capacity*. The trait approach assumes that a person who displays the capacity will be looked to for leadership. This assumption resembles the great man theory of leadership, which holds that a person will always emerge to meet the requirements of the situation. In social situations, some people are more able than others to assume the position of leader. In school, perhaps you remember one or two people who always seemed to be elected to every office—from hall monitor in the first grade to student body president in high school. In organizations, the manager who displays a competent and capable bearing is demonstrating the capacity to lead.

COMMUNICATION SKILLS In some groups the person who talks the most (and sometimes the loudest) is perceived as the leader. This is a poor method of determining leadership. Good talking and listening skills are important in leadership, however. The smooth communicator or the polished orator is often perceived as a leader. Rarely will a group deliberately elect an incoherent person as its leader. Of course, in the typical organization, leaders are seldom elected. They are usually appointed by other administrators.

The trait approach to leadership suggests that leadership is based on what someone is. The significance of this approach is that "manager" and "leader" may mean two different things. To be perceived as a leader, the manager must demonstrate the traits of leadership.

The Participative Approach

The participative approach to leadership represents the current thinking in many organizations.[15] The approach is firmly grounded in the work of Douglas McGregor, who proposed two sets of assumptions, which he called Theory X and Theory Y.

MCGREGOR'S THEORY X

1 The average human being has an inherent dislike to work and will avoid it if he or she can.
2 Because of this characteristic dislike of work, most people must be coerced, controlled, directed, and threatened with punishment to get them to put forth adequate effort toward the achievement of organizational objectives.
3 The average human being prefers to be directed, wishes to avoid responsibility, has relatively little ambition, and wants security above all.

MCGREGOR'S THEORY Y

1 The expenditure of physical and mental effort in work is as natural as play or rest. The average human being does not inherently dislike work. Depending upon controllable conditions, work may be a source of satisfaction (and will be voluntarily performed) or a source of punishment (and will be avoided if possible).
2 External control and the threat of punishment are not the only means for bringing about effort toward organizational objectives. Man will exercise self-control in the service of objectives to which he is committed.
3 Commitment to objectives is a function of the rewards associated with their achievement. The most significant of such rewards ... can be direct products of efforts directed toward organizational objectives.
4 The average human being learns, under proper conditions, not only to accept but to seek responsibility. Avoidance of responsibility, lack of ambition, and emphasis on security are generally consequences of experience, not inherent human characteristics.
5 The capacity to exercise a relatively high degree of imagination, ingenuity, and creativity in the solution of organizational problems is widely, not narrowly, distributed in the population.
6 Under conditions of modern industrial life, the intellectual potentialities of the average human being are only partially utilized.[16]

[15]D. Ewing, "Who Wants Corporate Democracy?" *Harvard Business Review*, 49, no. 6 (November/December 1971), 12–28, 148–49.
[16]D. McGregor, *The Human Side of Enterprise* (New York: McGraw-Hill Book Company, 1960), pp. 33–34. Used by permission.

McGregor argued that a manager adopts one of these two sets of assumptions in controlling the behavior of subordinates. As you can see, the Theory X manager is practicing something much like scientific management. The Theory Y manager, on the other hand, lets the subordinate participate in decision making. He or she assumes that each subordinate has *something* to contribute. However, this manager retains control. *He or she neither makes the decision unaided, as in the autocratic approach, nor allows the group to make the decision unaided, by voting, as in the democratic approach.* The Theory Y manager's task is to insure that everyone has the opportunity to participate. Sometimes this manager will retain final power (veto). Other times, the *final* power will be a matter of negotiation between the manager and the group.

The emphasis of participative leadership is on creating an environment in which each member of the work group feels comfortable enough to contribute ideas. This is done by offering recognition and encouragement to members. The advantage of participation is that each member perceives that he or she is a useful part of the team.

types of leadership techniques

Various techniques can be used to exercise leadership in the organization. In this part, five of the most common techniques are examined.

Leadership by Fear

Most leaders wield considerable power. The typical leader has the power to give and withhold raises, to hire and fire, to reward and punish. This is sometimes called *positional power*,[17] since it is held by a person who maintains a particular power position in a group. The leader can use this power to create fear and tension for subordinates. Consider the following dialogue:

Subordinate: What do you want me to do?

Superior: I want you to go and review the marketing plans Wilson submitted.

Subordinate: Okay ...

Superior: Remember, you better do this right or you'll feel it at salary time.

[17]B. Collins and B. Raven, "Group Structure: Attraction, Coalitions, Communication, and Power," in *The Handbook of Social Psychology,* eds. G. Lindzey and E. Aronson (Reading, Mass.: Addison-Wesley Publishing Co., Inc., 1968), IV, 102–205.

The implied threat is that if the task is not done the way the superior wants it done, the subordinate will be punished at review time with a negative recommendation. In this situation, most of us would probably comply with the manager's wishes, because our livelihood depends on pleasing the boss. Leadership by fear is an effective means of obtaining conformity and compliance from subordinates.

However, it can have extremely negative results. In the short run, we may comply with the manager's wishes, but in the long run, we are likely to mistrust him (or her). If we are made to feel that someone else is constantly controlling our behavior, we may well resent it. Furthermore, our own creativity and imagination will be stifled. If we are not *expected* to come up with new and innovative ideas, we probably will not. Leadership by threat can create a negative climate by destroying mutual regard and trust between superiors and subordinates.[18] Thus while it may be temporarily effective, its effectiveness tends to be short lived.

Leadership by Charisma

It is normal to *want* to follow people we believe in. Some politicians have a remarkable ability to inspire and motivate people. Those who have been inspired may leave classes, jobs, or families and travel to the far corners of the world to campaign for these politicians. Some people have suggested that such martyred leaders as Dr. Martin Luther King, Jr. and President John F. Kennedy had this exceptional ability to inspire people.

Many organizations also have leaders who are able to inspire their subordinates. They seem to have the knack of generating enthusiasm for achieving the organization's goals. This ability to inspire is called *charisma*. Charismatic leaders have four special qualities.

They are dynamic. Charismatic leaders are energetic, enthusiastic, and active.

They are concerned about the audience. Charismatic leaders are concerned about the welfare of the people they are talking to. They have the best interests of their followers in mind.

They are concerned about the task. Charismatic leaders demonstrate a high concern for the job to be done. They can persuade others to produce by calling attention to the significance of the task.

They are genuine. Charismatic leaders are honest and straight forward. They are rarely phony or insincere.

[18]C. Rogers, *Client-Centered Therapy: Its Current Practice, Implications, and Theory* (Boston: Houghton Mifflin Company, 1951), p. 21.

Charismatic leaders have the ability to encourage others to behave in ways "above and beyond." Some people really do not like the tasks associated with their position, but they put up with these tasks because they enjoy working for their supervisor.

Unfortunately, charismatic leaders are rare. Charisma is apparently an inborn trait. Obviously, it is difficult to train someone to be "charismatic." Since there are so few charismatic people, the chances are not large that a charismatic person will be chosen for a managerial position.

Leadership by Expertise

In many organizations, people are promoted to positions of leadership because they are experts at a certain task. Leadership by expertise is very important when the task is complex and difficult. The expert leader can furnish a particular type of direction that other kinds of leaders cannot furnish. When the task is not especially complex or difficult, the leader's expertise is less important.[19]

There are three kinds of expertise.

TECHNICAL EXPERTISE Technical expertise involves knowing more about the technical aspects of the task than anyone else. If it is an engineering task, the best engineer is the technical expert. If it is an accounting task, the expert is the best accountant. Technical expertise will vary among individuals, but the leader is normally expected to demonstrate at least a minimum of technical expertise.

INTERPERSONAL EXPERTISE Some leaders have particular interpersonal skills that are important in the organization. These skills include the ability to: (1) compromise, (2) offer guidance on decision-making structures, (3) provide humor, (4) encourage all group members to participate, and (5) develop talents in subordinates. While the technical expert provides the "hard" information necessary to accomplish the task, The interpersonal expert finds and develops the necessary abilities in other members.

POLITICAL EXPERTISE Because an organization is a highly structured social system, political expertise is an important attribute in leaders. Departments, units, and work groups will choose leaders who can dem-

[19]F. Fieldler, *A Theory of Leadership Effectiveness* (New York: McGraw-Hill Book Company, 1967), p. 111.

onstrate upward influence in an organization[20]—that is, who can secure rewards for their subordinates. We often think of the political expert leader as the front who projects a favorable public image for the group. The political expert leader is able to inspire cooperation by influencing agencies and offices that can offer rewards to group members.

Leadership by Persuasion

A leader often wins compliance by using rational discourse. This is called leadership by persuasion. The following dialogue illustrates this form of leadership.

Superior: George, how are you today?

Subordinate: Fine, Mr. Wheeler.

Superior: George, I have a couple of matters that need some action.

Subordinate: Okay, how can I be of help?

Superior: Two things, really. First, I wonder if you could show Art Whittier, the new man, the machine tool process on the first station. Then maybe you could go over to purchasing and answer some of their questions regarding that order we made for new parts. You know the shop better than anyone, so you should be able to answer their questions. Would you mind doing these things for me George?

Subordinate: Not at all, Mr. Wheeler. No problem. I'll get right on it.

Although there may be an element of charisma, fear, or expertise in the relationship between George and Mr. Wheeler, the primary mechanism that Mr. Wheeler uses to obtain compliance is a gentle form of persuasion. Under the appropriate conditions, persuasion can be one of the most effective and useful techniques available to the leader. However, for persuasion to succeed, four things are necessary.

THE SOURCE MUST BE CREDIBLE Before the subordinate will accept and comply with the request, he or she must accept the source (the superior) as credible. Thus, persuasion depends on a trustworthy and open relationship between the subordinate and the superior. In the example, Mr. Wheeler had probably established this credibility with George through his past behavior.

[20]H. Jain, "Supervisory Communication and Performance in Urban Hospitals," *Journal of Communication*, 23, no. 1 (1973), 103–17.

THE AUTHORITY OF THE SOURCE MUST BE LEGITIMATE   Normally, we perceive our immediate superior as a legitimate authority, by virtue of his
or her position. Occasionally, however, we may conclude that the person trying to persuade us is not a legitimate authority ("He has no
business telling me what to do," "She doesn't speak for the company").
When this happens, persuasion cannot be effective. Mr. Wheeler, being
George's immediate supervisor, is a legitimate authority.

THE REQUEST FOR ACTION MUST BE APPROPRIATE   Before the subordinate will comply with a request, he or she must see it as appropriate.
It must appear to be legal, rational, and realistic. If the request is
inappropriate, persuasion will not work. Sometimes communication
can be used to persuade a subordinate of the appropriateness of a
request. The subordinate may then comply. It does not follow that
legitimate authority will always make legitimate requests. The perceptive subordinate will tend to make judgments on both the request and
the source. In the example, George could certainly view Mr. Wheeler's
request as legitimate.

THE REQUEST MUST BE MEANINGFUL TO THE SUBORDINATE   For persuasion
to work, the request must be meaningful to the subordinate. He or she
needs to know what is being asked and needs to understand its significance. A general request for compliance ("All of you men better get this
done") is less likely to be effective than a highly specific request ("Larry,
you have done this for me many times; would you please do it again?").
The request for compliance must necessarily apply specifically to the
receiver. In the second example, the superior included a gentle stroke
to Larry's ego along with his request for compliance.

Leadership by Communication

Leadership by communication involves using, or attempting to
use, all of the channels of communication, trying to keep open all of the
avenues of interaction between oneself and one's subordinates. Such
terms as "openness," "mutual trust," "respect," "supportiveness," and
"honesty" characterize this form of leadership.

Communication is reciprocal. The sender adapts the message to
meet the needs of the receiver, as the sender interprets those needs.
The leader and the subordinate also have a reciprocal relationship. The
leader depends on the subordinate for effort, for information, and for
loyalty. The subordinate depends on the leader for information, for
support at appraisal and pay raise time, and for expertise. Each meets

the other's needs through communication. When communication channels are closed, little can be done to develop compliance to the organization's goals. To maintain this type of communication relationship, four things are necessary.

FEEDBACK Each person must be sensitive to the feedback given off by the other. We should also be aware of the feedback we give off ourselves. Feedback is the follow-up aspect of communication. The leader who fails to follow up by responding to suggestions, questions, and written memoranda will have trouble leading by communication.

LISTENING Let us briefly review listening as it relates to leadership by communication. Listening involves trying to interpret and identify with what the other person is saying. Subordinates will only offer ideas, contributions, and suggestions when they know that they will be listened to. One of the best ways for a leader to find out how things are going on the job is to listen to what subordinates are saying. This is not easy. The daily pressures of the job assignment and life within the organization make it difficult for most people to devote the energy necessary to practice good listening. However, once one *does* learn good listening skills, that talent will enable the person to develop as a communicator.

CONFIDENCE Confidence is closely related to McGregor's Theory Y assumptions. For leadership by communication to take place, both the leader and the subordinate must make *assumptions* of mutual confidence and trust. The leader must *assume* that the subordinate will follow through on his or her duties. The subordinate must *assume* that the boss will act fairly, never "stabbing him (or her) in the back," if an opportunity should present itself.

EMPATHY The concept of empathy is closely related to the concept of confidence. *Empathy* is the ability to understand and identify with another person's motives. It is the ability to recognize the various pressures and expectations placed on the other person. Of course, only when people are willing to share can others recognize these pressures and expectations. Some degree of *self-disclosure* is a necessary component in a superior–subordinate relationship if empathy is to be developed.

A CRITICISM The perceptive student who has experienced life in the "real world" of organizations may criticize this discussion of leadership by communication as requiring *too much* of both the superior and the subordinate. You may argue that most leaders do not have the time or interest necessary to establish this kind of communication relationship with subordinates. It is true that leadership by communication is difficult. However, the foregoing description was presented as an *ideal*. Although it may be difficult to achieve, it is a goal that you should seek if you want to practice good leadership.

important interpersonal skills in good leadership

The communicator's interpersonal skills help him or her to be a good leader. We have already examined those personality traits which cause one to be *perceived* as a leader. Now let us examine those acquired interpersonal skills which enable one to *function* as a leader.

Flexibility

Flexibility is the ability *not* to face each problem with a highly structured, rigid set of expectations. Each problem is both similar to and different from previous problems. Routine and innovative leader and group behavior will both be required to solve it.

The typical organization changes daily, according to administrative practices, conditions in the world outside, and the nature of each task and the people who must do it. The manager who approaches each problem with a fixed set of ideas about how to solve it may find that those ideas don't work anymore. Flexibility in exercising the tasks of leadership mentioned earlier in this chapter (creating, planning, and so forth) will enable the manager to generate *behavioral options*—that is, to create a range of alternative solutions to each problem. The following three guidelines may be helpful.

EXPECT INCONSISTENCY The leader is often required to interact extensively with people, and people do not always behave consistently. At the same time, they may expect their leader to behave consistently toward them. This places the leader in quite a dilemma. Consider the following dialogue:

Superior: George, you didn't secure the work area before you left for lunch. This is the first time that you've ever forgotten to do that.

Subordinate: I know, but I knew that you wouldn't get uptight about it.

Superior: Why did you leave the work area like this, anyway?

Subordinate: I had an important telephone call, and I meant to come back and clean it up. You're not going to come down on me, are you?

Superior: George, you know the rules. It's going to cost you five promotion points.

Subordinate: Hey, I heard some of the other guys did it and you didn't penalize them. Everyone makes mistakes once in awhile. Why single me out? And how come you get upset over it all of a sudden?

In this situation, the superior encountered inconsistent behavior from his subordinate. His approach was to apply the standard rules of the organization. The subordinate perceived this application of the rules as a change. He met it with resistance and accusations of unfairness. This kind of conflict occurs often in the organization.

RULES WILL BE BROKEN   Life in the organization often leads to the establishment of rules that are designed to structure individual behavior. At the same time, life in the organization often forces people to break the rules. This happens when the immediate press of events changes the conditions under which the rules were made. The implication is clear. Although the leader may know all the rules associated with his or her job, those rules will change—perhaps as early as tomorrow. The leader must be flexible enough to cope with these changes.

Spontaneity

Spontaneity is the ability to solve problems in a novel, yet appropriate, fashion. Sometimes it means finding new solutions to old problems. Other times, it means recognizing that a problem can be solved by the implementation of existing solutions. Spontaneous leaders are willing to experiment with new methods of doing things. Spontaneity is applied to both "hard" decisions—about things—and "soft" decisions—about people. The spontaneous leader will try out new ways of dealing with subordinates. If one technique does not work, the spontaneous leader tries another one. The spontaneous leader avoids falling into unproductive routines.

Evaluation

It is part of a leader's duties to evaluate subordinates. This is sometimes a daily task. It consists of talking with subordinates about their job performance. Often the evaluation is intended to improve the subordinate's work skills. Some leaders find it easy to pay a compliment but difficult to offer criticism, even if the criticism in constructive. But offering criticism and encouraging subordinates to accept constructive evaluation is part of the leadership task.

In chapter four some attention was given to the conduct of the appraisal interview. To be an effective evaluator, the leader must be aware of: (1) the task, (2) the subordinate's attitude, and (3) the subordinate's capability.

THE TASK To make an adequate evaluation, the leader must know what the subordinate is supposed to do. Normally, evaluation will require the leader to compare the subordinate's level of skill with an established criterion for success (see chapter five on small group skills). Given the extent to which task accomplishment was possible, how close did the subordinate come to accomplishing it? Such comments as "Good job" or "It looks OK" do not demonstrate sound evaluation skills. They are too general. Specific comments that compare the work of the person being evaluated to a standard with which that person is familar make for a good evaluation.

SUBORDINATE ATTITUDES Subordinates differ widely in their ability to accept criticism. If heavy criticism is going to induce a moderately successful worker to withdraw, it will become more *functional* if it is lightened just a bit. One's attitudes and values influence one's job performance.[21] A good evaluator can perceive the attitudes of subordinates fairly accurately and can choose the best evaluation strategy in each case.

SUBORDINATE CAPABILITY Not all workers are equally good workers. It is important to remember that the primary reason for doing evaluation is to improve job performance. Leaders need to develop skills that will enable them to determine which subordinates are working up to potential and which are not.

Encouragement

Encouragement is the ability to inspire the work group to work hard. It is also the ability to develop participation. In chapter five, much space was devoted to the value of participation in the work group. The leader's communication behavior can create a climate where participation can flourish. A climate that makes members *want to participate* is essential to effective group problem solving.[22] This is the point of the following dialogue:

[21]Lawler and Porter, "Antecedent Job Attitudes," pp. 139–55.
[22]A. Lowin, "Participative Decision-Making: A Model, Literature Critique, and Prescriptions for Research," *Organizational Behavior and Performance*, 3, no. 1 (1968), 80.

Superior: Kathy, I thought that you did a fine job on that tour you led for the divisional research people.

Subordinate: Thanks, Sarah.

Superior: Do you have any ideas about how we might eliminate some of that early scheduling difficulty we had on that tour?

Subordinate: Sarah, we have to solve some of that confusion in setting up these tours. We're wasting too many man-hours. We might be able to require more lead time between first scheduling and the actual tour. We might also assign Sally to that project. She's just finished the annual report and seems to have some extra time.

Superior: Both of those are very good suggestions, and I think we can implement both of them.

The interpersonal skill of encouragement is really an attitude on the part of the leader. The leader must want to keep the lines of communication open between himself or herself and the group. The arbitrary closing of a channel may preclude the participation and contribution that are essential to an effective work group.[23] Let us replay the same scene with the leader not practicing the skill of encouragement:

Superior: Kathy, the tour went OK ... no problems, huh?

Subordinate: No, none.

Superior: We're still having trouble scheduling these things. I just don't know what we're going to do about it.

In the second dialogue, there is very little encouragement for the subordinate to contribute good ideas. Managers who stifle ideas and close communication channels are practicing poor leadership.

Problem Orientation

The effective leader must be able to focus on the nature of the job rather than on the personalities of the workers. The leader should project a strong commitment to getting the job done right. At the same time, the leader must try to convince the workers of the job's importance to them personally. This skill enables the leader to play down personality conflicts. In routine work situations, people often get upset,

[23]Lowin, "Participative Decision-Making," p. 82; G. Hunt and C. Lee, "Organizational Climate: A Laboratory Approach" (paper presented at the annual meeting of the International Communication Association, 1976, in Portland).

tense, and difficult. This can create problems for the leader and the group, unless the group is encouraged to focus on the problem. The leader demonstrates this skill when he or she sends messages to the group members that remind them of the importance of getting the job done.

Tension Relieving

Conflict and tension are the by-products of just about any close work situation. A good leader will not be surprised when two or three subordinates engage in petty bickering or heated exchanges. This is human nature. However, the leader must be able to reduce the tension before it becomes harmful. Actually, the whole group must share the responsibility for reducing tension. However, the leader can use certain techniques to bring the work group back together.

HUMOR A joke intended to poke fun at one's self or at the group sometimes reduces tension—especially if it is related to the group's current task. However, the work group can turn into a wholesale joke session, if the leader does not maintain some control.

ROLE REVERSAL *Role reversal* occurs when the leader asks each side to state the other side's position. The situation can be taken one step further by having each side write down the other side's position, and then suggest how the conflict might be resolved. As each faction is able to perceive the strengths and weaknesses of the other, communication can sometimes be reestablished.

CREATIVE BRAINSTORMING *Creative brainstorming* resembles role reversal. Group members are encouraged to offer suggestions for improving a tense situation. Conflicting parties are encouraged to form a "committee of the whole" to generate a wide range of possible solutions to the conflict. The group will then attempt to implement the solutions that seem most appropriate.

Compromising

The last interpersonal skill to be considered here builds upon the skills already presented. Good leaders should be able to compromise when necessary. They should be able to compromise, not only with their subordinates, but also with their peers and with their own superiors. The ability to help work out compromises is an important tool in decision making.

Compromising skills enable the leader to develop a program, plan, or idea that *will work*. Compromising may mean working out an agreement between subordinates who disagree. It may mean trying to reach a settlement with the organization when the work group's official objectives have not been met. Or it may mean reconciling people who file official protests and grievances with the people whom they are protesting against.

In using compromise, the leader must work within the realm of the possible. Working out a compromise is really a process of give and take. Each movement toward agreement entails certain costs, e.g., increased labor cost, increased turnover. Compromise consists of accepting or rejecting an offer after one has calculated the potential costs. It therefore requires skill in calculating costs and expertise in proposing attractive alternatives.

the results of no leadership

To accomplish its task, the organization needs effective leaders. However, it does not always have them. In fact, one of the cries often heard in today's organization is that a leadership vacuum exists. Let us conclude this chapter by examining four conditions that result from lack of leadership.

Buck-passing

In the Truman Library, in Independence, Missouri, there is a replica of the Oval Office as it looked while Harry S Truman was president. On the desk the president used while he was in the White House sits a plaque that reads, "The Buck Stops Here." The responsibility for making decisions ultimately rests with the leader. The decision does eventually *have to* be made.

The techniques that the leader can use to gain input from group members have been considered extensively. These techniques are important. Wide consultation and participation are, without question, critical in decision making. Most theorists and practicing managers agree that participation by group members does improve the quality of decisions.[24] But when the leader uses participation as an excuse to avoid making decisions, he or she is *passing the buck*. Part of any leader's

[24]McGregor, *The Human Side*, p. 33–34; R. Likert, *The Human Organization* (New York: McGraw-Hill Book Company, 1967), pp. 42–60; R. Townsend, *Up the Organization* (New York: Alfred A. Knopf, Inc., 1970); Ewing, "Corporate Democracy"; Miles, *Theories of Management*, pp. 246–50.

duty is to make decisions, *after* appropriate consultation. Leaders who avoid this responsibility create a leadership vacuum. This is not to defend autocratic decision making. Rather, it is to say that once the avenues of consultation and participation have been exhausted, a decision must be made and implemented, and that this is the leader's responsibility.

It also makes for better relations with subordinates. Most of us would probably prefer to work for a decisive supervisor. We would like to be able to predict what our boss will do, as was mentioned in the discussion of consistency. We cannot do this if our boss is wishy-washy. Buck passers are not popular with their subordinates.

Filtering

Filtering in communication is the tendency to withhold the negative aspects of a message. It can occur in upward communication, when the subordinate withholds negative details from the boss, or in downward communication, when the boss withholds negative details from a subordinate.[25] It is downward filtering that sometimes results from lack of leadership.

It is difficult for most of us to tell someone something unpleasant. Leaders in the organization are no exception. However, this is one of their daily duties. If the negative aspects of the message are not communicated, an accurate exchange of information has not taken place.

The Need to Know

Some organizations apparently believe that the only people who should have certain information are the ones who are going to put it to immediate use. Many managers, even now, seem to accept this philosophy. These managers will only share information with a subordinate when the subordinate must have the information to do the job. At first, this may not seem like a bad policy, but it may be harmful in the long run. When employees must have information and cannot get it, morale and job satisfaction suffer.[26] And the best way to prevent duplication of effort is for the leader of each work group to *keep the members informed* about other groups' activities. Information sharing is perhaps not the subordinate's moral right, but it is certainly a practical idea—

[25]K. Davis, *Human Behavior at Work*, 4th ed. (New York: McGraw-Hill Book Company, 1972), pp. 123–24; W. Redding, *Communication Within Organizations* (New York: Industrial Communication Council, 1972), pp. 346–51.

[26]J. Tiffin and E. McCormick, *Industrial Psychology* (Englewood Cliffs, N.J.: Prentice-Hall, Inc., 1973), pp. 236–40.

one that can only serve the organization. When members have relevant information, it is much easier for them to consider the overall consequences of their actions.

The Ego Trip

It is natural, when one is appointed to a position of leadership, to associate feelings of high status with that position. Leaders in organizations normally receive higher pay, larger desks, bigger offices, and more responsibility than other employees. This is only reasonable. Since most leaders have a great many duties, they deserve commensurate rewards. The leadership vacuum appears when they allow their high status to interfere with their duties. Occasionally a leader will remain isolated, far removed from his or her subordinates. This can create barriers between the two parties. Some subordinates respond favorably to the leader who is able to "take off his coat and get his hands dirty." While this characteristic is certainly not a prerequisite for effective supervision, most of us do prefer to work for a leader who is, at the very least, *approachable*. The leader who can readily identify with subordinates is unlikely to be accused of ego-tripping.

FOR STUDY

1 What functions does leadership fulfill in the organization?
2 Identify four leadership tasks that consist primarily of communication.
3 Name some of the general approaches to leadership considered in this chapter.
4 How does one lead by communication? What communication behaviors help one to project good leadership?
5 What happens when there is no leadership in the organization? Is this potentially dangerous? If so, why?
6 Does it make good sense to allow subordinates to participate in making decisions that affect them? Why?

case six

The High School

Alton High School is located in Midway, Washington, a suburban community between Seattle and Tacoma. It serves about 2200 students and is staffed by 125 teachers. Its principal is Ms. Carol Cummings.

Carol Cummings has been principal of Alton for the last three years. She came to the district almost 30 years ago as one of the original teachers at Alton High. At that time, she had just graduated from Western Washington State University. In the beginning, Ms. Cummings taught history. She moved into administration nine years ago, when she completed her M.A. in educational administration at the University of Washington. Since Ms. Cummings came to the district very early, most of the teachers who joined the staff when she did have also moved into administration. The superintendent and all of the assistant superintendents are old friends. With this kind of influence, Ms. Cummings receives much more support at the head office than do any of the other principals in the district.

Ms. Cummings believes in running a tight ship. She holds herself accountable for everything that goes on at Alton, and she makes it a point to maintain control. Very little happens without Ms. Cummings knowing about it. For vice principal, she has appointed Barry Downey, a longtime English teacher, who has worked in the district for 27 years. He is nearly 55 years old and can hardly wait to retire, so that he can live year-round in his cabin in Idaho, where he now spends his summers. He welcomed the opportunity to get out of the classroom because, as he told one of his friends, "It was killing me." He is happy to carry out Ms. Cummings's plans for running the school.

Terry Jenkins, 27, is Ms. Cummings' administrative assistant. Ms. Cummings had Terry as a student in a history class about 10 years ago. Terry went on to college and got his teaching degree. He was hired to teach health but was promoted to A.A. when he obtained his administrative credential. Terry is intensely loyal to Ms. Cummings; he has told friends that he looks up to her as a mother figure. Much of Terry's job deals with student discipline and campus activities. He reports directly to Ms. Cummings by telephone every day on matters under his supervision.

A teacher or staff member who wants to see Ms. Cummings must get the approval of either the vice-principal or the A.A. Ms. Cummings does not schedule appointments directly with the staff. If something requires the principal's approval, it is given to either Terry or Barry. They make a recommendation and forward the item along to Ms. Cummings for final approval. Ms. Cummings considers that her primary job is to represent the school interests on the outside, especially to the district office. She has often said that she spent 20 years of her life as a classroom teacher and now she wants nothing to do with classrooms. She avoids direct contact with students as much as possible.

To her credit, Ms. Cummings has been very successful at raising money for the Alton educational program. She was almost single-handedly responsible for having the district's 9000-seat football stadium located on the Alton campus. When the Alton band was invited to compete in the national band competition last summer at the University of Michigan, she went to the district and came back with a $5000 grant that enabled the entire band to spend two weeks in Ann Arbor. The school library at Alton is among the best in the state. The campus has a completely equipped journalism facility that includes a printing press and a radio and television laboratory. The teachers' lounge is comfortably equipped with modern furniture and a work area that boasts the latest in business machines. Alton is the only high school in the district that provides a separate office for each faculty member.

Yet today Alton is seething with unrest. It was touched off by a student-produced radio program. Under the direction of Ms. Kaye Ball, the communications instructor, the students put out a documentary on the use of marijuana at the school. It was broadcast on the campus station at lunch hour. The program took a fairly objective stand on drugs all the way through but in the end, during a comment segment, came out for the legalization of pot and for getting police undercover officers off campus. It even went so far as to identify by name and appearance three local undercover narcotics officers.

Ms. Cummings was attending a meeting at district headquarters when the program was aired, so she did not hear it. But the next day she received a phone call from the chief of police. He asked rather pointedly if any taxpayer-owned facilities had been used in producing the program, which he called "subversive." Ms. Cummings had had no idea that the program was being produced. She was furious at Kaye Ball for letting it go on without her permission. That afternoon, both the Midway *Times* and the Seattle *Post-Intelligence* ran stories on the radio program. They had talked to Ms. Cummings first, but she had refused to comment. She was embarrassed about the incident and wanted to quiet it down as soon as possible. When the superintendent called a meeting for the next morning, it was difficult to tell if he was madder at the students for producing the radio program or at the Seattle paper for running the story.

Ms. Cummings took prompt action. She called Kaye Ball in, gave her an official reprimand, and placed a letter to that effect in her personnel file. She suspended the producer of the program for three days and canceled all noontime radio broadcasts for the rest of the semester. She insisted that each piece of copy for the school yearbook and newspaper be funneled through her.

Mr. Charles Harmon, the father of the suspended student, immediately contacted the Seattle Chapter of the American Civil Liberties

Union, who promptly brought a $500,000 damage suit against the principal and the school district. The suit claimed that the student's constitutional rights of freedom of speech and freedom of the press had been violated. The A.L.C.U. said that the student had been denied due process.

The situation has split the school. From the talk on campus, it appears that most students and staff support the suspended student and not the administration.

FOR STUDY

1 What terms would you use to characterize Ms. Cummings' leadership style? Is this style likely to produce good working relationships in the organization?

2 Consider Ms. Cummings' communication style. What do you see as her philosophy of communication?

3 What do you think might happen next? What must happen before the situation will improve?

4 Assume that you are operating as a communication consultant. What program would you recommend to improve communication at Alton High?

5 Discuss the relationship between communication and leadership. Can one's leadership style influence one's communication style? If so, how?

presentational communication

PART THREE

achieving
thorough planning

The next two chapters will present an overview of the important elements in public communication. This overview will focus on the skills you will need to become an effective public communicator in the organization. Chapter seven deals with planning the oral presentation. Chapter eight deals with the implementation of the plan. However, you should not think of these as two separate topics. The planning and implementation processes are both aspects of public presentation. This chapter and the next should be considered as a single unit.

It is important for you to remember that public communication skills are closely related to the skills we have already examined in this book. Good listening, good interviewing, and good leadership will all make you a better public communicator.

public communication: a definition

Communication is a dynamic phenomenon. It changes rapidly, as many scholars have suggested.[1] Some scholars believe that communication goes on all around us, and that by seeking to define it, we miss some of its significance.[2] It is therefore equally difficult to define public communication. But here goes:

> Presentational or public communication in any organizational setting occurs when one speaker is doing most of the sending and a number of listeners are doing most of the receiving.

[1] D. Barnlund, "A Transactional Model of Communication," in *Foundations of Communication Theory*, eds. D. Sereno and C. Mortensen (New York: Harper & Row, Publishers, Inc., 1970), p. 84; C. D. Mortensen, *Communication* (New York: McGraw-Hill Book Company, 1972), p. 15.

[2] R. Birdwhistell, *Kinesics and Context* (Philadelphia: University of Pennsylvania Press, 1970), p. 3.

chapter seven

Depending on the speaker's skill, public communication may be one-way (with little feedback going from the audience to the speaker), or two-way (with considerable feedback). In this book, public communication is generally referred to as *presentational* because this term is most commonly used in today's organizations. Other terms, such as "briefing," "oral reporting," and "oral outlines," are also sometimes used to refer to public communication.

This chapter begins with a discussion of the uses of the oral presentation. Next, the stages in its preparation are considered at length. The chapter concludes with a list of practical guideposts for people who must give oral presentations.

Presentational Communication: As Interaction

If there is one single idea central to both this chapter and the next, it is that *an oral presentation must be communication.* A good oral presentation will create mutual understanding between audience and speaker. Communicators in organizations often become *self-centered* in their attempts at interaction. They fall into the trap of giving presentations not for the benefit of the listener, but rather for their own benefit ("To please the boss"; "Because I have to"; "Let's get this thing over with, so that I can go on to something more important"). In chapter one, we introduced the idea of receiver-centered communication. It has been the spoken and unspoken theme of all the following chapters. Receiver-centered communication is also critically important to the oral presentation. Presentations should be designed to meet the specific needs of the audience regarding the topic under discussion. If the audience has no such needs, the presentation should not be given. Giving presentations for their own sake is not a good use of human talents. It wastes both the speaker's and the audience's time.

The concept of interaction implies that there will be some degree of give and take between the speaker and the audience. The speaker must be other-directed in planning and implementing the presentation. Being *other-directed* means considering the needs of the audience above all else in every phase of the oral presentation. This concept will reappear throughout this chapter.

Presentational Communication: A Managerial Tool

A good manager is proficient in a number of supervisorial and managerial tasks.[3] Similarly, a good managerial communicator is proficient in using a number of communication skills. These should include presentational communication. Perhaps only 5 percent of a manager's

[3] R. Likert, *The Human Organization* (New York: McGraw-Hill Book Company, 1967), p. 34.

time is spent in this kind of communication, but since many important decisions are made after oral presentations, it is important that a manager know how to make them.

In organizations, the oral presentation is an effective and fairly inexpensive vehicle for transmitting information to a number of people.[4] But in and of itself, it will not guarantee that the information will in fact be transmitted. That will depend on the skill of the speaker. There are many built-in obstacles that he or she must overcome. Some of these obstacles are related to the situation, some to the communicator, and some to the organization. All, in some way, involve the following premise: *Just because something is said to someone during a presentation, it does not necessarily follow that the listener has understood it.* Getting the audience to understand is a constant challenge for the public communicator.

The oral presentation is not the only vehicle for a manager who wants to reach a potential audience. Other vehicles include the interview, the small group, the memorandum, and the written report. Good managers know how to choose the most appropriate vehicle for transmitting information. This choice will depend on the manager's ability to assess the specific situation and his or her confidence in using a particular vehicle. In short, the choice to use the oral presentation should be a deliberate one, based on facts.

specific uses of presentational communication

The oral presentation is appropriate in many situations. Consider the following sample cases.

CASE A George is a first-line foreman in a large manufacturing plant. His duties include the supervision of nearly 70 machinists and maintenance personnel who are involved in the production of fuel injectors for jet engines. Rarely does George find it necessary to call his people together for a group meeting. He has learned instead that he works best in a one-on-one relationship with each subordinate. However, George must hold one group meeting each month. The plant superintendent has ordered that each month, on the last Friday afternoon, each foreman call his people together for a presentation on ways to improve safety in the plant. As a part of his job description, each foreman must develop and present a 15-minute talk on some aspect of

[4]A. Sanford, G. Hunt, and H. Bracey, *Communication Behavior in Organizations* (Columbus, Ohio: Charles E. Merrill Publishing Company, 1976), p. 12.

safety. In his presentations, George always discusses a safety problem that he has noticed during the month. He takes pictures of the problem, describes it in some detail, and ends his presentation by calling for solutions from the audience. If the men agree that one of the solutions is superior to the rest, George takes it to building maintenance. He always reports back to the men on the results at the next safety meeting. While other foremen dread making these presentations and complain that nothing ever gets accomplished, seven crucial safety problems have already been solved in George's department. Since George has been so quick to implement the workers' suggestions, they have been willing to offer them. The Friday afternoon safety sessions are popular with both George and his men.

CASE B   Bill is the sales manager of a small firm that manufactures seating equipment for sports arenas, hotels, schools, and so forth. A large city in an adjoining state is considering building a civic public hall. The city's planning commission has requested presentations from four suppliers of custom seating for the contract to supply the public hall. Bill, his assistant, Dave, and Don, who has the sales territory where the public hall is to be built, are flying to the meeting of the planning commission to make the presentation on behalf of their firm. Operating as a team, Bill, Dave, and Don tell the commission members what their firm can do to provide low-cost, high-quality seating for the public hall. They discuss the quality of the workmanship on their product, their record in supplying comparable buildings, and their firm's history of delivering on time. Along with their presentation, they show slides and samples of their firm's work. They also answer numerous questions from the members of the commission. When they planned their presentation, they decided to divide up the responsibilities, each man taking a particular area of expertise. This made each member of the team feel that he was contributing to the presentation. The presentation was a success—their firm was awarded the contract to supply the new public hall.

CASE C   Sharon has been training coordinator for the Miller Stationary and Printing Company for three years. Before becoming training coordinator, she worked as an interviewer in the personnel department. Her job requires her to plan, conduct, and analyze all training for Miller employees. She is currently working on a premanagement workshop for potential managers, a course on performance appraisal for middle-level managers, and a preretirement planning course for long-term employees who will retire in the next year. Sharon conducts most of the training herself, although her staff gathers information for her. A typical class will meet an hour a day for a week, but some of the more important ones—for example, the premanagement workshop—run 20 hours a week for nearly a month. Sharon has found that to be effective in training presentations, she must keep the trainees involved in what they are doing and present material that they can use back on the job or in their personal lives. Therefore, she has developed many demonstrations and activities to supplement her lecture material. Sharon has often been complimented by her superiors for her innovative and interesting programs.

CASE D   Jan is a sergeant for the Lakeview Police Department. She is presently serving as team leader of the midnight–8:00 A.M. shift. In that capacity, she is responsible for all of the activities of nine patrol officers on the street during those hours. At 11:00 each night, the officers meet at the Lakeview P.D. briefing room for roll call conducted by Jan. After calling the roll, Jan makes announcements about new rules, changes in departmental procedures, and recent crime trends in Lakeview. She also conducts a short course on some aspect of police procedure. When she was a patrol officer, many of her peers did not take these briefing sessions seriously. There was quite a bit of horseplay and goofing off. Jan promised herself that when she became team leader, she would make these sessions vital and interesting. She spends about two hours at the end of each shift preparing for the next day's briefing. She reads the chief's directives and memoranda thoroughly for information to pass along to the officers. She examines the crime statistics. She studies career development opportunities as they come up, so she can persuade officers to take advantage of them. And she talks with the other two team leaders to find out what is happening on their shifts. In this way, she has been able to gather lively and important information for each day's briefing. The officers have noted that much of the information that they later used on the street first came up during these briefing sessions. The officers no longer complain about having to attend roll call, and much of the horseplay has subsided.

These cases illustrate some of the many widely different types of situations where public presentations can be used to good effect. Like most other public presentations, they have one interesting common characteristic—their inherent public relations value.

Presentations as a Public Relations Vehicle

The public presentation is one of the primary public relations vehicles used by organizations. Public and in-house listener attitudes are formulated or altered through the public presentation. Think back to the last time you heard an outside speaker talk about his or her organization. Whether it was a local fireman discussing fire safety at your elementary school, or an engineer describing job opportunities in nuclear power to the engineering club at your college, chances are that you formed your attitudes about the speaker, the topic, and *the speaker's organization* based on what the speaker said.

PUBLIC IMAGE An organization's public image is composed of the *collective perceptions that its relevant publics have of it.*[5] These perceptions are most often formed through presentations given by official representatives of the organization and through press releases, which sometimes turn into news reports. Thus the public communicator represents the organization to which he or she belongs. Its public image is formed by how the communicator looks, what he says, and more generally, by how he handles himself.

IN-HOUSE IMAGE The same holds true within the organization. When a department head must outline the results of his or her unit's work output in a public presentation to the board of directors, the department's image is on the line. When the orientation supervisor for new employees gives a welcoming address, those new employees' image of the organization will be influenced by what they hear.

CREDIBILITY The concept of credibility has already been considered several times. It is also important in the public presentation. The credibility, or the trustworthiness, of the organization is often represented through the public presentation. Audiences normally assume that a communicator *represents* the views of his or her organization. Thus *what* an individual says to the audience may be taken for the policy of the organization on that topic *by that specific audience.* If that individual turns out to have been mistaken, the organization's credibility will suffer.

Functional Uses of the Public Presentation

Presentations are given for a wide variety of reasons. This section will present a classification system for the major types of public presentations given in organizations.

INFORMATIONAL PRESENTATIONS Informational presentations are used to transmit information to a group of people. There are five kinds of informational presentations.

Orientation presentations. New employees are usually socialized

[5] J. Thompson, *Organizations in Action* (New York: McGraw-Hill Book Company, 1967), p. 117.

to their new environment through a series of orientation communications. These often include one or more oral presentations, as well as a series of written handouts. These orientation presentations sometimes deal with specific themes, such as benefits, rules, and regulations. The orientation process may be brief—as when a personnel manager welcomes a new group of workers into the organization—or very elaborate, like the eight-week basic training program given a new member of the armed forces. In the latter situation, there may well be a whole series of oral presentations.

Training for a specific job. When members are given a new job in an industrial organization, they must be trained for that job through some form of oral presentation by a foreman or training officer. Occasionally, job training and orientation are accomplished in the same presentation. Even when on-the-job training is used, it is normally accomplished through dialogue between trainer and trainee. Showing someone how to *do* something is one of the most common topics for oral presentations in organizations. Job training is a continual process, so employees may hear presentations about how to do something throughout their tenure in the organization.

Status reports. Each subunit of the organization must be kept informed about what other subunits are doing. This is done by means of status reports. Status reports usually follow the organization's chain of command. That is, each supervisor reports on the status of his or her department to his or her supervisor. However, they also may be lateral —when peers report on their respective departments—or downward— when a subordinate tells the supervisor how things are going. Status reports are sometimes accompanied by memoranda and production reports. These contain supplementary written information. They may be given at a regular time (e.g., once a week or once a month). Or they may be given very informally—on the golf course or in the organization's lunchroom. The need for status reports is inherent in the organization. When they know what is going on in other units, individual members can coordinate, instead of duplicate, their efforts.

Reports to boards. Members of organizations are often called upon to give reports to relevant boards. Sometimes these boards will have authority over the presenter. Sometimes they will not. A city manager making a report to a city council committee would be the former situation. The same city manager making a report on the same subject to the local ministerial association board of directors would be in the latter situation. When we must make a report to a board that has the power to hire and fire or punish or reward us in some way, like the city manager in the first situation above, we are likely to feel tense. This situation is discussed at greater length in chapter eight, when the commitment-seeking presentation is considered.

General meetings. Some organizations still live by the old adage "If you are in trouble and do not know what to do, just call a meeting on it." Managers conduct meetings with each other and with their subordinates and attend meetings with their superiors. One of the main activities of these meetings is the transfer of information. This transfer of information requires that the individual know something about developing brief presentations.

COMMITMENT-SEEKING PRESENTATIONS   Some oral presentations given in organizations are intended to influence the listener. An oral report may be both informative and persuasive. The speaker may attempt to convey information about a particular topic while at the same time trying to change the listener's attitudes about that information. The theory and guidelines for developing the commitment-seeking presentation are covered in the next chapter. Some of the most important *types* are outlined briefly below.

Sales presentation. The most obvious type of commitment-seeking presentation is made by the salesperson trying to sell a particular product. But one does not have to be labeled "salesperson" to make a sales presentation. A manager requesting an increase in her department's budget for the upcoming quarter, a scientist presenting a request for work to begin on a new product, or a secretary who asks for a new typing table are all engaging in this form of communication. Think back over your work career. There were probably times when you developed a sales pitch to persuade your boss to give you something that you wanted, perhaps a raise or time off for an important date. On these occasions, you were making a commitment-seeking public presentation. This type of public presentation is widely used in organizations. Knowing how to get someone in authority to say "yes" is a practical communication skill that you should seek to acquire.

Motivating presentation. Sometimes a manager must appeal to subordinates to improve their performance. A commitment-seeking presentation that is intended to get someone to work hard or produce more is called a *motivating presentation.* The football coach who addresses his players at half time, trying to get them to overcome a 0–21 score, the circulation manager of the local newspaper who tells her people that more subscriptions are needed and that they must solicit them door-to-door, the lead carpenter who tells his subordinates that they must improve their work on the interior of a new home are all making motivating presentations.

Because human behavior is so complex, the motivating presentation often backfires. Some unsophisticated managers seem to believe that if they threaten or coerce their subordinates to work harder, they necessarily will.[6] This thinking is naive. People work or do not work for a variety of reasons. A manager who simply tells an employee to work harder is not saying or doing anything to change the *reasons why* the employee is not working.

Recruiting presentation. A public communication intended to get someone to join your organization, or to take a particular position within your organization, is referred to here as a *recruiting presentation.* The personnel manager recruits potential executives; the line worker tries to get his buddy to help him with a project. The basketball coach at the university makes a recruiting presentation to the family of the six-foot eleven, all-state high school center, trying to persuade them that Junior should further his education at good old State U. Getting someone competent to work is a constant challenge for most organizations. A manager must be a good recruiter.

Team approach. The team approach is actually a *methodology.* Unlike the three types of presentations just discussed, it is not limited to one particular situation. Organizations have recently recognized that the commitment-seeking presentation requires a wide perspective. To achieve this, the team approach is commonly used. Usually, three or four people, each with a different expertise, will form a team to make a public presentation. Its purpose is to persuade an in-house or public audience to adopt a particular idea. All of the members work toward this common goal. When a team is effective, members build on each other's knowledge and ideas to get much more information on the table than any one presenter could do. For example, an architectural firm might make a team presentation to sell its plan for a proposed shopping center. The team might be composed of a supervising architect, who would act as chair; a structural engineer, who would discuss the building; a civil engineer, who would discuss the roads to the shopping center; and an environmental engineer, who would report the results of the environmental impact study. Each member of the team would concentrate on his or her specialty, but all of them would work toward the same goal—selling the overall design to the developer.

Special types of commitment-seeking presentations. Because most organizations have their own way of doing things, one occasionally sees special types of oral presentations. Most of these are intended to encourage members to participate more fully. Two of these special types of presentations are *traditional addresses* and *confrontation meetings.*

Perhaps once a year, the president of the organization will call all

[6]D. McGregor, *The Human Side of Enterprise* (New York: McGraw-Hill Book Company, 1960), p. 24; H. Leavitt, *Managerial Psychology,* 3rd ed., (Chicago: University of Chicago Press, 1972), p. 56.

of the members together for a "state of the organization" address. Often these addresses are given on special occasions, such as Christmas or the anniversary of the company. They may sometimes filter down to the first level of supervision, as when the foreman calls all of the subordinates together to thank them for their efforts during the last month. Some people argue that the president's annual Christmas message wastes everyone's time and serves no useful purpose. But organizations, like any other social institutions, develop their own traditions, and traditions die slowly. Furthermore, violating a tradition can create conflict. What would happen in your first class next semester if the professor, instead of following the tradition of making the "this is what the course is all about" speech, gave a multiple-choice test? Traditions are important to both people and organizations. This is probably why most chief executives continue to speak to "the troops" on certain special occasions.

Some organizations allow members to hash out their differences in a no-holds-barred confrontation meeting. These meetings may be called rap sessions, encounter meetings, or gripe sessions, but the purpose is always the same: to resolve built-up conflicts. In a confrontation meeting, the disagreeing parties are called upon to present their respective sides of the question. The skilled presenter will use this opportunity to seek recruits to his or her position. After each side has had the opportunity to hear the opposite viewpoint, the matter is discussed and —sometimes—resolved.

the stages in planning a public presentation

This section will discuss the stages in planning a public presentation. Note that although the discussion is organized around five chronological stages, the *activity* itself does not fall neatly into these five stages. People plan differently. You might plan a public presentation one way while your classmate might do it another way entirely. The five stages are intended to serve only as a guide.

Stage One: Determining the Purpose

Before you begin to prepare a public presentation, you must have a clear-cut purpose in mind. *If a particular public presentation has no clear purpose, it should not be given.* Unfortunately, it is often given anyway. A purposeless presentation wastes everyone's time. Here *purpose* may be defined as *the specific reason why a speaker is addressing a particular group of listeners.* Actually, every public presentation has two purposes: the *speaker's* purpose and the *listener's* purpose. Sometimes these two purposes are compatible; sometimes they are not. In determining the purpose of your own public presentation, you should consider the following factors.

WHO IS THE MOST APPROPRIATE COMMUNICATOR? In planning a public presentation, the first question to ask is, "Who should be making it?" A group of government employees was once asked to identify the biggest problem they faced in making public presentations. Overwhelmingly, they agreed that the problem that came up most often was that their department had sent the wrong person to make a particular presentation—them! Getting the right person to make a specific presentation is really a question of managing human resources. The requirements of the situation (what is to be accomplished), the talent available (who is best qualified), the trust of the audience (who is most credible), and the pragmatics (just who can we get and what problems will we encounter if we send him) all must be considered. When a person is called upon to make a presentation, and that person does not feel comfortable or competent in the assignment, the organization's image may suffer. Since the public presentation will almost always be intended to reflect positively on the organization, the person giving it should be the one best qualified for the assignment. Deciding who is best qualified, then, is an important part of the planning process.

WHAT EXPECTATIONS ARE ASSOCIATED WITH THE COMMUNICATION? People formulate prejudgments about what they expect to happen in a given context. These prejudgments are called *expectations.* Expectations will or will not be confirmed by the succeeding events. In planning the public presentation, you should consider two sets of expectations— those of the organization and those of your supervisor.

Earlier, it was suggested that public presentations represent the image of the organization. Organizations often expect certain things of the person who is representing them. These expectations may be very specific; they may even be spelled out in a speakers' handbook. Or they may be extremely general and handed down by word-of-mouth to each person assigned to give a presentation. The first kind are clear-cut and difficult for an intelligent and thorough communicator to violate. The second kind are less obvious. Examples of these general expectations might be that communicators take promotional literature about the organization with them, that they stand when addressing any audience, or that they always wear a "dress-up" outfit when talking to a public group. Organizations vary a great deal in the degree of control they exert over public communicators. When you plan a public presentation, ask yourself, "What does my organization expect of me in this presentation?"

If your boss has assigned you to make a specific presentation, he or she may support it more strongly than if you developed this opportunity yourself. This a real "nitty-gritty" issue. If your supervisor supports the presentation, he or she may let you take work time to plan and deliver it. Without your supervisor's support, you may have difficulty presenting it at all. Just as you would ask yourself what the organization expects, you should also ask what the boss expects. Remember that you are *representing* him or her before a group. Your boss and you are on the line. Occasionally it will be enough simply to inform your supervisor of the upcoming presentation, describing the general direction it will take and the type of audience you are addressing. Other times, it will be necessary for you to work closely with the boss in planning the presentation.

You will note that we have not even touched on the most important set of expectations. These are the expectations of the audience. Audience expectations are so crucial to the success of any presentation that they will be considered separately later.

WHAT IS THE CONTEXT OF THE COMMUNICATION? You should consider the context of the presentation early in the planning process. Ask yourself these two questions:

When is it to be given? A famous coach once said that 90 percent of success in baseball is timing. The same holds true of public presentation. When you plan a presentation, review the events surrounding the time frame in which it is to be given. Average presentations can have significant impact when they contain the right words at the right time. Finding the right message means becoming familiar with the events that have occurred before you begin to speak. The effectiveness of the Gettysburg Address and the "I Have a Dream" speech by Dr. Martin Luther King, Jr., were both tremendously enhanced by timing.

Where is it to be given? Location is the other half of context. To answer this question, you must take a close look at your audience. Above all, will you be speaking on the audience's turf or on your own? Addressing a captive audience, such as a group of students called into the principal's office for disobeying rules, is quite different from addressing an audience that has invited you to speak on its own territory —for example, a women's club that has invited a member of the city's planning commission to speak in its clubhouse. A third alternative is to speak in a neutral location. An example would be a church service held in a national park, where both the minister and congregation are visitors. The variable operating here is power. Who has the power, the communicator or the audience? If you have it, you have many more options available. Getting the audience to be responsive is probably easier when you are familiar with the territory. This is not a rigid rule, but it should be considered in planning a presentation.

NOW: THE SPECIFIC PURPOSE   You are now ready to move to the next step: stating the purpose of the presentation. Exactly *why* is this presentation being given? To establish the *why* you must have information about: (1) the significance of the occasion, (2) your listeners' preconceived ideas about the event, and (3) the history of the occasion. Getting the information means asking questions of others and reading any available relevant material. Then try your hand at formulating a purpose statement.

There are two things that you should do after the purpose has been established. You should check out your thinking with others, and you should remain flexible.

Check it out. Thus far, your planning has been an individual effort. But after you have made all the decisions already mentioned, check with a colleague. See if your thinking is consistent with his or hers. By having someone else check your logic and analysis, you are developing more information to use in planning.

Be flexible. Because people change and audiences are fairly dynamic, skilled public communicators follow this rule. No purpose, no plan should ever be cast in cement. Your plan should be flexible enough to allow for some degree of change and, ideally, improvement.

When you have finally established the purpose of your public presentation, you are ready to write it down. That way you can keep it in front of you, available for refinement and modification. Purpose statements can vary greatly in length and structure. Here are two examples:

- *Statement 1:* This presentation is being given to the Millerville Recreation Commission to report a study conducted by city staff on the attitudes of community citizens regarding a proposed family swimming program.
- *Statement 2:* New teachers will be welcomed through a presentation by Albert E. Miller, principal of Sunny Hills Terrace High School, at the annual luncheon to mark the beginning of the school year.

Each of these purpose statements specifies the context of the presentation along with the reason why it is being given. Both are clear and concise. Once the purpose has been established and written down in a statement, it is much easier to plan the rest of the presentation.

IDENTIFYING SPECIFIC AUDIENCE OUTCOMES The final step in determining the purpose of the presentation is to establish specific desired outcomes. A specific desired outcome is a goal or objective. You might think of each outcome as a statement that summarizes one thing *that you want your audience to retain* or *do*. Take Statement 1. The outcomes of that presentation might be:

- *Outcome 1:* To have the audience (the members of the Recreation Commission) become familiar with the methods used to conduct the study.
- *Outcome 2:* To have the audience understand the major findings of the study.
- *Outcome 3:* To have the audience attempt to identify some of the reasons why the findings of the study emerged as they did.
- *Outcome 4:* To persuade the audience to implement the results of the study into their planning and decision making about the recreational needs of the community.

In short, the outcomes are the information that you want your audience to retain or the behavior in which you want them to engage. You will use these outcomes as an outline when you build your presentation. Identifying specific outcomes is nothing more than implementing the purpose statement that you developed early in the planning process. The purpose statement, if you will remember, was the general reason that motivated you to communicate in the first place. The outcome is a specific breakdown of the general purpose into manageable parts. At this state, your outcomes should remain flexible, because they may be modified a little later in the planning process.

Now you have completed the preliminary work in the planning of the public presentation. Keep in mind that all of the decisions that you have made thus far are still tentative. Events can happen—a change in the composition or attitude of the audience, a change in the profitability of the organization—that may oblige you to alter your *presentation plan*. If your plan is dynamic, this should not be difficult. By the time you actually appear in front of your audience, your presentation will probably reflect hours of change and modification.

Stage Two: Assessing the Audience

Most of the work you have done so far on your presentation plan has been related to content and rationale. If you were literally following the advice put forth in this chapter, you would have systematically ignored the audience. Of course, you would not really do this. The audience would have been and would continue to be in the back of your mind throughout the planning of the presentation. But now you must turn all of your energies toward considering the audience and its expectations.

Because the public presentation by definition has more than one listener, all of the difficulties that we normally encounter in person-to-person communication are multiplied. It is imperative that we know "where the audience is coming from." For use in workshop sessions, a brief worksheet can help a public communicator assess his or her audience. (See figure 7–1.) This worksheet lists some of the most important things that you should consider in analyzing the audience's preattitudes (its attitudes prior to the presentation). The categories included on the form will be discussed. They are followed by several other factors that you should also consider in assessing an audience.

DEMOGRAPHIC CHARACTERISTICS OF THE AUDIENCE Every audience has a set of unique demographics associated with it. *Demographics* are those general factual categories which can be used to describe any group of people—in this case, the group of listeners to whom you will be directing the public presentation. Among those categories which might be included in a demographic analysis of the audience are average age, range of age, socioeconomic level, and level of aesthetic and cultural understanding and sensitivity. Knowing these facts about your listeners will help you to understand exactly who will be sitting in the room listening to your presentation.

When your presentation is directed to an audience within your own organization, you may have built up a pretty strong *sense* of these demographic factors simply by working with the people for a long time. Some communicators have addressed the same group of middle-level managers or first-line foremen every month for the last five years. In this situation, you may not need to do as thorough a job of audience assessment as you would if you were appearing before a group for the first time.

In doing a demographic assessment, you may sometimes be obliged to draw generalizations about a particular audience. These generalizations may eventually prove to be unjustified. Just because an audience is young, will it always be politically liberal? Will a middle-class audience always behave in a certain way? Obviously not. To make such blind assumptions without planning for error would be foolish. It would go against everything we know about human behavior. The reason for doing this assessment is not to make hard-and-fast, unchangeable assumptions about the audience. Rather, it is to gather information that will enable you to judge the tone and appropriate level of treatment in planning your public presentation. If you are making an infor-

FIGURE 7–1   Audience analysis worksheet

Demographic Characteristics

   Age: Economic Status:

   Educational Level: Political Status:

   Occupational Type: Other Influences:

General Audience Attitudes

   What are their political orientations?

   What are their social orientations?

   Where do they get their information?

   What constituencies do they serve?

Specific Audience Attitudes Toward Proposal

   What do they think of your proposal?

   Sources of their attitudes?

   What attitudes can be changed?

   What strategies may work?

Specific Audience Attitudes Toward Communicator

   What do they think of you?

   What are your strengths (with listeners)?

   What are your weaknesses (with listeners)?

   Possible sources of credibility?

mational presentation, you need to know the intellectual level of the audience. If you are trying to be persuasive, you need to know what types of arguments will work best. But any conclusion that you draw about your audience is, at best, an educated guess. Since you cannot be sophisticated enough to assess every member of a large group accurately, it is necessary for you to come up with some kind of *profile*. This profile will be a workable document that can aid you in the planning process. It should help you to forecast *reasonably* accurately how the audience *ought* to behave toward you and your proposal.

Let us assume for a moment that you are representing your organization in a presentation at the local YMCA. If you knew the location (the local Y) and only one other fact—that your audience is to be composed of 14–16 year olds—you probably would have enough data to begin the planning process. The more demographic data you have about a specific audience, the more accurate your predictions are likely to be because you will know where you are directing your communication messages.

GENERAL AUDIENCE ATTITUDES   Once the demographic characteristics of the audience have been determined, it is possible to make some guesses about its general attitudes. Although such terms as "liberal" and "conservative" are too general to be very descriptive, they help you to characterize your audience as either "willing to change," a purported characteristic of liberals, or "resistant to change," a supposed characteristic of conservatives. Some popular stereotypes—business leaders are conservative; college professors are liberal; policemen are more conservative than social workers—are based on common perceptions of these general attitudes. To determine the general attitudes of your audience, ask yourself the following two questions: (1) Given the demographic data that I already have about the members of this audience, how are they likely to behave? (2) If they do behave as predicted, is that behavior likely to influence their acceptance or rejection of my proposal? The answers to these questions will provide additional input to the presentation plan. Remember, though, that at this point you are really just guessing. You will probably make some good guesses and some bad ones.

SPECIFIC AUDIENCE ATTITUDES TOWARD PROPOSAL   Where does your specific proposal stand with members of this audience? Have they heard about it before and have they formed an opinion on the ideas that you plan to talk about? If the listeners already have their minds made up against your proposal, you may be in trouble. If they are already 100 percent in favor of your ideas, you would probably do better not to talk to them at all. You might change their mind. Most audiences will proba bly fall somewhere between these two extremes. Audiences generally have some idea what you are going to talk about and some opinions, positive or negative, on the subject. In the audience assessment stage of the planning process, it is necessary to make some educated guesses and, if possible, to collect some first-hand data, to determine how much information the audience already has about the proposal. If the audience is knowledgeable about your ideas, it would be foolish to waste time transmitting a lot of information. You can move straight into arguments directed at gaining commitment. If the audience appears to know very little about the proposal, you must spend some time filling in the background. Sounding people out, making telephone calls, and asking people for their experiences with this particular audience are all ways of determining specific audience attitudes toward your proposal.

SPECIFIC AUDIENCE ATTITUDES TOWARD COMMUNICATOR Where do you stand with this specific audience? Have the members of the audience formed some knowledge of or attitudes about you from past experience? If you have power over the audience (e.g., if you supervise them), you are in the driver's seat. If the audience has power over you, you may be at a disadvantage. If the audience does not know anything about you, it is up to you to offer it enough information about yourself to build some degree of credibility. You can do this by providing biographies or data sheets, or simply by asking the person who is going to introduce you to describe your particular qualifications on this topic. Audiences respect credible communicators.[7] If you have credibility with a specific audience, you may be able to persuade it, or at least a significant part of it, to believe what you say about your proposal. A frank and honest assessment of your own assets and liabilities with respect to your audience is an important aspect of the planning process. Know your weaknesses ahead of time. You may be able to strengthen them through expert planning.

CONSTITUENCIES SERVED BY THE MEMBERS OF THE AUDIENCE Most of us, at one time or another, have found ourselves serving as someone else's representative. If members of the audience are serving specific constituencies, there are really two audiences—the one in the room and the phantom audience that is being represented. Speaking only to the audi-

---

[7]K. Giffin, "The Contribution of Studies of Source Credibility to a Theory of Interpersonal Trust in Communication," *Psychological Bulletin*, 68, no. 2 (1967), 109; K. Andersen and T. Clevenger, "A Summary of Experimental Research of Ethos," *Speech Monographs*, 30 (1968), 62.

ence in the room and neglecting the extended audience may not be the best strategy. Grasping exactly who the real audience is is an important part of the planning process.

SPECIFIC AUDIENCE CHARACTERISTICS When you considered the context of the public presentation, you may have discovered that the audience had some unique characteristics (e.g. they are all school teachers, Chicanos, Presbyterians, ex-convicts). If the audience has any unique characteristics, they should be considered in the planning process.

IMPORTANCE OF ASSESSING THE AUDIENCE Assessing the audience may seem at first like a difficult job. Indeed it is. There is always the risk of spoiling your whole plan by guessing wrong in one area. Some people take shortcuts to avoid having to assess the audience at all. They may rely on one all-purpose presentation that can be used with any audience or on general presentations that make no reference to the specific audience. This is certainly not a good example to follow. Difficult as a thorough assessment may be, you should do it, because it adds crucial data to the planning process. You will use these data to make a two-way exchange with the members of the audience by communicating with them at their own level.

REVISITING THE PURPOSE OF THE PRESENTATION After the initial assessment of the audience has been accomplished, you must ask yourself two questions: (1) What does the audience expect me to say? (2) Is the purpose that I have developed consistent with the expectations of the audience? There is nothing inherently wrong with violating audience expectations, but you should do it deliberately and for a good reason. Revisiting and reanalyzing the purpose of the presentation will enable you to check back on your earlier decisions. If your purpose appears to be consistent with your reading of audience expectations, fine. If not, ask yourself if you have a good enough reason to violate these expectations. Since your plan was left flexible, it should not be difficult to make minor adjustments.

Let us stop and see how far we have come in planning our public presentation. We have developed our purpose statement thoroughly. We have considered expectations and context, and we have tried to develop audience outcomes consistent with those expectations and that context. We have then made a complete assessment of the audience, including its demographics, attitudes, and expectations. We are now ready to begin to search for materials that will help us to support and document our presentation.

In the search stage, we are trying to find materials that will enrich and develop the audience outcomes contained in our presentation. There are three major cognitive activities associated with this search.

RESEARCH *Research* consists of going to where the information is stored and looking for the appropriate data to support one's position. Unlike the research scientist, who is supposed to remain objective in the search for information, the public communicator usually searches subjectively. Most often, the only useful information will be that which supports specific audience outcomes. When the public communicator knows basically what he or she wants to say, the research is specific and narrow. Some of the locations for research will now be described.

Company files. Probably the best place to find information about an organization will be its filing system. A famous organizational theorist has written that the history of an organization can be found in its files.[8] Files can provide useful and accurate data for the communicator. Specifically, they can tell you what the organization has done in the past to deal with a particular problem or issue.

Company or public library. Large organizations sometimes maintain complete libraries with lists of relevent sources in the areas of the organization's specialty. Public or university libraries are less useful because they are less specialized. Such a narrow topic as "the XRE process for purifying milk" or "labor relations in the aluminum industry" is too specific for most public libraries.

Documents. In the United States, many organizations, especially the federal government, spend thousands of dollars publishing documents on just about any topic. The documents published by your own firm are probably in the files. Other documents may be found in company libraries and in special depositories. Probably the most useful document is the *annual report.* Almost every firm publishes one. Although annual reports are sometimes vague and general, they do provide a wealth of information about the firm's activities over the past year. By examining a series of annual reports, you may be able to perceive historical trends in the organization without having to go to the files.

Original data. There are many methods of generating first-hand information. Among the most common are survey and questionnaire studies, interviews, and personal observation. The following example shows how observation can be used.

[8]M. Weber, *Essays in Sociology,* trans. H. Gerth and C. Mills (London: Oxford University Press, 1946), p. 212.

You have been asked to report to the management committee on worker satisfaction in your work unit. You have checked the files and have found only a very general study of job satisfaction done many years ago. You have interviewed some people, but all they said was that, although things don't seem to be too good, they haven't noticed any problems. Finally, you have gone through the last five annual reports —which present only a glowing profile of the workers' motivations and attitudes. But during the course of your daily work, you have noticed that the workers seem angry at the conditions in their lunchroom. Each day the workers come in and find that the lunchroom has not been cleaned, and that the food and snacks in the vending machines are sometimes weeks old. True, the social science research on job satisfaction does not say very much about dirty lunchrooms as a cause of worker dissatisfaction. But intuitively you have made the connection. In your report to the management committee, you might talk about this condition, saying that it is something that you have noticed. You would not give it the same validity as you would give to a job satisfaction research project.

Reporting the obvious is something that sophisticated behavioral scientists have trouble doing. If you are called upon to make a public presentation, be sure to look around. Try to make some judgments about what you see. Add the data you come up with to the other documentation you use to support your position.

ANALYSIS When you have found the information you need, the next step is to analyze and evaluate it. Examine your material carefully. You will probably find that some of it can be used effectively with all groups, some with only certain groups, and some not at all. You will eventually want to feature your best material by drawing attention to it during your presentation. At this point, you may discover that you do not have adequate information to support the audience outcomes you have developed. If this happens, go back to the last step and do some more research.

SYNTHESIS Now you must decide how you are going to put together your best data to support your audience outcomes. Look at all of the information that you have uncovered. See if any trends or general ideas emerge. Keep asking yourself, *What does this information mean to me? What will it mean to my audience?* A word of warning: After doing considerable research on a particular question, you may uncover information that might prove threatening or embarrassing to your audience. For example, you may find that specific members of the audience are responsible for creating a particular problem. If this happens, you have a decision to make. You can either level with the audience and risk reprisals later, or you can soft-pedal the information. Either response may be acceptable, depending on the situation.

SEARCH AS DEDUCTION A complete search for information should be as deductive as possible. You should start by collecting general information on the topic and then narrow the search down to specific information. This specific information will provide the necessary documentation for the presentation. By approaching the search for data in this manner, you will be forced to go through the mental discipline of building a strong case to support the proposition. In the end, you should have the necessary specifics without losing the big picture.

REVISITING THE PURPOSE AGAIN Now go back again to the purpose that you developed early in the planning process. Have you done enough research to build a presentation that achieves both this purpose and the preliminary audience outcomes? If not, you need to do further work. Since you phrased your preliminary audience outcomes tentatively, you can adjust and modify them if the results of your search seem to warrant it. If you are convinced that you have done the appropriate background preparation, you are now ready to develop the public presentation.

Stage Four: Development

Now you must decide on the final audience outcomes that you will seek to achieve through presentation. Will they be primarily informational? If so, make a list of the facts that you want your audience to retain. Will they be commitments? If so, formalize each commitment in a declarative statement called a *proposition* and develop the reasons why your listeners should accept each one. Last of all, go back to your original purpose. This was the reason why you were going to speak. Remember that the original purpose was established *before* you had done much background work. It may be that the original purpose must now be modified after your efforts. If the final audience outcomes are consistent with the original purpose—no problems. However, it is quite possible that there will be some inconsistency. This inconsistency should result primarily from the later thinking that you did after you developed the original purpose. Once you have developed your final outcomes, it is late to make any adjustments. Generally, you will want to go with them.

Your final outcomes should be clear, concise, and supported with data. Let us consider each of these points.

CLARITY There is no need to be complicated at this stage. State simply and clearly what you want the audience to know or do. For example, suppose that you are making a report to your boss and peers about the status of the upcoming vote for collective bargaining in the work unit. Your outcomes might be stated as follows.

I want the audience to be aware that

1 Fifty-five percent of our employees will probably not vote for collective bargaining, according to the prediction of the personnel department manager.
2 Three national unions are competing to represent our employees.
3 We have decided to maintain a hands-off policy among management personnel about this issue.
4 The vote will be coming up in two weeks, and the results will be available three days after the polls close.

These four outcome statements are clear and straightforward. In the next chapter, you will learn that these clear outcome statements should be the *main points* in your presentation.

CONCISENESS State your final outcomes in a few words or phrases. Keep it simple. That is the best way to keep the channel open between you and the listener.

SUPPORT The information that you have gathered provides the support for the outcomes. Each outcome statement is developed using evidence and data. If you want the audience to retain a concept or accept a commitment, the documentation provides the *reasons why.*

A FINAL WORD ON AUDIENCE OUTCOMES You may think that the author is practicing overkill in his emphasis on audience outcomes. This emphasis is deliberate. A good measure—perhaps the only real measure—of the success of a public presentation is the degree to which the members of the audience do retain the main outcomes. Since you have selected and developed the outcomes with the audience in mind, you want to make sure that the audience has heard and understood them. They must be repeated, emphasized, and summarized. Making a presentation that the audience neither understands nor is interested in is one of the biggest calamities that can happen to a public communicator.

Stage Five: Refinement

Thus far, you have established the audience outcomes for your presentation and have developed reasons why the audience should accept the ideas they represent. Now you are ready to put on the final touches. To do this, ask yourself four questions.

DOES THE PRESENTATION DO WHAT I INTENDED IT TO DO? Even now it is not too late to make changes. Sometimes we get so caught up with the details of the planning process that we miss the overall purpose of the presentation. We speak in order to "do something" to a specific audience. Whatever that "something" is (to inform, to persuade), you need to determine whether or not your presentation does it. Go through all of the planning decisions you have made so far and review them in terms of the original reasons why you decided or were chosen to speak. It is difficult to submit one's own work to this kind of hard criticism, but you must do it if you want to know whether your solution (the final presentation) does in fact solve the problem (the original reason why you were moved to communicate).

IS THE PRESENTATION UNDERSTANDABLE? Since you have kept the attitudes and orientations of your specific audience in mind throughout most of the planning process, it should not be difficult to go back now and determine whether they will be able to understand the proposed presentation. Are the terms defined? Does the plan flow well? Have you tied up all the loose ends? If you go back through your plan challenging each idea as a member of the audience might, you will probably be able to make your presentation a lot more understandable.

ARE THE INTENDED OUTCOMES OBVIOUS? Examine your plan as objectively as possible. Ask yourself if the outcomes are stated in such a way that they are obvious to a potential listener.

WHAT GENERAL IMPROVEMENTS CAN BE MADE IN THE PRESENTATION PLAN? There is always room for improvement. Refinement really means fine-tuning your work to such a degree that it cannot help but hit the mark. Needless tinkering with the plan is not recommended, but changes that clarify and simplify should be made.

Now check out your plan with others. This will give you a wider perspective on your thoughts. After you have done this, your plan should be in pretty good shape, but a few more points must be mentioned.

Considering Possible Contingencies

In any type of planning, what you are really trying to do is to account for any possible contingency. Planning a public presentation is no exception. Of course, it is virtually impossible for one plan to take every possible contingency into account. But you may want to brainstorm a few contingencies to see if your plan allows for them. Some of the most obvious contingencies are:

1 Suppose that you have assumed that your audience is moderately well informed on your topic. When you arrive to talk, you find that the audience has absolutely no information whatever. Can your plan meet this contingency?

2 Suppose that you had planned on a 20-minute presentation. When you arrive, you find that you are slotted into a five-minute time period. Can your plan meet this contingency? (The opposite situation sometimes occurs, too. What if you had assumed a five-minute time period but were given 20 minutes?

3 Suppose that you had misjudged the orientation of your audience. You had assumed that they would be objective toward you, but when you arrive, you find that, for some unknown reason, they are hostile to you and your proposal. Can your plan meet this contingency?

4 Suppose that you had misunderstood the reason why you were to give a public presentation. You thought it was for one reason, and the audience thought it was for another. Can your plan meet this contingency?

Such contingencies occur rarely, and good planning can sometimes neutralize them when they do occur. A skilled communicator will have a plan that can take care of these and other unexpected situations.

A Review

Two ideas should be reemphasized. The first is to *be your own strongest critic.* If you can criticize your plan, and can then improve it based on your own analysis, this should build both your self-confidence and your image when you eventually interact with the audience. Second, *do not let your plan become rigid.* To be workable and useful, a plan must be flexible. Each planning decision is made when it must be made, but all these decisions are always being reviewed.

In conclusion, figure 7–2 offers a review of the stages in planning a public presentation. Each stage feeds back to the earlier stages in such a way as to encourage adjustments and improvements at each point in the planning process.

some guideposts in planning the public presentation

Many of the chapters in this book conclude with a set of practical guideposts intended to help the student use the material presented in the chapter. Here are five guideposts for you to use in the planning process.

1. *In most situations involving the public presentation, there are few absolutes.* It is more a matter of making what seems to be *the best*

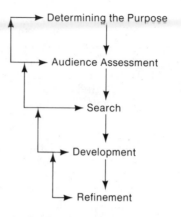

FIGURE 7-2   Stages in planning the presentation

choice and going with it. Experts disagree on the best methods for giving public presentations. This is because the subject itself is nebulous. This, in turn, is because audiences are composed of people, and people are unpredictable. So building effective presentations is not an exact science. Some people can violate all of the rules and still be very effective. Others who follow each rule seem doomed to failure. It is difficult for the student to know what to do. The only meaningful advice is simply to do a thorough job in your planning, choose what you think will work best, and try to implement it. It is a rare situation when A will work and B will not. Most often A may work somewhat better than B.

2. *Always keep the audience in mind.* Because public presentations are a form of communication, and the audience is the receiver, a good communicator will remember the audience at each stage of planning. A communicator who violates just about every other principle, but remembers this one, still has some chance of success.

3. *Because effective presentations can be built in a number of ways, do not stick with tradition solely for tradition's sake.* There is nothing wrong with tradition. Textbooks on public speaking describe the traditional techniques for making presentations. These traditional techniques may work well for you, or they may not. Be suspicious of any approach that suggests that there is only one way to build an effective presentation. Skilled communicators understand the theory of good public communication, but they do not "do it by the book" at the expense of their own creativity and talent.

4. *Given the many possible routes to effectiveness, be experimental—try things out.* This guidepost follows from the preceding ones. A good public communicator will be flexible enough to try out new ap-

proaches and techniques. When you try something and it does not work, try something else. Being experimental means trying out different alternatives until you generate a planning formula that works for you. Your style may be substantially different from someone else's, but if it works for you, it is justified.

5. *Planning presentations is time-consuming, hard work.* A management consultant once asked a group of managers who often had to make public presentations what they considered to be the absolute minimum planning time required for a ten-minute presentation. As a group, the managers replied that they would feel uncomfortable if they spent less than two hours on planning. They added that they would recommend one hour of planning time for each five minutes of speaking time. That is a great challenge when other duties are competing for our time. Although the research on the topic is limited, many people say that the more they have prepared for a presentation, the more confident they feel when they face the audience.

FOR STUDY

1 Identify some of the uses of presentations in the organization.

2 Why should a manager be able to make a public presentation? Name three situations calling for a presentation in a manager's typical day.

3 Name the stages in planning public presentations.

4 Public speaking instruction has, for many years, emphasized audience analysis. Why is audience analysis important? What function does it fulfill in helping to make a successful public presentation?

5 Where might one go, within an organization, to gather data to make a public presentation? Name some other potential sources of information.

The Nursing Administrator

Nancy Culver works in the nursing department of Langley Hospital in Portland, Oregon. After receiving her B.S. from Portland State University, she worked first as a psychiatric nurse and then moved into an alcohol-abuse program. After that, she was the lead nurse in a large pediatrics department. At present, however, she is assistant director of nursing services.

Nancy's supervisor is Mary Gonzalez, head of nursing services at Langley. Some time ago, it came to Mary's attention that Nancy has a talent both for handling people and for getting the job done on time. These are vital administrative skills, and Mary decided to make use of them.

Nancy was given her first administrative task about three years ago, when she was appointed to serve on the ad hoc committee to study physician-nurse relations at Langley. During the committee meetings, Nancy was appointed to serve as spokesperson for the group. In that role, she had numerous opportunities to talk with the press and members of the public. Later, when the committee presented its findings to the hospital board of directors, it was Nancy's job to report to the board on the results of the various surveys. Since an entire three-hour meeting was devoted to these data, Nancy had to do a lot of planning and analysis to make sure that her presentation fit well into the time slot, and that the audience would remain interested in what she had to say.

After this assignment, Nancy served on the self-study committee that prepared the report for accreditation of the school of nursing at the hospital. She also served on the all-hospital committee to examine Langley's role in the community. In this last assignment, Nancy was given numerous opportunities to go out and talk to groups of people from the community. These talks had two purposes—to let the general public know what Langley was doing and to learn from the public what they wanted Langley to do in the future. When Nancy had completed this last assignment, Mary Gonzalez invited her to join the director's staff as an assistant. Nancy accepted at once. Although she thoroughly enjoyed working with patients, she felt that administrative work offered a greater challenge to her abilities.

In her job as Mary's assistant, Nancy often acts as a spokesperson for the nursing staff at the hospital. When an issue comes up, such as the possibility of a shorter work week for nurses or a shortage of trained nursing personnel, it is Nancy's duty to formulate a response that represents the position of the nursing staff. Since she also represents management, she occasionally has to oppose the stand taken by the nurses' union. However, since the union and Mary Gonzalez' office are both working for better conditions for nurses, they seldom conflict.

When the newspapers or local television stations call for a response to a current medical story, the hospital public relations representative often refers them to Nancy for the "nursing perspective." This happened recently, when the Associated Press ran a story to the effect that there are 125 percent more males attending nursing school now than there were five years ago. When this story broke on the Portland wires, Nancy was immediately called for a quick rundown on the number of male nurses at Langley. She told the reporters that she would check and get back to them. Within an hour, she called each reporter with the following statement:

```
We at Langley Hospital have 12 male nurses
currently employed on a regular full-time basis. We
employ six males part-time as the need arises. In
the Langley School of Nursing, we have 25 males
compared to just eight five years ago. It is the
position of the administration at Langley that many
more men are needed in the field of nursing. We want
to do all that we can do to encourage qualified men
to make nursing their career.
                    Nancy Culver
                    Assistant Director
                    Nursing Services
```

Nancy's most important task is representing the nursing department at the regular hospital board of directors meetings. Since Mary Gonzalez wears two hats at the hospital (she is both the director of nursing services and chief administrative officer of the nursing school), she must be away often. Much of the day-to-day business of running the department of nursing services has fallen to Nancy. At board meetings, the hospital's chief administrator, the director of medical services, the director of patient services, the chief of administrative services, and Nancy—all present status updates on the progress of their respective departments. When the situation calls for it, each is given an opportunity to respond to questions related to his or her unit. But a board member's most important duty is to make a presentation to the board outlining the annual budget of his or her department. These presentations are planned to highlight recent changes in the budget or new programs that require funding. The presenter must be able to answer questions raised by other board members.

Nancy makes it a point to put a lot of effort into these presentations. She goes over each line in the nursing services budget to see if anything being recommended this year represents a major change over last year. If it does, she prepares a response explaining why the change is being proposed. When there is some question whether a particular item will be approved, she develops arguments in favor of that item aimed at particular board members. For example, this year's proposed budget showed an increase of nearly 25 percent for in-service education and training. Nancy knew that such increases always receive careful scrutiny. So she did her homework. She found that, because of inflation, training costs were increasing at a rate of nearly 15 percent. Furthermore, Langley Hospital had been forced to hire many nurses who did not have B.S. degrees. These nurses needed the incentive of tuition reimbursement to return to college. Finally, since medicine was changing so rapidly, many nurses were afraid that they couldn't keep up in their fields. When the board considered the nursing budget, sure enough, one member questioned the 25 percent increase in training. Nancy went into a defense of the increase that lasted 20 minutes. The board must have been moved by her presentation, for it approved the increase—one of the few increases it did approve in this year's budget. This kind of thoroughness and preparation have helped to mark Nancy as a person "on her way up at Langley."

FOR STUDY

1 What skills and attributes that were discussed in this chapter enabled Nancy to succeed in her job?

2 What do you consider to be the essential steps in preparing a public presentation? Did Nancy do these things?

3 It has been suggested that the public presentation is important in the organization because so many important decisions are associated with it. Identify some situations in the organization that call for a public presentation.

4 Audience analysis might be defined as the ability to structure arguments that have significant impact on the listener. What things did Nancy do to analyze her audience?

5 This chapter devoted much space to ways of meeting audience expectations. Why are these important in influencing the potential success of a public presentation?

effective implementation

This chapter deals with the activities associated with putting your presentation plan into practice. This is called *implementation.* Implementation involves actually facing your listener and attempting to achieve your audience outcomes. The plan is the working document of the presentation. Implementation is simply *the making of the presentation in front of the listener.*

As you learned in the previous chapter, the ability to plan an effective public presentation depends on the ability to make the best choice from among a number of alternatives. This ability is also important in implementation. Good implementation means making those choices which enable you to communicate most effectively with the listener. This chapter will present a number of alternatives and demonstrate where each alternative might be best used.

The first part of the chapter will focus on the informational public presentation. The second part of the chapter will focus on the commitment-seeking presentation. The chapter opens with a discussion of those concepts from communication theory which are relevant to the public presentation. Outlining, introductions and conclusions, and visual aids are discussed next. The chapter then discusses the listener as a receiver of persuasive messages and the steps in gaining commitment from the listener. Style and delivery are then examined, and the chapter closes with two final observations related to implementation.

concepts from communication theory

Making effective presentations is a *communication challenge.* There are a number of concepts from communication theory that should help you to meet this challenge. But before beginning to examine these concepts, a word about communication theory itself.

chapter eight

This, as you have no doubt discovered, is a "how-to-do-it" book. Thus far little space has been devoted to the theoretical assumptions from which many of the ideas presented in this book were derived. Other books discuss these assumptions at length.[1] Nevertheless, a good communicator should know not only what works well, but why. The science of communication theory studies why particular kinds of communication behavior work in certain situations and why others do not. Some basic ideas from communication theory are now considered.

Communication Overload

In many ways, people resemble a computer. They can *process* so much information and *store* that information in their cognitive structure[2]—but only so much. Both people and machines have what is called a *channel capacity*. When that channel capacity is reached, the same thing happens to both the person and the machine—they break down.

Let us examine the concept of channel capacity in more practical terms. Think back to your first week at your present college or university. If you were like most of us, you went through a series of orientation and registration sessions as soon as you arrived on campus. You probably heard from the dean of students, the financial aid officer, the student body president, the president of the Panhellenic society, the athletic director, and so forth. After eight or nine such speeches about the college and its numerous opportunities, you had so much floating around inside your head that your image of the school was composed of many loosely fitting, sometimes disjointed pieces of information. There may have been a point, even though you were vitally interested in the subject—your future in the university—at which you reached saturation and simply turned off. When we reach this point of saturation in our communication behavior, we are said to be experiencing *communication overload.*

When a listener reaches overload, that listener turn offs any further information. When the listener has turned off, any effort at communication on the part of the sender is a waste of energy. Each person has a different channel capacity. Some of us are able to process much more

---

[1] A. Sanford, G. Hunt, and H. Bracey, *Communication Behavior in Organizations* (Columbus: Charles E. Merrill Publishing Company, 1976); R. Farace, P. Monge, and H. Russell, *Communicating and Organizing* (Reading, Mass.: Addison-Wesley Publishing Co., Inc., 1977); and B. Johnson, *Communication: The Process of Organizing* (Boston: Allyn & Bacon, Inc., 1977).

[2] K. Sereno and C. Mortensen, *Foundations of Communication Theory* (New York: Harper & Row, Publishers, Inc., 1970), p. 46.

information than others. In any public communication situation, your audience is likely to represent a great variety of channel capacities.

In implementing the presentation, you must have some notion of the channel capacity of the audience. A presentation that attempts to communicate too much information will fail. The audience will (1) withdraw, (2) tune out, or (3) become angry. Since you have planned the presentation with the audience in mind, you will probably already have a good idea of the composition and abilities of the people represented.

In transmitting information, ask yourself these three questions:

1. *Can the information be processed rapidly?* If the information is simple and straightforward, you should have little difficulty operating within the channel capacity of the audience. Remember, however, that ease of processing must be considered from the receiver's perspective, not the sender's. Obviously, the information is old to the sender but new to the receiver.

2. *Does the information come at an appropriate rate for comprehension?* Information that comes so fast that we have difficulty understanding it will not be processed. Slowing down may improve audience comprehension.

3. *Are the relationships made clear?* Sometimes when we communicate, we assume that our audience has all the necessary background information to understand what we are saying. Often this is not so. Without this background information, the audience must work so hard to fill in the details that it will miss much of the information you want to transmit. The good public communicator will fill in all of the background details for the listener.

Redundancy

In transmitting information, it is sometimes necessary to be intentionally redundant. *Redundancy* means transmitting the same information a second or a third time, using the same or different channels. People often miss information the first time. This occurs because they are not paying attention or not concentrating, or because the sender has made some communication error. If, as a listener, we have missed part of the transmission, the rest of the exchange is difficult to follow. Planned redundancy enables the communicator to build in methods for making sure that the information reaches its destination.

There are some easy ways to be redundant. One is simply to say the same thing over again. This may seem a bit basic, but it serves our primary goal, which is to get the information across to the audience. Slides, visual aids, and pictures can also be used to reinforce the message. Visual aids are considered later in this chapter.

In making choices about planned redundancy, you should consider *listener preference.* One of the first scientific studies to deal with organizational communication was conducted by Thomas Dahle in 1954.[3] Dahle sought to learn what communication channels listeners preferred that the organization use. Among the choices Dahle studied were the grapevine, bulletin boards, written channels (memoranda, reports, newspapers), oral channels (presentations, interviews), and written channels supplemented by oral channels. His results indicated that generally workers *prefer* oral communication supplemented by written communication. These data were consitent across a number of organizations. Dahle's results are significant because it was the members of the organizations themselves who told the researcher that they wanted this planned redundancy.

Perception

Because each of us is the product of many influences (e.g., personality, learning, environment), each of us experiences just about any event a little differently. What we take out of an event is our *perception* of that event. Given our differences, the chances are that your perception and mine will be quite different. This may be demonstrated by the following example:

The author once attended a live performance by a contemporary entertainer who happened to be one of his favorites. Upon leaving the performance, he turned to his companion and said that he was very impressed by the performance, because the entertainer had worked so hard to please the audience that he seemed physically exhausted after the show. Just then, the author overheard another member of the audience say "This guy is really washed up. He can't even pull off a 90-minute show without almost passing out from exhaustion. He's over the hill." The two of us, even though we had experienced the same event (the show), had perceived it differently.

Each member of your audience will perceive things differently. Your perception of the facts you have included in your presentation plan will probably be different from the perceptions of most of your listeners. And not all members of your audience will hear the same speech. Some of them will think they heard A, some will think they heard B, and still others will think they heard neither A nor B. Obviously, the effectiveness of your transmission will depend on what the listeners think they have heard.

[3]T. Dahle, "Transmitting Information to Employees: A Study of Five Methods," *Personnel,* 31, no. 2 (1954), 243–46.

Physical and Psychological Noise

In their early research on communication, Caude Shannon and Warren Weaver determined that certain *interferences* in the channel may block the transmission of information.[4] Later researchers called these interferences *noise*. Noise can be physical or psychological.

PHYSICAL NOISE When we have to strain to hear what is being said, it is usually because there is physical noise. Physical noise can be a real problem in organizations. The first-line foreman who must make a presentation to his subordinates over the roar of machines and shop sounds is trying to deal with physical noise.

PSYCHOLOGICAL NOISE Many stimuli compete for our attention at any given time. Thus we sometimes have difficulty concentrating on any one stimulus. As we attempt to focus on one idea, another creeps in. For example, suppose you are listening to the manager make a presentation on the profit-sharing program in your organization. But this presentation is being given at 11:45 A.M., and you did not eat breakfast and are starving. The information being transmitted must fight for your attention with other types of stimuli, specifically being hungry and wanting lunchtime to get here quick. Psychological noise prevents us from devoting our complete attention to a stimulus and so makes us miss part of what is being said.

When you make a public presentation, try reduce physical and psychological noise for the listener. You should be aware of both kinds of noise and *expect* them both to interfere with your transmission. But the more interesting and vivid your public presentation, the better your chances of overcoming noise.

Feedback

At its most basic level, feedback is the *response* a listener makes to a message. Feedback research suggests that information is more easily transmitted when the communicator adjusts the message to the listener, based on feedback from the listener.[5] A communicator who gets blank stares can improve the interaction by making the message clearer. It is through the feedback process that two-way communication can be achieved. It is the sender's responsibility to monitor the impact

[4]C. Shannon and W. Weaver, *The Mathematical Theory of Communciation* (Urbana: University of Illinois Press, 1949), p. 38.
[5]H. Leavitt, *Managerial Psychology*, 3rd ed. (Chicago: University of Chicago Press, 1972), p. 119.

of his or her message on the listener. To do this, the sender must observe the listener closely for the outward manifestations of that impact. This is done by observing facial expression, eye movements, other physical movements, and extent to which the listener is paying attention.

Serial Effect of Communication

This book (and many other sources) stress the idea that communication is dynamic. The effects of the public presentation do not stop in the briefing room. People talk outside of room about what took place within. Sometimes people who were not in the room will talk about what went on. People add to and take away from what was said. Communication travels in all directions, and there is no telling where it will end up. Public communicators say things that will eventually become part of the organization's grapevine. These things may be misinterpreted, sometimes causing conflict and confusion. This is unavoidable. It is a fact of organizational life that must to be faced.

outlining the public presentation

Before you finally implement your plan, you must pull it all together and put it into a manageable package. This manageable package is called the *presentation outline*. There are many ways to outline a presentation. We shall consider five of the more basic ones. Whichever method you use, make sure as you develop your outline that all of the audience outcomes, determined much earlier, are reflected in it. The main points of your outline may be those same specific outcomes.

Topical Outline

In the topical outline, you place the subjects that are similar together. Related points are grouped. An example of a topically organized presentation follows.

OUTLINE 1
Topic: Market Trends

I We need to become familiar with new developments in the marketplace.
  A New electronic gear
    1 semiconductor
    2 transistor
  B New alloys
    1 copper
    2 zinc

II We need to become aware of new customer attitudes.
  A Wants more personal service
    1 from the company
    2 from the salesperson
  B Is harder to sell
    1 shops around more
    2 very hesitant to waste money
      a inflation has made it necessary for him to get the most for his money
      b uses old products until they cannot be used any longer
  C Seems to understand why he uses our product
    1 is well informed
    2 does not buy useless products
III We need to become aware of the competition.
  A Must know who the competition is
    1 their strengths
    2 their weaknesses
  B Must be prepared to meet the competition
    1 need to know how we stack up against them
    2 need to know how we can improve

This outline is a simple way to organize your ideas before implementation. The important thing to remember about this technique is that all the items under the Roman numerals must be related. In the topical as in any other outline the items under main points should follow logically.

Step Outline

The step outline and the chronological outline are closely related. The step outline is used when specific steps must be taken to accomplish a particular task. Often the steps will follow one another chronologically. By using this outline, you are saying that one step must be taken before the next. An example of a step outline follows.

OUTLINE 2

Topic: Making a Sales Contact

  I Getting clearcut profile of the customer
    A Background reading
    B Examine past buying habits
    C Talk with other salespersons
 II Setting up the first appointment
    A Convenient to customer
    B He needs to know the purpose
III Initial face-to-face contact
    A Firm handshake
    B Initial greeting

IV Building sales rapport
  A Establish eye contact
  B Maintain a good sense of humor
V Exploring customer's needs
  A Find out what product he presently buys
  B Find out whom he buys from
  C Find out if customer is considering change
VI Building our products
  A Express strengths
  B Show samples
VII Calling for action
  A Request trial by customer
  B Promise follow-up
VIII Closing sale
  A Make out order
  B Tell customer you are at his disposal

In the step outline, the communicator can tell the listener exactly what to expect next. It works very well when the topic can be broken down into steps.

Chronological Outline

The chronological outline is appropriate when there is an obvious time dimension associated with the topic. To use the chronological outline, the communicator may choose to start with the most recent event and move backward or vice versa. An example of a chronological outline follows.

OUTLINE 3

Topic: The History of Lindenville

I Founding of the community in 1820 by migrants from Massachusetts
  A Establishment of settlement: 1822
  B Establishment of first church: 1823
II Period of moderate growth: 1820–1855
  A Enlargement of school system: 1831
  B Creation of city charter: 1840
  C Beginning of road system: 1847
III The Civil War and politics split the town: 1855–1870
  A The Baptist congregations split over slavery issue: 1860
  B Lindenville boys fight for both the North and South: 1860–1868
IV The age of industrialization: 1870–1900
  A Many people employed in new steel firm: 1876
  B New growth generated by new industry: 1880–1900
V The age of education: 1900–1930
  A Lindenville State College founded: 1905

  B Linden College founded by State Methodist Convention: 1915
  C Two Lindenville high schools built: 1920–1930
VI The depression and war years: 1930–1946
  A The depression hits Lindenville hard: 1930
  B Lindenville citizens support the war effort: 1940–1946
  C New defense plant built in Lindenville: 1943
VII Lindenville enters the postwar age: 1946–1950
  A Many veterans employed locally: 1946–1950
  B Housing boom created by returning veterans: 1946–1950
  C New city hall and civic complex built: 1955
  D City increases services to younger and older citizens: 1955–1960
VIII Lindenville today: 1960–1977
  A Population increase to 45,000
  B Employment center for many surrounding areas
  C New banks, commercial and industrial development undertaken

The chronological outline makes a fine road map for the presentation, because it enables the listener to associate a particular time period with the information being transmitted. The only problem is that relatively few topics can be so neatly structured into specific chronological periods.

Problem–Solution Outline

The problem-solution outline can be used effectively in either informational or commitment-seeking presentations. It consists of the development and explanation of a problem followed by the proposed solution. You may want to use it in the commitment-seeking presentation to persuade the listener that your solution is better than any other. In the informational presentation the speaker attempts to analyze objectively, offering, perhaps, a number of solutions. An example of a problem–solution outline follows.

OUTLINE 4

Topic: The Problem of the Freeway System in Los Angeles

  I Experts contend that there are too many cars using the Los Angeles freeway system.
  A Tremendous pressure on road surface
  B Extremely high maintenance costs
  II Too many cars have created air pollution.
  A L. A. has the worst smog problem in the U. S.
  B Many deaths have been attributed, at least partially, to the air pollution.
  III Too many cars have created noise pollution.
  A On the L. A. freeway system, at 8:00 A.M. or 4:00 P.M., it is dangerously noisy.

   B People who live by the freeways must tolerate tremendous noise levels.

IV Psychologists report that driving the freeway systems places people under dangerously high stress levels.
   A People seem to get higher blood pressure readings when they drive on freeways.
   B Those who drive the freeways five times a week or more are three times more likely to have a heart attack than those who do not.

 V Therefore, we should build no new freeways in Los Angeles, and we should find alternative ways of moving people.
   A Mass rapid transit
   B People movers
   C Alternative use of freeway space

By using the problem–solution outline, the communicator can lay out the problem effectively for the audience. The problem may also be developed in narrative form. In this case, the communicator describes it by telling a story.

Advantages-vs.-Disadvantages Outline

Like the problem–solution outline, the advantages-vs.-disadvantages outline can be used in both informational and commitment-seeking presentations. In the informational presentation, the speaker objectively offers both advantages and disadvantages without taking a position. In the commitment-seeking presentation, the communicator will argue that his or her proposal has more advantages than disadvantages for this particular audience. An example of the advantages-vs.-disadvantages outline follows.

OUTLINE 5

Topic: Rubber-Wheeled vs. Steel-Wheeled Vehicles for Mass Rapid Transit

   Advantage I: Rubber-wheeled vehicles offer flexibility.
     A They can be used over existing roads.
     B They can be integrated with existing transportation systems.
   Advantage II: Rubber-wheeled vehicles cost less than steel-wheeled vehicles.
     A They are more readily available.
     B They have lower short- and long-term costs.
   Advantage III: Generally, rubber-wheeled vehicles have greater public acceptance than steel-wheeled vehicles.
     A The public is used to rubber-wheeled public transportation systems.
     B Less time will be required to train the public to use this system.

Disadvantage I: Steel-wheeled vehicles have the potential for much greater speed over long distances than rubber-wheeled vehicles.
A High speeds are possible with steel-wheeled vehicles.
B On existing track, some people feel that even on short runs, steel-wheeled vehicles will prove faster.
Disadvantage II: Steel-wheeled vehicles are much more durable than rubber-wheeled vehicles.
A They can normally run much longer and more often without replacement.
B New experimentation is driving down the cost of replacement and maintenance all the time.

Therefore: Looking at the global question, at present rubber-wheeled vehicles have greater potential for public transportation in our city than steel-wheeled vehicle because they offer greater flexibility and public acceptance for less cost than other systems.

Some Final Words About Outlining

These outlines are intended merely as guidelines. Each one will work under certain conditions and not under others. The purpose of any outline is to provide a system that helps you to present your ideas in a way that is clean and easy to follow. It is difficult to follow a communicator who jumps around from one idea to the next. If you will keep the listener in mind and figure out the clearest possible way to present your ideas, you should be able to develop an outline that works for each presentation you give.

developing the introduction and conclusion

Developing the Introduction

What you say before you begin talking about the main material on your outline constitutes your *introduction.* The introduction should provide the proper foundation for the rest of your message. You may have heard about the student who was going to give a talk on raising plants. Before he began, he walked up to the front of the room, blew up a brown paper bag, and then popped it. After the sound had subsided, he turned to the audience and said, "Now that I have your attention, I want to talk with you about my hobby, raising plants." This was not a good introduction. It did not constitute a proper foundation, because it had nothing to do with the topic of the presentation. It was simply tacked on for effect. Introductions should lead *gracefully* into the main ideas. A good introduction should do the following things.

IT SHOULD RELATE THE TOPIC TO THE AUDIENCE The introduction is your first opportunity to acknowledge the presence of the audience. After you have made this initial contact, you are faced with the challenge of attempting to interest the audience in the subject of your talk. The introduction gives you an opportunity to tell your listeners what is in it for them. Think back to the presentation plan developed in the previous chapter. You will remember that you developed this plan because you wanted to do something for the audience. The introduction is the place where you begin to do it. Thus you would not simply say, "Tonight I am going to tell you about the history of labor relations in our industry." Instead, you might say, "We all face the challenge of the modern labor relations movement in our daily lives as managers. It occurred to me, as I was planning this talk, that we might all benefit from a lively historical perspective on labor relations as they affect us." This second introduction generates immediate interest by getting the listener involved with the subject.

IT SHOULD ESTABLISH COMMON GROUND BETWEEN AUDIENCE AND COMMUNICATOR The audience will pay attention to a communicator who seems to be a person like themselves. When we find people who reinforce our own value systems, we are likely to give them a forum.[6] Your task in the introduction, then, is to establish areas of mutual interest ("things we both have a stake in") and areas where you resemble your listeners. A good introduction demonstrates that the communicator is trying to keep the best interests of the audience in mind.

IT SHOULD PREVIEW THE REST OF THE PRESENTATION When we sit down to hear a presentation, most of us want to have some idea of what to expect. When we know more or less what topic is going to be discussed and for how long, we can relax and listen. The introduction gives you the opportunity to preview your presentation for the audience. In an organization where listening to a presentation may take people away from their jobs, the preview, at least in terms of the time commitment, is important. If we know that we are going to be listening to the speaker for 25 minutes, it is easier for us to concentrate on what is being said. The preview also gives the communicator the opportunity to cover the main points of the presentation. This will alert the audience to the direction the speech is going to take.

IT SHOULD MAINTAIN LISTENER RAPPORT *Rapport* between the listener and the speaker might be defined as that characteristic which allows them to build a mutually satisfying relationship, at least for the duration of the presentation. There is no magic formula for creating rapport. For

---

[6]A. Monroe and D. Ehninger, *Principles and Types of Speeches* (Glenview, Ill.: Scott, Foresman & Company, 1967), p. 232.

the most part, it seems to emerge when the audience perceives the communicator as sincere and as genuinely concerned about their interests.[7] The introduction gives you your first opportunity to begin to build rapport. In the introduction, you will probably want to do and say things that will make the audience respect you and your position.

IT SHOULD LEAD GRACEFULLY INTO MAIN IDEAS Since the introduction is built on the main points of the presentation, it should provide an easy transition to those main points. If you structure your introduction properly, you will arrive at your first main point with the groundwork already laid.

The introduction, like everything else about the presentation, should be a unified package. The entire package is designed to meet the purpose of the presentation, which you established earlier. Not every introduction will do each of the things already described. There may be good reasons for not doing some, or even all, of them. But most good introductions will do most of these things.

Developing the Conclusion

The *conclusion* is what you say after you have finished discussing the main points of the presentation. It is the last opportunity you have with the audience, so you must make sure that you have accomplished everything you set out to do. In the commitment-seeking presentation, the conclusion gives you one last chance to argue for your position. In the informational presentation, it gives you a chance to review the core of your information. A good conclusion accomplishes three tasks.

IT PROVIDES A CHANCE TO SUMMARIZE INTENDED AUDIENCE OUTCOMES The conclusion enables the communicator to restate and summarize the audience outcomes. Remember that the outcomes are what you want your listener to know or do. You may want to be so blunt as to state them directly. For the informational presentation, the conclusion allows you to review the facts that you want your listener to retain. For the commitment-seeking presentation you may well restate your most important arguments, giving the reasons why listeners should accept them. It is almost always a good idea to include a summary in the conclusion.

IT PROVIDES CLOSURE *Closure* is a word from communication theory. It is the listener's psychological sense that the communication has been completed. If the listener feels that there are loose ends still hanging, he or she may feel uncertain and dissatisfied about the results

---

[7]K. Giffin, "The Contribution of Studies of Source Credibility to a Theory of Interpersonal Trust in Communication," *Psychological Bulletin*, 68, No. 2 (1967), 104–20.

of the presentation. You should use the conclusion to provide closure for your audience. Review the presentation and ask yourself, "Does the listener know what to do next?" If you think that the answer might be "No," you may not have provided closure. To do so creates frustration for your listener, which will affect your credibility as a source.

IT MAINTAINS RAPPORT At the final stage of the presentation, it is crucial to maintain rapport. You are trying to achieve good public relations, and the audience is your public. You must leave a good lasting impression and insure that the channel of communicaiton remains open between you and your audience. This rapport must be maintained through the question-and-answer period. You should be genuinely interested in the inquiries and appear enthusiastic in your interactions with the audience.

The general comments that apply to the introduction also apply to the conclusion. That is, not every good conclusion will do each of these things. The tasks described do not constitute a checklist. Rather, they are suggestions that can help make the conclusion contribute to the overall effectiveness of the presentation.

visual aids

Transmitting Information with Visual Aids

It is sometimes easier to transmit information when the audience can visualize it. Devices that make this possible are called *visual aids.* A visual aid can be anything that helps the listener to visualize information. The use of visual aids is a skill that is developed through practice. But it is worth the time investment, because visual aids are a valuable tool. Although they are most often used in informational presentations, they can also be helpful in persuasive speeches. You can often build credibility with listeners through the judicious use of visual aids.

In deciding whether to use visual aids, you should ask yourself the following questions.

DOES THE VISUAL AID HELP THE COMMUNICATOR? The speaker who intends to use a motion picture for a visual aid, only to find that he does not know how to operate the vintage projector (circa 1940), is not going to be helped by the visual aid. The first question to ask yourself about a potential visual aid is whether it will help you. If you can use the visual with some confidence *and* competence, the tool will work for you. Otherwise it may do more harm than good.

CAN THE VISUAL AID BE SEEN BY ALL THE MEMBERS OF THE AUDIENCE? For the visual aid to be effective, it must be seen. The most important factor here is its size. If the room where the presentation is to take place is large, the visual should be big enough so that the listeners in the back of the room can see it. Small visual aids may work well in a small conference room, but they are usually useless in large auditoriums. If you are not sure whether your visual can be seen, test it out in a room comparable to the one where you will give your presentation. Normally such items as 8 X 10 photographs, newspaper clippings, and 8–½ X 11 memoranda have to be enlarged for use in large rooms. Often a communicator will use an overhead projector to cast a small object onto a screen. This accomplishes the enlargement quite well, but it does make extra "hardware" for the communicator to carry around.

DOES THE VISUAL AID PROVIDE ADDITIONAL INFORMATION? The major reason for using a visual aid is to help you to transmit information more easily. If the visual aid does not do this, there is no reason to use it. The listener should be able to grasp what the visual says, and how it is related to your message, without straining.

DOES THE VISUAL AID SUPPORT THE COMMUNICATOR'S MESSAGE? If the listener must ask a neighbor what a visual aid says, both your impact as speaker and the impact of the information is diminished. Occasionally careless communicators use visual aids that contradict their message. At first this may seem like an unbelievable mistake. But it is easier to make than you might think. When you choose a visual aid, you do so because the aid has special meaning to you. You see something in it that makes you want to use it. However, someone else may see something entirely different. During an informational presentation, a perceptive listener may uncover something in a graph or chart that destroys or significantly damages your case. When the listener points this out—and he probably will—your credibility will be damaged. To avoid this, examine each visual aid thoroughly before you use it. Ask other people to look at it for something you may have missed. If a visual aid is the least bit ambiguous, don't use it.

ARE THE VISUAL AIDS INTERESTING? The visual aid should be meaningful enough so that the audience will be interested in it on its own merits. Boring photographs or complicated graphs or charts contribute little to a presentation. The use of visuals demands some creativity. The decision to use a visual, like everything else in the communication process, should be made with the audience in mind. If the listener is interested in your visual, that interest can be carried over to the entire presentation. In this way, the visual can contribute to the overall effectiveness of the speech.

DOES THE VISUAL AID BUILD THE COMMUNICATOR'S BELIEVABILITY? Your appearance, your style, your message, and how you carry yourself before the audience all contribute to your believability. The general impression you create in the minds of your listeners should be improved through your use of each visual aid.[8] Imagine that a recruiter for a large company comes to your school. If the speaker has a slick presentation, you make certain judgments about the firm. If the recruiter fumbles over the slide tray, does not have a bulb for the projector, and puts the slides in upside down, you also make assumptions regarding the organization.

Types of Visual Aids

Almost anything can be used as a visual aid if it can meet the criteria just listed. Here we will consider some of the most important types of visual aids.

FILMS Motion pictures can be productive visual aids. Be careful, however, not to let the film take over the presentation. Because the film commands our attention so easily, it may be difficult for the listener to concentrate on what the speaker is saying during, and perhaps even after, the showing of the film. Achieving maximum impact means selecting the best film, showing it at the most appropriate time, and using sound judgment about what you say when the film is over. Libaries, corporate training offices, and the public relations departments of large firms are all good sources of industrial films. More and more large organizations are forming their own units to produce visual aids. It is a safe bet that the more "hardware" conscious large organizations become, the more industrial films there will be on the market.[9]

---

[8]See V. DiSalvo, C. Monroe, and B. Morse, *Business and Professional Communication* (Columbus, Ohio: Charles E. Merrill Publishing Company, 1977) for additional material on the effective use of visual aids.

[9]Titles of films are listed in *National Information Center for Education Media Index to 16mm Educational* (New York: R. R. Bowker Company, 1969); William Wachs, ed., *Film Guide for Marketing Executives,* Rutgers University Sales and Marketing Executives International, 630 Third Avenue, New York, New York 10017; and *Films for Personnel Management: An Annotated Directory of 16mm Films, Filmstrips, and Videotapes,* Educational Film Library Association, Inc., 17 W. 60th Street, New York, New York 10023.

FILMSTRIPS Filmstrips are used widely in training and in presentations on new products and ideas. They are not as costly to manufacture or rent as films, and they are generally effective. Since the speed of most filmstrips can be adjusted, the communicator can maintain a control that is not possible with films.

CHARTS Charts are often used to show an enlargement of some object or detail. The working parts of an internal combustion engine or the steps in the refraction process in the manufacture of eyeglasses could easily be illustrated with charts.

GRAPHS A *graph* is a particular kind of chart that shows the relationships between at least two variables, ideas, qualities, or concepts. The two most widely used forms of graphs are the bar graph (figure 8–1) and the circle graph (figure 8–2). In figure 8–1, the variables being compared are the numbers of male and female students in college in three different years. In figure 8–2, the variables being compared are the percentages of the state tax dollar going toward education in three different years. The value of the graph is that it enables the listener to perceive immediately certain trends that it would take much longer to describe in words. It is also easier to make comparisons with graphs.

FIGURE 8–1 Bar graph

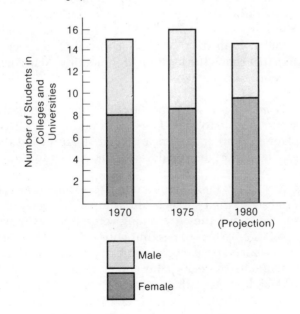

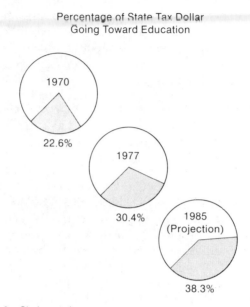

FIGURE 8–2   Circle graph

PICTURES A picture is probably the best way to help a listener visualize a situation. Slides shown on a motion picture screen are excellent. If slides cannot be used, a good size picture to display in a typical 20- X 30-foot briefing room would be 11 X 14 or 14 X 18 inches. Anything much smaller than this may be too small. One special kind of picture is a map that shows the location of something. Maps help to give the listener a sense of perspective.

MODELS A *model* is a working representation of something. It is a miniature done to scale to show how it compares with other objects. Architects, planners, and engineers are good at expressing their ideas by means of models. Portable models are the easiest to use.

WRITTEN HANDOUTS Public communicators sometimes pass out written material about their subject. This is usually a good idea. It gives the listeners a sense that they are taking something away with them from the presentation. When to pass out your handouts is an important issue. Some experienced public communicators have found that if they pass out the handouts too early, the audience spends so much time looking at the handouts that they miss the point of the presentation itself. If the information can be transmitted by means of handouts alone, why have a presentation at all? The handout should supplement the speech. Perhaps the best way to use handouts is to announce early in the presentation that there will be a handout later and then wait until near the end of the presentation to distribute it.

A Final Word on Visual Aids

In using visual aids effectively, there are a few important issues to keep in mind.

TIMING   Use the visual aid at the most appropriate moment in the presentation. One experienced public communicator who worked for an architectural firm was supposed to give a talk about his proposal for a new civic center complex to the members of the planning commission. His firm developed a scale model of the civic center for him to use during the presentation. Unfortunately, he brought the model into the planning commission meeting uncovered. Before the meeting started, all of the commissioners gathered around to examine the model carefully. When it came time for the man to talk, the members of the commission pounced on him before he could even get his first point out. They bombarded him with specific questions about the model based on their earlier observation of it. This speaker missed the opportunity to display his model at the most appropriate moment to meet his own objectives. Again, it is generally best to use visual aids near the end of the presentation.

SETTING   The setting of the presentation should be such as to allow for maximum effective use of the visual aid. The key here is appropriateness. A set of miniature models is not appropriate for a public auditorium. A large-screen motion picture complete with a stereophonic sound system is not appropriate for a small conference room. Your choice of visual aids should be dictated by the setting in which they will be used.

TOPIC   If the topic must be illustrated somehow for the audience to understand it, use visual aids. If the topic is easy to follow, you may not need them. Remember that your primary goal in the informational presentation is to make your audience understand. If that understanding can be facilitated through the use of visual aids, use them.

SPECIFIC AUDIENCE   The decision whether or not to use visuals may vary with the audience. By now you know that each audience will have a different level of knowledge about a given topic. If the members of your audience have been briefed on the topic and are familiar with it, there is obviously no reason to use visuals.

Visual aids can be a tremendous help to the communicator when they are used well. You should not be afraid to use them, nor should you use them just because "it would be nice." In deciding how best to use visuals, consider timing, setting, topic, and your specific audience.

the listener as a receiver
of persuasive messages

The first part of this chapter was devoted primarily to presentations intended to provide information to an audience. The second part will focus on presentations intended to gain commitment from the audience.

Relationship Between Informational
and Persuasive Communication

The distinction between informational and persuasive communication is a fine one. The difference is really one of degree and has more to do with the communicator's intent than anything else. Even in a wholly informational presentation, there is an element of persuasion at work—the speaker is attempting to persuade the listener that the information being given is accurate. And in a wholly persuasive presentation, there is nearly always some type of information exchange.

Some Typical Audience Dispositions

In persuasive communication, you are attempting to change the disposition of your audience. In order to do this, you must understand what your audience's natural disposition is. In this section, we shall consider typical audience dispositions.

AUDIENCES WANT TO MAINTAIN A SENSE OF EQUILIBRIUM If there is one idea that emerges out of 30 years of attitude change research, it is the idea of *equilibrium*. The concept goes something like this. Each individual, within his or her cognitive structure, wants to maintain a state of equilibrium (e.g., balance, consistency). Most of the stimuli we encounter tend to reinforce our view of the universe, or help us to maintain equilibrium. However, when a stimulus distorts or casts doubt on our view of the universe, our equilibrium is challenged.[10] We can then

[10]L. Festinger, *A Theory of Cognitive Dissonance* (Evanston, Ill.: Row, Peterson, 1957), pp. 121–23.

(1) change our view of the universe, (2) devalue the message or stimulus that has cast the doubt, (3) devalue the source of the stimulus, and/or (4) withdraw from the situation entirely. The following example will clarify this idea.

George works in a large organization. For strong religious reasons, he does not believe in labor unions. But the plant where George works is a closed shop, which means that he must join the union. George opposes unions because he believes that they restrict individual freedom, and that they place the welfare of the group ahead of the welfare of the individual. But since George has started working, he has seen that the union has accomplished many positive things. It has been responsible for improvements in plant safety, increased insurance and salary benefits, and a clause in the contract that provides tuition allowances for union members who must send dependents to special schools. Since George has a daughter who is developmentally disabled, he has taken advantage of this last benefit. All of these things have forced George to reevaluate his view of labor unions. He is now in a state of disequilibrium, because what he has learned and experienced regarding unions is not consistent with his initial view of them. The equilibrium theorists argue that George will have to *do something* about this condition to reduce the imbalance. By reevaluating he is gaining equilibrium. People must be in a state of equilibrium and will go to great extremes to maintain or regain it.

Shrewd persuaders capitalize on this need for equilibrium by offering information that challenges the listener's balance. They then try to show that the most acceptable method for regaining balance is, in reality, their proposal. Since different listeners use different techniques to regain equilibrium, this approach can backfire.

There are two major equilibrium theories of attitude change. These are cognitive dissonance theory and consistency theory.

Cognitive dissonce theory was originally developed by Festinger. It deals with *cognitive elements*—bits of knowledge, opinions, or beliefs about oneself, one's own behavior, and one's surroundings.[11] The theory describes what happens when these elements are inconsistent with one another. Charles Kiesler, Barry Collins, and Norman Miller explain cognitive dissonance theory as follows:

> In this theory, three possible relationships among elements are posited: (1) they may be irrelevant to one another (the knowledge that I smoke heavily and the knowledge that it is raining in Algeria); (2) they may be consistent with one another (the knowledge that smokers are regarded as

[11]Festinger, *Theory of Cognitive Dissonance.*

more masculine) referred to by Festinger as a consonant relationship; and (3) they may be inconsistent with one another (the knowledge that I smoke heavily and the knowledge that smoking causes cancer) referred to by Festinger at a dissonant relationship.[12]

The relationship between the cognitive elements need not necessarily be logically consistent. It can be psychologically consistent as well. The more inconsistent the relationship is, the more dissonance is created. The source of the dissonance may be (1) logical inconsistency, (2) cultural mores, (3) opinions of others, or (4) past experience. According to Festinger,

1. The existence of dissonance creates psychological tension or discomfort and will motivate the person to reduce the dissonance and achieve consonance. [This resembles the basic hypothesis of all of the consistency theories.]
2. When dissonance exists, not only will the person attempt to reduce it, but he will actively attempt to avoid it by staying away from situations and information which would increase dissonance.[13]

Consistency theory was developed through the work of Fritz Heider, Charles Osgood, and Ted Newcomb.[14] Consistency theory holds that a person strives for consistency within his or her cognitive framework. Kiesler, Collins, and Miller point out that "each consistency theory postulates a basic need for consistency."[15] Some consistency theories focus on the need to be personally consistent. Consistency theories emphasize the need to maintain consistency between attitudes, between behaviors, and between attitudes and behaviors. In other words, our thoughts should be consistent, our behaviors should be consistent, and there should be some consistency between our thoughts and our behaviors. Like cognitive dissonance theory, consistency theories assume that the presence of inconsistency produces psychological tension or discomfort. In order to get comfortable, one may be forced to rearrange one's perceptual world.

There are numerous examples of the need to maintain consistency. They include the manager who thinks he or she is an autocrat and has the habit of controlling the behavior of others, the salesperson who uses the product he or she sells, the teacher who goes to summer school to learn. William McGuire describes some of the ways in which

---

[12]C. Kiesler, B. Collins, and N. Miller, *Attitude Change: A Critical Analysis of Theoretical Approaches* (New York: John Wiley & Sons, Inc., 1969), pp. 191–92.

[13]Kiesler, Collins, and Miller, *Attitude Change*, p. 192.

[14]See F. Heider, *The Psychology of Interpersonal Relations* (New York: John Wiley & Sons, Inc., 1958); C. Osgood and P. Tannenbaum, "The Principle of Congruity in the Prediction of Attitude Change," *Psychological Review*, 62 (1955), 42–55; T. Newcomb, *The Acquaintance Process* (New York: Holt, Rinehart and Winston, 1961).

[15]Kiesler, Collins, and Miller, *Attitude Change*, p. 55.

a person striving for consistency may encounter inconsistency.[16] (1) A person may be forced to occupy two conflicting social roles. An example would be a personnel manager who must provide services for employees but becomes their adversary at contract negotiation time. (2) A person's environment may change but not that person's attitude. An example would be a strong prolabor worker who gets promoted to first-line supervisor but still has the attitudes of the line worker. (3) A person may be pressured into behaving in ways that conflict with his or her attitudes. An example would be a truck driver who must deliver liquor inspite of religious beliefs in its abstinence. In this final situation a persuasive message will have limited impact.

This brief discussion was intended only as an introduction to equilibrium theory. In formulating a plan for a persuasive presentation, a legitimate strategy for trying to move the listener toward your position might be either to point out some possible inconsistency already present in the cognitive structure of the listener or to attempt to create one yourself by what you say. When you point out an inconsistency and then provide a technique for reducing it—one that falls within the framework of your proposal—you are using well-established principles of persuasion.

AUDIENCES ARE SUSCEPTIBLE TO EMOTIONAL ARGUMENTS   Aristotle, writing many years before Christ, developed a paradigm of persuasion that is still useful today. Aristotle suggests that a communicator can persuade a listener by means of (1) his or her own trustworthiness (ethos), (2) the logical appeal of the message (logos), or (3) the emotional appeal of the (pathos).[17] Of these, the most effective is the last. Although we like to picture ourselves as highly logical and rational listeners, almost all of us are moved by emotional arguments. You only have to turn on the television set to recognize that the advertising industry generates millions of dollars by structuring appeals to the emotions of the public. Although we are moved by many kinds of emotional appeals, a few of them are used over and over again by communicators in organizations.

"It's for the good of the organization." This appeal is often used when public communicators direct persuasion to in-house listeners, attempting to get them to work hard. It appeals to the values of the group over the values of the individual.

"If you do your best for the organization, you'll be treated right." This appeal, often directed to members of organizations, is based on the

[16]W. McGuire, "The Current Status of Cognitive Consistency Theories," in *Cognitive Consistency: Motivational Antecedents and Behavior Consequents,* ed. S. Feldman (New York: Academic Press, Inc., 1966), pp. 1–46.
[17]L. Cooper, *The Rhetoric of Aristotle* (New York: Appleton-Century-Crofts, 1932), pp. 121–24.

idea that the organization will take care of its own. It attempts to paint the organization as a benevolent patriarch. We have a natural desire to trust those who hold power over us. We want to think that if we put forth our maximum effort and energy, we will be rewarded. Fair play and a sense of justice are important bases for many emotional appeals.

"A good day's work for a good day's pay." Perhaps as a holdover from the traditions of Calvinism, many people believe that they should work hard. The assumption is that there is an inherent value in hard work. Most people in our society do put in many hard hours to earn their paychecks. But along with hard work comes the idea that people who work hard should be well paid. This idea is rooted in a sense of equality. For example, at the emotional level we want people to be treated fairly. We become upset if someone doing the same job we are gets more money than we do.

"Don't make waves." This emotional appeal might be subtitled, "The organization, right or wrong." Many of us tend to go along with the program and resist the temptation to make trouble for our organization. In many subtle forms of communication—such as complex and unreadable grievance procedure memoranda and bulletins that praise the service of long-term employees—organizations use this appeal to keep the worker in line.

The perceptive student can find fault with these and most other emotional arguments. Yet we are continually being bombarded with arguments directed to our sense of justice, equality, patriotism, loyalty, love of family, love of community, and so forth. Why? The answer is obvious. Emotional appeals help to sell products, fill churches, get people elected, and get people hired. They work.

Neither this or nor any other book on communication is going to advise you to make a presentation using only emotional arguments. Such a presentation would eventually backfire, because your listeners will *eventually* see you as insulting them by appealing only to their emotional instincts. However, the good persuader knows how to use well-selected emotional arguments, conceived with a particular audience in mind, as part of a well-developed persuasive plan.

AUDIENCE BEHAVIOR IS GOAL DIRECTED The proposition has been advanced in the motivation literature that all behavior is *goal directed*.[18] This position is widely accepted among motivation scholars. *People behave as they do for a reason, and that reason is the specific goal for which they are striving.*

[18]V. Vroom, "Industrial Social Psychology," in *The Handbook of Social Psychology,* eds. G. Lindzey and E. Aronson (Reading, Mass.: Addison-Wesley Publishing Co., Inc., 1968), IV, 260; J. Gibson, J. Ivancevich, and J. Donnelly, *Organizations: Structure Processes, and Behavior* (Dallas: Business Publications, Inc., 1973).

Each member of an audience will have different goals (e.g., individual recognition, economic well-being, security), and the strength of these goals will vary. We all share certain goals (e.g., safety, esteem, physiological well-being),[19] but the relative strength and importance of these common goals will also vary from one individual to another. When you made the audience assessment discussed in chapter seven, you should have considered the goals of your audience extensively. It provides basic survival skills for members of organizations. The literature on motivation describes five goals that, to some extent, can be generalized to all members of organizations.[20]

Self-preservation. When we are threatened, be it psychologically or physically, we react strongly. We have a tremendous built-in goal to protect anything we have from anybody who might threaten it. Threats of layoffs, mass firings, and so forth, generate these feelings of self-preservation. We also want to protect what we have achieved through the organization—things such as power and prestige. The desire to protect ourselves can lead to tremendous battles, as when opposing sides confront one another, each threatening the other's territory.

Economic well-being. People work for many reasons, but especially to support themselves and their families. The need for money motivates most listeners. Money is also related to other goals, because the people who earn the most money are normally those with the highest status. Therefore, the threat of losing money may threaten many other goals as well.

Getting Ahead. People want to succeed at their jobs. While not all of us are driven to achieve power, prestige or wealth, most of us do measure success at least partly by how well we do our job and by the status associated with it. When opportunities for advancement are denied us, we may get defensive or angry, especially if we believe that the denial was unjust.

Doing a good job. A group of motivational theorists have suggested that we want to do a good job—to turn out good work.[21] We are driven by a need to *achieve.* If the situation (e.g., the structure of the organization, our supervisor's attitude) prevents us from doing good work, one of our basic drives is thwarted.

[19]A. Maslow, *Motivation and Personality* (New York: Harper & Row, Publishers, Inc., 1954), p. 128.
[20]There is a great deal of literature on motivation, and you should become familiar with it. See, for example, V. H. Vroom, *Work and Motivation* (New York: John Wiley & Sons, Inc., 1964); F. Herzberg, B. Mausner, and B. Snyderman, *Motivation to Work* (New York: John Wiley & Sons, Inc., 1967); J. Campbell and others, *Managerial Behavior, Performance, and Effectiveness* (New York: McGraw-Hill Book Company, 1970).
[21]D. McClelland and others, *The Achievement Motive* (New York: Appleton-Century-Crofts, 1953); J. Atkinson, *An Introduction to Motivation* (New York: Van Nostrand Reinhold Company, 1964), p. 12.

Recognition for good work. We all need to be recognized when we do good work. Here the idea of justice is important. We do not want underrecognition for doing a big job or overrecognition for doing a small one. Recognition should be fair and earned.

Remember that your listeners are goal directed. Learn which goals are the most important to them. If a proposal helps a listener to achieve one of his or her goals, that proposal has some chance of being accepted. Finding out what your audience's goals are, and demonstrating how your proposal will enable the audience to attain them, is good persuasive strategy.

THE AUDIENCE REFLECTS THE ATTITUDES OF THE HIERARCHY As people rise in an organization's hierarchy, their attitudes tend to reflect the position they hold.[22] A person who is promoted to manager will probably become more management oriented. As we rise in the hierarchy, our perspective often changes; we think in terms, not of a single department, but of the whole organization and its environment. The tendency to view things globally may be illustrated by the difference between a group vice president and an executive vice president to whom the group vice president reports. The group vice president sees only the group (of things) he or she is responsible for, while the executive vice president knows the problems of all groups. Thus, the group vice president will advocate what is good for his or her group, which may or may not be right for the other groups. This is a case of representing a constituency.

When you plan and implement a persuasive presentation, you must make certain assumptions about your listeners. The important assumption here is that your listener will reflect the attitudes appropriate to his or her position in the hierarchy.

steps in gaining commitment from the listener

In planning a persuasive presentation, you can follow the general principles discussed in chapter seven. However, there are also some special points to consider. The steps about to be outlined tell how to build a persuasive presentation that gets results.

[22]E. Lawler and L. Porter, "Antecedent Job Attitudes of Effective Managerial Performance," *Organizational Behavior and Human Performance*, 2, no. 2 (1967), 140.

Build Credibility

In the persuasive presentation, you are trying to give the audience a reason to believe what you say about *this particular topic.* Therefore, your *expertise* must be apparent. If you have no expertise, don't give the speech. If you do have expertise, tell the audience what your expertise consists of. It may be difficult for you to bring yourself to describe your own qualifications. If so, you can provide your audience with a data sheet or have someone describe your qualifications in an introduction.

Since many persuasive presentations are given to an in-house audience, your listeners may already know why you are (or are not) qualified to speak on a given topic. Then again, they may not. If there is any doubt, remind them by saying, "You will remember that I have been working in this area for six months" or "Let me remind you that our recommendations are based on nearly 800 man-hours of background work." This will show the audience that you have given the presentation some thought and that you are qualified to make it.

Fit Your Proposal into Your Audience's Range of Acceptance

People have a range of things that they will accept about a specific idea.[23] On any given topic, a person will accept an argument that falls within this range of acceptance but will reject an argument that falls outside that range. For example, suppose you strongly believe that capital punishment deters crime. Your range of acceptance on capital punishment might look like the continuum represented in figure 8–3. Given this range of acceptance, you would probably not accept the argument that capital punishment is morally wrong and should be abolished. This argument would fall so far out of your range that if you heard it you would probably turn off the communicator. However, you might listen to an argument more to the center of your range of acceptance—for example, that capital punishment has been shown to be

[23]C. Sheriff, M. Sheriff, and R. Nebergall, *Attitude and Attitude Change: The Social Judgement–Involvement Approach* (Philadelphia: W. B. Saunders Company, 1965).

FIGURE 8–3   Attitude range

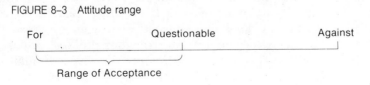

ineffective in lowering the homicide rate in states that execute capital offenders.

The persuader who uses arguments that fall outside the listener's range of acceptance is wasting everyone's time. In planning a persuasive presentation, try to calculate your audience's acceptance range, based on the results of your audience assessment. Most persuasion theorists believe that it is easier to get the listener to move a little way toward your proposal than a long way. It is probably impossible to move the listener greatly with a single presentation. Your chances are far greater in a campaign, because there you have the audience's attention over a long period.

Structure Arguments
Geared to the Specific Audience

The persuasive presentation should be geared to the specific audience. If the audience has any special characteristics—if it is composed entirely of Republican teachers, Chicanos, or firefighters, say—you may be able to build on that. If through your own background you can closely identify with the audience, do so. Each argument posited should be structured to appeal to this particular audience. For each argument, ask yourself, Will it work with this audience? On any given topic, most of us have some raw nerves—areas where we are particularly vulnerable to persuasion. By thoroughly planning and developing directly related arguments, you can learn to hit those vulnerable areas by designing your proposal in such a way that it strongly identifies with what the listeners do or do not believe.

Deal with Opposition Arguments

Experts disagree as to whether the persuader should attempt to answer opposition arguments. Some experts feel that by giving the other side of the question equal time, you risk providing the ammunition for your own defeat. Others hold that persuasion really consists of encouraging rational decision making, and this implies covering all possible alternatives. The latter position is the only appropriate one for the communicator in the organization. Because organizations must use rational decision-making processes, which encourage search behavior, you are responsible for discussing alternatives to your proposal. The best way to do this is to demonstrate that your proposal solves the problem more effectively than any other approach. The communicator who creates the impression of dealing with every possible counterargument will probably impress the audience as being an expert. There is another strong argument for dealing with the opposition case. It helps you to prepare. Going through the mental process of developing counterarguments and attempting to refute them is the kind of hard preparation you need to succeed.

If you will remember to (1) build credibility, (2) develop arguments within your listeners' range of acceptance, (3) structure specific arguments, and (4) deal with counterarguments, you should have a successful persuasive presentation.

those loose ends: style and delivery

Even the most sophisticated and thorough plan must be implemented effectively to be successful. Successful implementation depends on two things: style and delivery.

Style: Toward the Effective Use of Language

We all use language every day. Most of us develop a style that others can understand when we are communicating informally. However, that same ease and informality sometimes escapes us when we must talk in front of a group. Some people get tongue-tied, nervous, and tense—all fairly typical reactions—and their language reflects this uncertainty. The best style to use in giving a presentation in an organization is one that enables you to transmit information clearly and easily to the audience. There are four things to remember in selecting the best style.

AVOID BEING TECHNICAL One of the worst things you can do in making an organizational presentation is to use needlessly technical language. This is a common fault. Each discipline and occupation develops its own vocabulary. If you are a member of that occupation, you probably understand the language. If not, you probably will not. Most of the time audiences in particular organizations understand the language used there. Nonmembers generally will not understand the language. The best approach in selecting words and phrases is to avoid technical language and jargon. The clearer the words, the greater the likelihood that you will be understood.

KEEP THE LISTENER IN MIND In choosing language, remember that you are talking to a specific listener. That listener has to understand the language if the presentation is to be successful. Any audience represents a wide range of levels of understanding. For some people, comprehension will be no problem regardless of the level of language used. For others, it is necessary to speak simply. It is probably best to aim at the lower end of the comprehension scale represented by your audience. There is some danger of appearing condescending if the level of language is too low, but this is better than aiming too high and missing half the audience.

BE EXPERIMENTAL   Sometimes you can increase your listeners' interest by using such techniques as repetition, flowing phrases, and quotable passages. Obviously, a straightforward, informative presentation under tight organizational constraints may not lend itself to much flowing artistic language. But try to vary the style a bit and add a few unusual phrases. This can help you to capture and retain the interest of your audience.

BE APPROPRIATE   The situation, the message, and the audience should dictate the style of the presentation. In short, *be appropriate.* It is not necessary to use language that will make you look like a scholar. Rather, let the level of treatment be dictated by the subject and the listeners.

Delivery: Toward Being Communicative

Perhaps you are one of those people who judge the effectiveness of a communication solely on the basis of how the speaker sounds. After reading these two chapters, let's hope you will change your method of evaluation. Delivery is an important component of good communication, but it is less important than some of the other topics we have considered in these two chapters. In the brief discussion of delivery that follows, we will examine some of the major problems that you may experience in this area. Then we will look at a few suggestions for improving your delivery.

SOME COMMON PITFALLS IN DELIVERY   Delivering a presentation is not a skill one acquires overnight. It takes time and a great deal of practice. There are a few classic pitfalls that inexperienced communicators seem to fall into.

"And ah" transition. Some nervous communicators are under the impression that they must constantly fill up the airways with sounds. They string their words and phrases together with "and ahs." When an entire speech is connected with "and ahs," it becomes one long paragraph. No one would string together written sentences like this, but people often do it when they speak. There is nothing wrong with pausing and letting the airways clear up once in a while. By avoiding the use

of "and ahs" you will make your presentation flow much more smoothly.

Mumbling. Nervous communicators also occasionally fall into the habit of mumbling. Some mumblers go so fast that it is difficult to understand them. Other mumblers will neglect to pronounce all of the syllables of their words. If you mumble, your audience will have difficulty focusing on your message.

Musical accompaniment. Some communicators jingle their keys, change, and other objects in their pockets while they talk. This can distract the listener, and it rarely adds much to the presentation. A few people will thump a table or rock the podium to provide a percussion section to their musical accompaniment. This is simply a habit—one that can easily be broken once you are aware that you are doing it.

Pacing. Walking around in front of the audience is another common mistake. There is nothing wrong with a little activity, but when it becomes excessive, it can create problems. In your own experience you may have noticed a speaker who paces back and forth in front of you. The pacing was for no apparent reason; it was just a nervous mannerism conveying tension from speaker to audience. Your movements should support your message. If they do not, they are unnecessary and should be avoided.

WHAT IS GOOD DELIVERY? To determine how good your delivery is, ask yourself the following questions.

Is it appropriate? The situation, message, and audience will dictate the appropriateness of the delivery. It should be such as to help you to transmit your ideas clearly and succinctly.

Is it listenable? The best delivery is one that is easy to listen to. This means that the rate, pitch, and volume should be geared to comfortable listening levels.

Is it free from unnecessaries? Avoid unnecessary movement, distractions, and so forth. Things that get in the way of comprehension should be identified and removed.

Is it straightforward? In the organizational setting, the most widely used form of delivery is the straightforward businesslike approach. For most situations, this is probably the most viable technique. Simply tell the audience plainly what you want them to hear. Straightforwardness is really the key to effective delivery.

final observations

There are two things that should be mentioned before we move on. They are general observations that you may want to keep in mind when you think about giving presentations.

Expect Stage Fright

Some people avoid making public presentations because the mere idea gives them stage fright. They are not alone. Few of us relish the idea of getting up in front of a group. The ability to control stage fright is a learned attribute; it comes with experience. Stage fright is no reason to avoid giving presentations. Instead, you should expect the stage fright, the butterflies in the stomach, the clammy hands. These things —though you may not believe it—can work to your advantage. Stage fright, assuming that it is not so severe as to make you physically sick at the very thought of getting up in front of people, can keep you alert and perceptive to what is going on around you. The tension can help you to generate good ideas and to make sure that you have planned everything thoroughly. Take comfort in knowing that almost everyone gets stage fright, and most of us survive the malady.

Presentations Are Just One Method of Communicating in the Organization

Public presentations are only one of several techniques for transmitting ideas in organizations. As we saw in chapter seven, they can pose major problems, and they should be supplemented with other forms of communication if information is to be transmitted successfully. These other forms of communication include group meetings, person-to-person communication (interviews), and memoranda. Presentations are only one part of the picture.

FOR STUDY

1 What concepts from communication theory can help us to give effective public presentations? Analyze the public presentation as a communication event.

2 What approaches can be used to organize a public presentation? Under what conditions would each approach be used?

3 Before one attempts to use visual aids in a public presentation, what things should one consider? What makes a good visual aid?

4 Define persuasion. Under what conditions would one want to use persuasion in the context of the organization?

5 To gain commitment from a listener, what steps should a communicator take?

case eight

The Planning Department

The Planning Department of the city of Ocean View, California, is responsible for coordinating the master plan for the city. The department must view and approve all major changes in the master plan as well as plans for any large developments. When a builder or developer has a project in mind, he or she must submit an official copy of the plans to the department for study. After the planners have had the opportunity to read the plans, they visit the site, study it for its appropriateness, and then hold a public hearing on the project. At the public hearing, anyone who has anything to say about the project can be heard. A member of the staff acts as hearing officer to conduct the meeting. When the meeting begins, a staff member from the Planning Department presents the department's findings and recommendations about a particular project to those attending the public meeting. The public can comment directly at the meeting or can write opinions on the department's recommendations.

In addition to conducting public hearings, members of the Planning Department meet with community groups to explain various components of the city's master plan. This is a vitally important function, because Ocean View falls within the jurisdiction of the California Coastal Commission. The Coastal Commission is a state-mandated body that reviews and monitors the development of the coastline. Before the owner can do anything to any piece of coastal land situated within two miles of the shoreline, he or she must have the approval of both the Planning Department and the Coastal Commission. Since there is a strong working relationship between the two units, the recommendation of the local group carries a lot of weight with the state agency. Many citizens feel that the Coastal Commission has taken away much of their individual freedom regarding their property, therefore, there is a continuous need for the planners to meet with the public, to explain the approval process and the purposes of both planning bodies.

Not all the planners like having to meet the public. They were trained as environmental engineers or city planners, and until now they have never had to learn to deal with an audience. Now approximately 25 percent of their job involves some form of public contact. While some of the planners will go the great extremes to get out of giving public presentations, two of them developed their own effective approach.

Mark Hanson and Stella Taylor have been working as a planning team for the past two years. When they find out that they are scheduled to make an appearance in front of a public group, they follow a five-point preparation plan: (1) They find out all they can about the group they will be talking with. To do this, they call up the group's spokesperson and talk with him or her about the group's expectations as well as its history

251

and purpose. (2) After this initial investigation, they meet together to plan a strategy session in which they discuss alternatives for conducting the public presentation. (3) Next, they collect all of the visual aids they need for their presentation. The visuals are handled by a special unit in the Planning Department, and it is necessary for the presentation team to meet with the visuals unit to describe what they need in the way of maps, graphs, and so forth. One of the factors Mark and Stella always consider is the size of the room in which they will be making their presentation. They try to select visuals that are appropriate for the meeting room. (4) Now they develop a complete outline and structure. In preparing this outline, they take every precaution to make sure that the audience's expectations have been met. One part of the outline also specifies who will be talking when. Mark is good at explaining succinctly the history and purpose of the coastal plan and the city's master plan. Stella is good at handling the audience's questions in a friendly and relaxed manner. They capitalize on their respective abilities during the planning sessions. (5) Finally, Mark and Stella always arrive in the room at least half an hour before they are scheduled to begin. They do this to make sure that visuals have been set up properly, and that the microphone and other sound equipment works. If there is any problem, they will have time to solve it.

Since they have been working together as a team, Mark and Stella have been selected to make several important public presentations. Part of their success is attributable, perhaps, to the methods *other* planners use when they must make a presentation. Most of them have a single method of presentation, which they make no matter what the occasion. They always take the same maps and arrive at the hall only a few minutes before the meeting is to begin. Once in a while, word gets back to the manager of the department that some of his people are not making a very good impression on the public. Apparently it is not uncommon for a planner to be asked a question only to have to respond, "I don't know" because he or she was not prepared.

At public hearings, planners must present specific information about a particular problem. For example, they may have to present a soil samples report or discuss such matters as slope density and erosion rate. Most of the planners discuss these matters as if everyone in the audience understood all the technical terms. By talking with members of the public, Mark and Stella have discovered that many people do not have the foggiest idea what these terms mean. When they present the Planning Department's recommendations to the public, Mark and Stella are careful to define their terms clearly in everyday language. This approach has made their reports much more interesting than those of their colleagues, not only to the public, but also to the press. Since they have been working as a team, Mark and Stella's reports have received much better treatment in the Ocean View *Tribune* than the reports given by other planners. Their success in making presentations has created a bit of a problem for them, however. It seems that their colleagues are continually calling upon them to make presentations for the department. "You do it so much better than we do," they hear whenever they are asked to take over colleague's presentation. But Mark and Stella, who both sometimes miss "real planning work," have told their supervisors that instead of having them make all the presentations, the rest of the planners should learn to improve their own techniques.

FOR STUDY

1 Briefly identify what you consider to be the major components of Mark and Stella's success in making presentations. Relate these components to the material presented in this chapter.

2 What methods did Mark and Stella use to analyze their audience?

3 If Mark and Stella used successful techniques, apparently their colleagues did not. Which of the other planners' practices should be improved?

4 What sort of training program would you recommend to improve the presentations in the Planning Department? How might your program be implemented?

5 Why do you think that the image of the Planning Department suffered from ineffective public presentations? Do you judge some organizations by the quality of their outside spokespersons?

written communication

PART FOUR

writing:
Developing Effective Messages

So far, this book has focused almost exclusively on oral communication. This next-to-last chapter deals with writing. Although writing is an important skill for members of organizations, it is treated relatively briefly in this book for two reasons. First, there are already two excellent works that deal with writing in the organization.[1] Second, in most contemporary organizations, writing remains the most common methods of communication, and therefore much more energy is devoted to improving writing than to improving oral communication. That is why this book has emphasized oral communication. However, both are equally important. You must learn how to write as well as speak if you want to be a good organizational communicator.

The chapter begins by reviewing some of the important issues associated with good communication. Next, the major types of organizational writing are discussed. The problems that can occur in writing are then examined, and a section is devoted to ways to solve these problems. The chapter concludes with a discussion of the various forms of written communication. Many examples and illustrations are included to show you some of the basic differences between good and bad organizational writing.

writing in the organization:
a beginning perspective

Organizations usually maintain full and elaborate historical accounts of their activities. Often these records take the form of files and

[1]R. Lesikar, *Business Communication Theory and Practice* (Homewood, Ill.: Richard E. Irwin, Inc., 1967); N. Sigband, *Communication for Management* (Glenview, Ill.: Scott, Foresman & Company, 1969).

chapter nine

documents.[2] Recently, because of extreme governmental, consumer, and legal pressures, organizations have had to be careful to document the reasons why they behave as they do. Consider the following example.

Over the last five years, the XYZ Corporation has provided the federal government with (1) a lengthy report on its effort to hire minorities and women into management positions; (2) its records of its political activities and contributions; (3) an environmental impact study on the effects of a new plant on the surrounding community; (4) a summary of recent collective bargaining meetings; (5) a detailed analysis of the ways in which the organization is planning to meet new federal fair employment guidelines; and (6) an analysis of its wage and salary structure in the light of new minimum wage laws. To the state government, XYZ has had to provide (1) written evidence that it is not polluting state streams and creeks; (2) a report on its efforts to buy from minority-owned businesses; (3) documentation that it is using high-quality steel and other raw materials in the manufacture of its major products; (4) a report on its activities to secure state construction contracts; and (5) a detailed analysis of its plans for developing a piece of land it owns within the state's master plan for the coastal region. By the city government, XYZ has been told to (1) document its efforts to hire members of the community hard-core unemployed; (2) report on its involvement in a high school career programs (3) submit a technical report on the sulfur content of the waste emitted at one of its plants near the city park; and (4) provide the city council with a report on the economic impact on the city if the corporation continues with plans to move its headquarters to another state.

These 15 requirements are typical of the pressures placed on today's organizations by governmental and regulatory groups. Even more formal and informal requests come from private, educational, and consumer groups. The remarkable thing about most of these requests is that few of them have anything to do with the major task of the organization-making a product or providing a service. Yet to meet all of these requests, which are sometimes really demands backed by court injunctions, requires a great deal of time. Given the pressures under which most organizations operate, it is easy to see why they would want to have complete documentation on just about anything they do. To provide this documentation, people must *write down* a large amount

[2]M. Weber, *Essays in Sociology,* trans. H. Gerth and C. Mills (London: Oxford University Press, 1946), p. 171; J. Thompson, *Organizations in Action* (New York: McGraw-Hill Book Company, 1967), p. 18.

of information and store it in some kind of system that enables them to retrieve it easily and quickly.

Besides all this, consider the enormous amount of material that is written down daily as a part of the organization's regular routine. It is easy to see why most organizations are swimming in a sea of proposals, manuals, reports, computer tapes, copies, letters, memoranda, and files.

The Problem: Overreliance

Early in this book, it was suggested that some organizations fall into the trap of overreliance on the written word. Given the circumstances just described, this overreliance is understandable. However, *written messages only become communication when they are read and understood.* Just because someone writes something about a subject, it does not necessarily follow that this person has communicated. Some scholars therefore conclude that the major communication problem facing American industry is the assumption that communication has really taken place.

This chapter has two goals. The first is to encourage you to think about ways to reduce the volumes of written material by learning when writing can be most effectively used. The second is to make you a more proficient communicator by showing you how to make your writing understandable and readable.

The Key: Good Choices

Successful written communication, as with oral communication, means making good choices in what we encode. Written communication is the official medium of interaction in organizations (e.g., letter of appointment or resignation). However, even in official documents, making good choices means keeping the reader's level of understanding in mind. Let us now turn our attention to a few of the basic principles of good writing. These principles may be applied to all forms of writing used in organizations.

principles of sound writing

All of the principles of good communication have at least some application to writing. Many of the following ideas have been introduced elsewhere in this book. Here they are reexamined as they pertain to written communication. Other ideas are new. All will help you to improve your writing abilities.

   1. The reader will interpret a piece of writing according to his or her personal experience. People will read information from the perspective of their own background.[3] The two most important components of this background are the situation and the personality of the reader. Consider the following memorandum from a sales manager to employees:

```
To: Sales Staff

From: Bill Jones, Sales Manager

Re: Sales Quota

We have been down in sales over the past few months.
We have not been putting forth the effort that we
did this month last year. I want all of you to give
maximum attention to your jobs . . . or else.
```

This memorandum contains three ambiguities. (1) It is not clear who "we" are. (2) It is not clear what "increased effort" means to the sender. (3) The "or else" is clearly a threat, but we do not know whether it means that people will be fired, be demoted, lose their Christmas bonus, or what.

   Each member of the sales staff will interpret this memorandum according to his perception of his own immediate situation. If one salesman has noticed some of his colleagues missing appointments or getting started late in the day, he will interpret the memorandum to mean that the boss is trying to crack down on the *others* in the department. If one salesman's territory is so far away from the home office, where the memorandum was written, that he is completely out of touch with what goes on there or in other sales territories, he may not understand the memorandum at all. To him, it is not communication, especially if he has been meeting the quota and making sales appointments. If for some good reason, such as sickness or family problems, one sales-

   [3]W. Schramm, "How Communication Works," in *The Process and Effects of Communication,* ed. W. Schramm (Urbana: University of Illinois Press, 1954), p. 211.

man has missed quota for the last month, he may assume that the manager's memorandum is intended specifically for him. As he reads it, he may conclude that the supervisor is coming down on him unfairly. This may eventually hinder his work performance. He may become so upset that he stops trying even to meet quota.

In all three cases, one simple, three-sentence memo has done more harm than good, because people place their own interpretations on what they read. It is impossible for the writer to foresee every possible interpretation. However, good writers examine their work for ambiguities. When they find one, they do their best to remove it. This will reduce, though it cannot completely prevent, misinterpretation.

2. Writing does not provide the opportunity for immediate feedback, so the writer should explore ways to generate reader reaction. Early in this book, we mentioned that oral communication provides a sense of give-and-take between the sender and the receiver. This is not true of written communication, because the receiver will often read it out of the presence of the sender. If feedback does come, it is often so delayed that the writer cannot judge the initial impact of his or her message on the reader. One of the most critical failures in organizational communication occurs when administrators fail to respond to a proposal or a written idea generated by someone in the organization. If you have a sound idea about ways to improve worker productivity in your unit, you are encouraged in most organizations to write it down for consideration. But if you never get a response to your suggestion, you may *never make another suggestion again.* This is a waste of enthusiasm and talent. It is one of the classic reasons why organizations are continually experiencing breakdowns in upward communication.[4]

It is impossible to guarantee feedback in every piece of written communication. But written communication becomes two-way interaction only when feedback has taken place. Some of the ways in which feedback can be generated are (1) by using cover sheets on memoranda that ask the reader to evaluate the course of action being recommended; (2) by installing a telephone system which enables readers to ask questions about a written document, and (3) by checking out the reader's reactions orally. These techniques do not guarantee feedback, but they do make it easier.

[4]A. Sanford, G. Hunt, and H. Bracey, *Communication Behavior in Organizations* (Columbus, Ohio: Charles E. Merrill Publishing Company, 1976), p. 361.

3. As in all forms of communication, there is no one best way to write something, but rather a few ways that will probably work well. This theme, too, should be familiar to you by now. We will only touch on it here. Some writers labor for hours over a single letter or memorandum attempting to get just the right phrase or word. While this perfectionism may be admirable, it is not efficient. It takes up too much time. Writing is a matter of *communication*—of getting information across simply and straightforwardly. If in 15 minutes you can write a memo that communicates the same ideas as your co-worker's memo that took two hours to write, then you are ahead in the game —because you have an hour and 45 minutes to devote to other activities.

Good writing in the organizational setting is a matter of trade-offs. You will have to trade off some of your concern for perfection against the utility of getting the message out quickly and clearly. Remember that the reader is facing just as many demands on his or her time as you are—if not more.

4. Choose the simple and straightforward over the complex and abstract. This idea builds upon the previous one. Some writers seem to want to sound sophisticated. This is not necessary in most organizations. Look at the two business letters reproduced as exhibits 9–1 and 9–2. Both writers are trying to make the same point. However, the first writer's main ideas get lost among all the long words and ponderous sentences. Good writers edit and refine their work until it transmits their main ideas clearly. Read the first business letter with the mind set of an editor who wants to clean up the written message. Then read the second letter. Which one is more effective? Why?

Some writers fall into the trap of using technical words in a non-technical context. These writers say *interface* for "meet," *input* for "giving ideas," and *ramifications* for "effects." U.S. News and World Report, in a humorous article on bureaucracy, collected a series of complicated passages that illustrate the errors described in this section (exhibit 9–3). Remember: Try to keep it simple. Good writers write in English, not in jargon.

5. The reader should not have to search for the central idea. The point of your message must be clear; the reader should not have to search for your main ideas. Two principles of journalistic writing are applicable to organizational writing because they enable us to express the main ideas clearly. The first principle is the concept of the *lead paragraph.* The first paragraph of a newspaper article must communicate six crucial pieces of information: *What? Who? Why? Where? When? How?*

EXHIBIT 9–1 . Wordy Business Letter

Mr. George C. Gerber, Manager
Community Development Office
City of Jonesberg
100 Civic Center Place
Jonesberg, Anystate 99999

Dear Mr. Gerber:

After much analysis and forethought, members
of the staff and I have come to the following
important and significant conclusion. Our firm
will be able to handle the advertising account for
tourism with great ease. As you have already been
made aware, Walters and Cochran is a local firm
which specializes in small accounts such as yours,
but an important firm when it comes to providing
superior and outstanding services to our clients.
All of our customers report that they are very happy
with the service we have provided them and the image
we have created for them in the local media. We can
do the same for you.

You are probably wondering what services we
will be able to offer you and rightfully so. We will
increase the exposure of the city of Jonesberg in
all phases of the media. We intend to show to
everyone what a good place Jonesberg would be for a
summer vacation. By working hard, we will attract
new businesses to the city. Our staff thinks that we
can get a number of national magazines to do stories
on the new city neighborhood parks plan, the
dial-a-ride transportation program, and the new
convention center. We also want to get a lot of
publicity for the Jonesberg Founder's Day
Festival, which, as you know, is held each May 20th.
With much hard work, individual initiative, and
close contact between members of your staff and the
account executives of Walters and Cochran, we
should be able to get the job done.

If you have any questions, we stand ready here
at Walters and Cochran to straightforwardly and
openly respond to any of your inquiries. Here at
Walters and Cochran we stand ready to offer any
assistance which you should deem necessary.

Sincerely,

Nancy M. Cochran
Senior Account Executive and
Managing Partner

EXHIBIT 9–2   Precise Business Letter

Mr. George C. Gerber, Manager
Community Development Office
City of Jonesberg
100 Civic Center Place
Jonesberg, Anystate 99999

Dear Mr. Gerber:

After discussion my staff and I have concluded that our firm is capable of handling the Jonesberg advertising account. As you may know, Walters and Cochran is a local firm that specializes in providing superior service to small accounts.

We feel that most of our clients are happy with the image we have created for them in the local media. Should it be necessary, feel free to contact any of our clients about the service we have provided them.

You may want to know what specific services Walters and Cochran can provide for Jonesberg. We feel that we can:

1. Increase Jonesberg's exposure in all phases of the local and national media.
2. Project a positive image of the city as an ideal location for a summer vacation.
3. Help attract new businesses to the city.
4. Encourage a national magazine to do stories on the new neighborhood park plan, the dial-a-ride system, and the convention center.
5. Increase the publicity given to the annual Founders' Day Festival.

With some intiative and close contact between our respective staffs, we should be able to improve significantly the recognition level of the City of Jonesberg.

If you have any questions, please call me personally. My staff and I are ready to provide any assistance.

Sincerely,

Nancy M. Cochran
Senior Account Executive and
Managing Partner

EXHIBIT 9–3   Government Language

TRANSLATING BUREAUCRATESE—*

Government reforms come and go, but the language of public officials remains impenetrable. Some examples from official statements—

Interior Department: "Directly impact the visual quality of the present environment."
Translation: *Spoil the view.*

Food and Drug Administration: "Innovative processes should be considered to better integrate informed societal judgments and values into the regulatory mechanism."
Translation: *Think.*

Senator Hubert Humphrey (Dem.), of Minnesota: "Our exhaustees did indeed continue to have labor-market trouble long after the original benefit termination."
Translation: *It's hard to find work after jobless benefits are used up.*

Senator Carl Curtis (Rep.), of Nebraska: "There are not many people here to hear this, but somehow we are all present when we ourselves speak. So we are never absent when we talk."
Translation: *Few listen when Senators debate.*

CIA: "Health alteration committee."
Translation: *Assassination squad.*

Census Bureau: "Data users who make inferences about the nature of relationships between unrelated adults of the opposite sex who share the same living quarters are cautioned that the data shown here on this subject are aggregates which are distributed over a spectrum of categories including partners, resident employes and roomers."
Translation: *Couples who live together don't always sleep together.*

National Park Service: "No person shall prune, cut, carry away, pull up, dig, fell, bore, chop, saw, chip, pick, move, sever, climb, molest, take, break, deface, destroy, set fire to, burn, scorch, carve, paint, mark, or in any manner interfere with, tamper, mutilate, misuse, disturb, or damage any tree, shrub, plant, grass, flower, or any part thereof, nor shall any person permit any chemical, whether solid, fluid or gaseous, to seep, drip, drain, or be emptied, sprayed, dusted on, injected upon, about or into any tree, shrub, plant, grass, flower."
Translation: *Don't hurt the plants.*

House Committee on Aging: "Budgeting restraints and the socioeconomic climate must also be considered in evaluating recommendations and deciding how they should be prioritized."
Translation: *If there's no money, don't spend it.*

*Source: U.S. News & World Report, October 26, 1978, p. 26. Reprinted from "U.S. News & World Report." Copyright 1978 U.S. News & World Report, Inc.

EXHIBIT 9-3 Cont.

Even after they leave Government, critics claim, bureaucrats continue to speak their own language. Cited as evidence: this sign on a door of the building that houses the National Association of Retired Federal Employes:

REAR ENTRANCE
Do Not Enter

If all of this information is communicated early, an editor, and later the reader, can shorten a story without losing critical information. The second principle is the concept of the *inverted pyramid of writing* (figure 9-1). According to this concept, all of the vital information in a news story should appear in the first few paragraphs. The assumption is that the reader may have limited powers of concentration and time and so may not complete even the most interesting story. If one does stop reading the inverted pyramid story after the first few paragraphs, one has still picked up most of the important details. Contrast the inverted pyramid with the climax order of presentation (figure 9-2). Here the piece of writing builds toward the main idea in the final paragraph. The problem is that the reader will miss the main idea if he or she does not "hang with you." Remember, your main purpose is to communicate ideas. Therefore, you must get the main idea out early. You can elaborate it later.

5. *The short is generally preferable to the long.* Professional journalists are encouraged to say what they have to say in the shortest possible way. However, for some reason many of us seem to think the longer, the better. According to almost every survey on the subject, most executives and managers report that they do not have enough time to do the reading expected of them. The same is true of educational and civil service workers. Here we have two opposing forces at

FIGURE 9-1 Inverted pyramid of writing

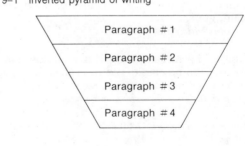

266

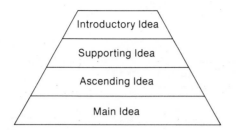

FIGURE 9–2   Climax order of presentation

work. The first is the writer's tendency to expand and embellish his or her writing. The second is the executive's need to limit his or her reading time. What happens? *Often a complete communication failure.*

Occasionally in formal proposals and reports, writers will recognize the need for precision by inserting a short executive summary at the beginning. If an executive does not have the time to read the entire report, he or she can still get the important ideas from the summary. Some organizations prevent their members from writing too much by giving them only limited space to write in. One big city police department provides its officers with small report forms. Officers who need more space must obtain a special form from their supervisor. Since each report is read by at least two levels of supervision above the officer, this system saves everyone many hours of work time.

When you write, save your reader's time. Get the main idea across as early as you can, using as few words as you can.

basic types of writing in the organization

Informational Writing

TRANSMITTING INFORMATION   The purpose of informational writing is to transmit information either within or outside the organization. Informational writing tells people how they fit into the structure of the organization, how to do their jobs, and how they can grow within the organization.[5] Examples of two types of informational writing appear in exhibits 9–4 and 9–5.

[5]See Sanford, Hunt, and Bracey, *Communication Behavior,* pp. 191–208, for a complete discussion of the techniques used to transfer information.

EXHIBIT 9–4 Letter to Transmit Information

Mr. John Barker
329 Blinker Dorm
Middletown State University
Middletown, Texas 74563

Dear Mr. Barker:

The purpose of this letter is to inform you that you have been selected to receive the George C. Baldwin Scholarship for your senior year at Middletown State University. As you may know, the scholarship is presented annually to the senior in the College of Agriculture with the highest cumulative grade point average for the first three years at the university.

As the winner of the scholarship, you will be able to complete your last year with your tuition paid from scholarship funds held in trust. Your name will also be inscribed on the commemorative plaque that hangs in the entryway to the College of Agriculture building.

Let me take this opportunity to congratulate you on your good work here. Good luck as you enter your senior year.

Sincerely,

Dr. Gregory A. Harris, Dean
College of Agriculture

EXHIBIT 9–5 Memorandum to Transmit Information

To: Members of Special Trim Department
From: Larry Jennings, Dept. Foreman
Re: Overtime Today

We will be working 92 minutes of overtime today. Please continue at your work station after the final whistle.

These two written messages are very different, but each fulfills the requirements of the situation for which it was developed. In the first, the requirement was to inform the student that he had won the award and to congratulate him. The Dean's letter accomplished both of these purposes. In the second example, it was only necessary to transmit information to the employees about the overtime scheduled for that day. The workers needed to know how long they would be working, and this notice, tacked up in the usual places in the department, met that need.

There are times when the need for information conflicts with other needs within the organization. Thus members may need information about a particular situation or event, but the leadership team may decide that other needs (e.g., the need for secrecy) take precedence. When this happens, some people do not get the word, and hurt feelings and misunderstandings—directed at management—result.

EXPOSITORY WRITING Organizations use the written channel to give instructions, convey directions, and provide guidelines to members and nonmembers. These are all examples of expository writing. The need for expository writing occurs when extensive and elaborate information must be communicated. Expository writing often clarifies complicated ideas, defines difficult concepts, or outlines a series of instructions. Often it attempts to make general information very specific. Expository writing is demonstrated in the following example where the dean is giving instructions to students about how to qualify for a resident hall counselor position:

To: Students Seeking Interviews for Resident Hall
Counselor Positions

From: George Dunton, Dean Of Students

Re: Procedures

All students who want to be interviewed for
resident hall counselor (RC) positions must meet
the following general qualifications. To be
considered the student must (1) be a senior, (2)
maintain 3.0 cumulative grade point average, (3)
have had experience in extracurricular activities,
(4) have been a student at the college for at least
two years, (5) have had dormitory living
experience, and (6) be recommended by at least
three full-time faculty members.

> If you meet all of these qualifications, there are
> four things that you must do immediately to insure
> that you will be interviewed for an RC position.
>
> 1. Pick up an application from the dean of
> students, fill it out, and return it as soon as
> possible to the dean's office.
> 2. Direct the registrar to send the dean of
> students a copy of your grades at this and any other
> college you have attended.
> 3. Schedule an appointment for a screening
> interview on the sign-up sheet in Campbell Hall.
> You will be notified if you cannot be interviewed at
> the time you have requested.
> 4. Ask three members of the faculty of this
> college to write letters of recommendation on your
> behalf. Please ask them to write their impressions
> of your creativity, responsibility, maturity,
> dependability, and personality.
>
> If you are selected as an RC, you will be considered
> part of the university staff, and you will qualify
> for certain fringe benefits, including tuition at a
> reduced rate. You will be eligible for free room and
> board and will receive a monthly stipend of
> $400.00. You will be expected to be on duty for 30
> hours per week and to be on call 24 hours a day,
> including weekends, when the dormitories are open.
>
> Should you have any questions concerning the RC
> program, please call Mr. Steve Parker of my staff at
> 4361, and he will be happy to respond.

Here the writer needed to meet many *informational* objectives. A simple memorandum or letter would not have been sufficient. Thus, the expository communication was necessary. Reports, manuals, and policy handbooks are examples of expository writing.

Persuasive Writing

Persuasive writing is used in an organization when a member must change the attitudes of some person or group within or outside the organization. Examples of persuasive writing would include letters of application, advertising and marketing campaigns. Following is an example of a persuasive circular:

```
ATTENTION!!

FELLOW APPLIANCE DEALERS

The Maywood Appliance Shop and Arnold's Hardware
Store have joined forces in a purchasing
cooperative that can save you hundreds of dollars.
You are welcome to join us. Here's how it works. . . .

        • We buy for all stores in the co-op. This way we
          get the merchandising and service breaks
          normally reserved for the large stores.

        • We buy the best available line of products.
          Since we will not be limited to only one
          company, we can buy the best product on the
          market for the best available price.

        • We can move quickly. Since we have a good cash
          reserve, we are not tied to our current cash
          flow position. We can take advantage of
          bargains when we first hear of them.

        • We can exchange merchandise among ourselves.
          By getting large quantities of products for
          many stores; we can keep a good inventory
          within our network without any one of us
          needing to expend large sums of money on
          warehouse space.

If you are interested, give us a call at 212-6672 or
243-9897, and one of us will come over to your store
and talk with you about the co-op. Remember, there
is no need for a large capital outlay, and we small
dealers can wind up getting the same breaks as our
large competitors.

                        Sam Jelison, Manager
                        Maywood Appliance Shop

                        Arnold Black, Owner
                        Arnold's Hardware Store
```

Almost all organizations use those principles of persuasion considered in chapters seven and eight to reach potential customers through advertising and public relations. At the same time, managers will initiate a persuasive campaign to encourage subordinates to be aware of such things as waste and productivity. To illustrate, the following notice appeared on the bulletin board in a California plant:

THINK SAFETY

We all benefit from safe surroundings.

The Safety Committee

Here the approach was simply to identify with the needs of the employee by demonstrating that all members of the organization are affected by safety. This is a fairly typical persuasive strategy used in organizational writing. Other strategies would include (1) pointing out something wrong or inconsistent in the current situation and proposing a solution and (2) developing a logical series of arguments for changing the situation.

Interrogatory Writing

Interrogatory writing asks for information or makes a request. An example would be the following letter:

Mr. George Mills
Hoover Electric Co.
Glendale, Calif. 92346

Dear Mr. Smith:

We are writing you to ask for clarification on two important points dealing with the bid for the electric work that you submitted for the Westvista housing project.

Would you please document the following two aspects of your bid:

1. The bid is not clear as to whether or not you plan to use subcontractors. If you do, would you please so inform.

> 2. There has been some confusion over the carrier for your construction insurance. As soon as possible, we need some information from your carrier on the type and amount of your coverage.
>
> As soon as you provide this information for us, we will be able to process your bid. Let me add a personal note. The bid, apart from these two areas, looks quite good, and I would estimate that our chances of success on this project are excellent.
>
> Sincerely,
>
> Wayne C. Moran,
> Project Director

Requests for clarification, further information, and documentation are common in most organizations. Good interrogatory writing requires two special skills. The first is the ability to be precise in stating the kind of additional information desired. The second is the ability to decide (or find out) whom the request for information should be directed to. If you make a request of the wrong person, one who is not empowered to grant it or who does not know what you are asking about, the request is so much wasted effort. Finding out whom to write to is a big factor in successful interrogatory writing.

Technical Writing

Organizations use technical writing to describe and define their service functions and their products. Sometimes members of an organization will use technical writing to document how something is done for internal purposes, as when they write manuals, guidebooks, directives, and so forth. Other times, the organization will use technical writing to explain to someone else what it does, as when it writes a report to governmental officials or a consumer's manual to accompany its product.

The major problem with technical writing in most organizations is that it is sometimes too technical for the average reader. By nature, technical writing has a limited readership. If too few people can understand it, however, the written message is useless for all practical purposes. People in organizations develop their own special language and codes, and these are often incorporated into their writing. When this happens, the writing becomes so highly specialized that it is intelligible

273

only to members of that one organization. Granted, most technical writing is going to be sophisticated, but it is still necessary to make it comprehensible.

common malfunctions
of written communication

In this section, we will examine some of the most common problems that occur in writing. The following discussion is based on the work of Lesikar, who first developed the list of malfunctions that will be used here.[6] However, the general background for these ideas was provided by the work of Alfred Korzybski, who developed a way of looking at the relationship between human behavior and language called *general semantics.*[7]

The malfunctions of written communication cause confusion and uncertainty on the part of the reader. The writing problems considered here are really problems in thinking that hinder all types of communication, but particularly written interaction.

Two-Valued Thinking

Some people write as if there was only two alternative courses of action in a given situation. They say, "Shall we go home or stay here?" "It is either black or white." "It is always too hot or too cold in Indiana." The flaw in this kind of thinking is obvious. The either/or orientation does not allow for any middle ground. It sets up each situation with only two alternatives.

Sometimes there really are only two alternatives. You will either get married or not, you will earn a million dollars in your lifetime or not, and so forth. But in most social situations, there are many more than two options available. Suppose you see someone in the office who appears to be gaining weight, and you say to a co-worker, "Sally is really getting fat." But your co-worker replies, "Sally is much lighter than Bill. Bill is fat." To the co-worker, a fat person may be one who tips the scales at over 250 pounds. To you, a fat person may be one who has a roll or two of extra flesh around the middle. There are many degrees of "fat" and "skinny" and many physical conditions in between.

[6]Lesikar, *Business Communication,* pp. 80–100.
[7]A. Korzybski, *Science and Sanity: An Introduction to Non-Aristotelian Systems and General Semantics,* 3rd ed. (Garden City, N.Y.: Country Life Publishing Co., 1948).

People sometimes use two-valued thinking in their professional writing. Lesikar gives the example of a supervisor who uses the word "lazy" in an appraisal review. The dividing line between the word "lazy" and another word, such as "industrious," may not be all that clear-cut. An employee who is productive for four hours of an eight-hour work shift would be considered lazy by some people. But contemporary studies show that the average worker is only productive for about two and a half hours of an eight-hour shift, what with interruptions, conversations, and time away from the work station. By today's standards, the employee who puts in four good hours would have to be considered industrious.

The point that both Lesikar and Krozybski are making is that difficult problems can arise when writers use words that reflect a two-valued orientation. Words like "good," "bad," "wrong," "right," "weak," "strong," "intelligent," and "ignorant" can all be criticized on this basis.

Fact–Inference Confusion

Some things are pure facts. Larry Brown is the vice-president of our firm. Sally Karney has joined the Los Angeles Chapter of the Public Relations Society. However, in most social situations pure facts are relatively few. When no pure facts exist, we must make inferences about the circumstances we encounter and act as though the inferences were facts. An *inference* is a judgment based on a calculation that we make after observing a situation. Suppose we have been away on a business trip. When we return, we see Jim Snyder, the assistant sales manager, sitting at sales manager Bill Motley's desk. We also observe that Bill's name tag has been taken off the door. We *infer* that Jim has been promoted to replace Bill. We do not know for sure, but that is our best guess.

Actually, however, there are many possible reasons why Jim is occupying Bill's desk. Perhaps Bill is ill. Perhaps Bill has been given temporary duties elsewhere. Perhaps Jim is playing a practical joke. Until we get more information to check out our initial inference, we may treat it as a fact, but we should remember that it may not be one.

Inferences are a necessary part of our existence. We would be severely limited in our communication behavior if we could only write and talk about proven facts. The problem arises when we do not recognize the difference between a fact and an inference. Sometimes we communicate this fact–inference confusion. For example, look at the following memorandum:

```
To: Supervisors

From: John Hart

Re: Supervision of Students

Student workers are only employed part-time and are
not to be considered regular workers. We must be
direct in our supervision of them. It is necessary
to keep very close tabs on their work. Make sure
that you are aware of all of their projects and
about their progress or lack of progress on them.
```

This memorandum contains an inference made by the supervisor and communicated to his fellow supervisors as if it were a fact. The inference is that all the student workers need close supervision. But it would be impossible for Mr. Hart to have observed the behavior of all the student workers. Mr. Hart probably observed the behavior of some students and made an inference about *all* students on those observations. In the literature of general semantics, this kind of inference is called an *allness* reaction.[8]

Given Mr. Hart's view of student workers, he does not leave room for the individual student who may be entirely capable of working independently. To compound the error, he has formalized his inference by officially communicating it through a memorandum. This will create problems for two reasons. First, the memorandum contains what amounts to a factual error. It implies that no student is capable of working independently or of making a worthwhile contribution. Second, the memorandum has become part of the historical record of the event. As such, it will be generally believed. Later, if specific examples are uncovered proving that Mr. Hart's judgment was only an inference —and a false one at that—it will be next to impossible to reverse its effects. Remember that written communication *documents* and *records.*

We cannot hope to communicate effectively without making inferences. We must draw conclusions based on the available data. However, good written communication will *recognize* that inferences are being made and will allow for the possibility of error. John Hart's memorandum should have read:

[8]I. Lee, *Language Habits in Human Affairs* (New York: Harper & Row, Publishers, Inc., 1941), p. 181.

```
To: Supervisors

From: John Hart

Re: Supervising Students

I have noticed that some of our part-time student
workers need more direct supervision than some of
our regular workers. We should identify these
students and monitor their activities closely. If
you have not been doing so, please note which
specific projects students are working on. As you
observe student productivity, please supervise
carefully those workers who do not appear to be
working hard.
```

Blocked Mind

A blocked mind usually belongs to the reader, not the writer, but it does affect the way in which your message will be interpreted. A person whose mind is blocked operates on limited information and refuses to accept any data that refute his or her initial conclusion. It's the old "don't bother me with the facts" syndrome. An example of the blocked mind in operation might be provided by your neighbor, who refuses to buy an automobile from General Motors. Her reasoning is simple. When she graduated from high school, her first car was a Buick. Over the next three years, she had nothing but trouble with the car. Her initial rationale for not buying another General Motors car was based upon data (e.g., the ineffective Buick). But for the next 20 years, this woman has maintained the same opinion of the Buick, as well as all the other G.M. products. She has steadfastly ignored any further data, specifically any current scientific evidence about improvements in General Motors cars. This is the blocked mind at work.

Leaders in organizations can also demonstrate the blocked mind. Such contemporary trends in management as Management by Objectives (MBO), Human Resource Accounting (HRA), Management Information Systems, and zero-based accounting have come into use much sooner in some organizations than in others because some administrators have been more willing than others to accept the data about these new procedures. This is not to suggest that people who value the status quo are necessarily demonstrating the blocked mind. People with blocked minds are those who reject new information that may force them to reassess their first impressions.

The blocked mind can hinder written communication in the organization. Just because a report or memorandum lays out the facts about an issue, it does not necessarily follow that the reader accept it as definitive. People cannot simply put their preconceived prejudices aside when they are reading new information. These prejudices act as a filter through which information must pass. People read what you write with their own preconceived ideas. If these ideas are strong, your written message, if contradictory, will not get through. More simply, the reader sometimes reads with his or her mind already made up. Lesikar suggests that to unblock one's mind, one should always leave room for additional data.

Static Viewpoint

THE PROBLEM DEFINED   Often we falsely assume that the way we describe or experience something is the way it will remain. When we make this assumption, we are demonstrating a *static point.* It is an error in communication to assume that circumstances will remain constant. Consider the following directive, which appeared on the bulletin board of a large western manufacturing organization:

Employees:

No employee who has had a suspension or who has had disciplinary action during the last three years will be eligible to take the promotion examination. The only individuals who will be eligible to take the examination will be those who have a good record in attendance and cooperation.

H. J. Gilbert
Plant Manager

The intent of the directive is plain enough. The plant manager is trying to compile a roster of test takers who have maintained a good conduct record while working in the organization. However, the directive embodies a glaring communication error. It assumes that an employee who once demonstrated bad conduct, even three years ago, will continue to be a disciplinary problem for the rest of his or her tenure in the organization. It assumes that such an employee is incapable of supervising the behavior of others. In short, the directive assumes that people cannot change. Yet people do change drastically. Country and western singer Merle Haggard, baseball player Ron Le Flore, former presidential aide Charles Colson, and San Francisco social reformer John Maher are all examples of people who made worthwhile contributions to society after having served time in jail. And as people change, so do organizations. During the oil crisis of the early 1970s, the recreational vehicle industry was in serious financial trouble, because the current assumption was that there would no longer be an endless supply of gas. Now the industry has made a strong recovery. The Chrysler Corporation has undergone many financial crises through the years but has recovered each time to produce automobiles and to place in the list of the largest American corporations. The evidence is overwhelming— people, conditions, and organizations change.

Since things do change, our language and thinking should reflect this change. But the nature of written language is such that when we write something down, we seem to be saying that this is the "way things are." John Smith is a Republican. The University of Minnesota has a beautiful campus. General Foods is the leader in the prepared breakfast food industry. How are we to resolve this problem?

THE CONCEPT OF DATING The theorists in the field of general semantics have given us a device that we can use in our writing to account for change. It is called *dating,* and it works like this: John Smith is a Republican in 1964. The University of Minnesota has a beautiful campus in 1957. General Foods is the leader in the prepared breakfast industry in 1979. Dating enables us to put a time frame around a particular statement. It sets the parameters for the statement. You cannot realistically date every statement you make in formal writing. But you should recognize that almost every message you send for (or receive) is transmitted within a time frame. This time frame strongly influences the events that are described in the message. You should not only be aware of this time frame, but should also specify it in your writing. Consider the following example:

```
To: All Employees

From: Harry Chousi, Personnel Department

Re: Fringe Benefits

As of today and until 10-1-78, the following
conditions will apply: (1) We will have Global
Health Insurance Major Medical coverage. At
```

> present, the Global bid appears to have the best
> program for employees at the most competitive rate.
> (2) The pension contribution rate will change from
> 7 1/2 percent to 8 percent for the next year. Over
> the next two-year period, this change will mean a
> tax savings to employees, due to new provisions in
> the federal income tax laws. These two conditions
> are being continuously monitored. Changes that
> will improve the financial position of our
> employees, and which are consistent with union
> contract clauses, will be made.

This memo structures the information being transmitted to employees within a specific time frame.

Failure to Discriminate

Good communicators recognize that people are different. Not only are people different, but organizations are different, and social contexts are different. Good writers allow for these differences. However, this is sometimes easier said than done.

STEREOTYPING It is much easier for us to react to a *class* than to a specific example. Look at the word "manager." To each of us, that word carries a different connotation. For some of us, a manager is someone who is able to do the job and pull off an assignment. For others, a manager is someone who is able to relate well to other people and inspire subordinates to work hard. For others still, a manager is someone who is in control and always has the situation well in hand. All of these meanings are appropriate in the sense that they all describe what a manager might be. We fail to discriminate when we react in the *same way every* time we encounter the word "manager," and react in the *same way* to *every* manager we see. Let us assume that our meaning for the word "manager" is someone who projects the image of being in control. Then every time we encounter a manager, we assume that he or she is in control of things. We have assumed, first, that managers as a *class* act in this way, and second, that *every single member* of the class has the characteristics we attribute to that class. This is known as *social stereotyping.*

AWARENESS Some people argue that stereotyping is always harmful. It is true that such categories as "black," "woman," "WASP," and "hick" are not descriptive. However, in and of itself, stereotyping is neither good nor bad. A better way of thinking about the tendency is to examine results. If we stereotype constantly, and the process prevents us from responding appropriately to specific cases that do not fit the stereotype (e.g., a boss who is not capable or a mother who is not kind), we are facing a problem. We do ourselves and others a disservice when we place them in an unsuitable category. All of us stereotype at one time or another, but the key is being aware that we are doing it. We need to leave room for differences, for the single example that does not fit. Lesikar offers good advice in the following passage:

> We can look for differences in all things about which we communicate. So the next time you hear someone make a reference to labor leaders, students, bookies, or cab drivers, keep in mind stereotypes will not fit them all. And the next time you hear a general judgment of all members of a category such as "women are fickle" or "Italian men are romantic" index these statements yourself. Ask yourself, "Which women are fickle?" and "Which Italian men are romantic?" By doing so, you will be gaining a more realistic understanding of the reality about which we communicate.[9]

ways to correct malfunctions

In the last section, we considered some of the glaring errors that can occur in written communication. Now let us see how these errors may be resolved.

This section discusses five techniques for improving the quality of your writing.

Adaptation

When you studied the public oral presentation in chapters seven and eight, you learned that it is important to meet your audience's needs and expectations. The same concept applies to written communication, but it is stated in a slightly different way. *Written communication must adapt to the reader.*

ADAPTING THE PURPOSE   When you write something in an organization, you have, or should have, a fairly clear purpose in mind. That purpose must be accomplished through the written document. However, that purpose must also be accomplished for your specific readers. Therefore, your purpose must be adapted to your readers. Look at these two memoranda:

[9]Lesikar, *Business Communication,* pp. 54–55.

To: Elementary Teachers at Patrick Henry School

From: Joe Systroming, Principal

Re: Extra Duty During School Carnival

All teachers will be expected to stay after school on Friday, October 30, to help with the school carnival. The carnival will start at 1:00 P.M. and will conclude near 6:00 P.M. I want to see all Patrick Henry teachers around at the end to help with cleanup, to meet parents, and to supervise the behavior of our students and visitors.

To: Elementary Teachers at Patrick Henry School

From: Joe Systroming, Principal

Re: Extra Duty During School Carnival

I know it is that busy fall season again, and you are all trying to get the school year off to a good start. My purpose here is to remind you that our annual school carnival is coming up on Friday, October 30, from 1:00 to 6:00 P.M. It has been the tradition in the past that teachers here at Patrick Henry remain "on duty" during the carnival. I would ask you to do so again, and I want to assure you that this is the only "extended day" of the fall semester. We need you all to remain on campus to meet parents, help supervise our students and visitors, and help with cleanup after the carnival. I am confident that all of you on staff will pitch in and make our school carnival a success.

Although the same general message—"you are going to have to stay after school and help with the school carnival"—was communicated in both memoranda, the second one reflects the writer's effort to identify with (or perhaps only to acknowledge) the needs of the specific reader. The principal tried to let his readers know that he was aware of the pressures they faced. He attempted to allay their fears that this kind of

Highly formal	Highly informal
Structured	Unstructured

FIGURE 9-3 Formality Continuum

overtime assignment might occur again. In short, he tried to adapt his purpose to the reader.

ADAPTING LEVEL OF TREATMENT Another form of adaptation involves the level of treatment given a particular piece of information. Obviously, you use one level of treatment with a group of third graders and another with a group of law students at the state university. Here the level of treatment is determined by your assessment of your readers' intelligence and reading ability. But level of treatment might also be classified along a formality continuum (figure 9–3). If you are writing to a group of old friends with whom you often communicate, you may be informal in your approach. If you are writing to strangers, you will probably be more formal. Consider the following two directives. The first was written by the new manager of a department, the second by an old hand whom everyone knows.

```
Employees:
I want to take this opportunity to welcome you back
after the Christmas holidays. I trust that you all
had a good rest and that you enjoyed the time with
your family. Let us all keep in mind the Christmas
spirit of good will and brotherhood throughout the
year. I offer you my personal wish for a good and
prosperous new year.
```

```
Employees:
Welcome back!
From all I've heard, you all had a great holiday and
enjoyed the time with your families. As we begin a
new year together, let's keep in mind the Christmas
ideals of brotherhood and good will. Good wishes
for a healthy and happy 1978.
```

In the second message the writer was confident enough of his friendship with the readers that he could take the liberty of being informal. This informality allows the writer to build on the relationship with the reader, thereby producing a message that is breezy and casual, yet still fulfills a purpose—welcoming back employees.

Adaptation means taking into consideration the purpose of the message, the needs of the reader, and the relationship that exists between the writer and reader. All three factors will dictate the writer's approach. If the writer ignores one or two of these factors, the message will probably not be well adapted to the reader.

Word Choice

Early in this chapter, you learned that a good writer uses a simple, straightforward approach. This can be done through one's choice of words. There are times when long or technical words are appropriate. However, short, single words are usually preferable, because they communicate one's ideas more effectively. Let us examine the choice of words in the following two letters:

```
Mr.Jerry Jacobs
Sales Manager
Hilter Corporation
Bayside, California 98761


Dear Mr. Jacobs:


We are concerned about the trend by members of your
sales staff to provide less than adequate service
in the follow-up of our account. Your salespeople
have been quite irregular and sporadic in their
visitation procedures of our personnel. They do not
seem observant of our needs and appear quite
unfamiliar with your products and our product
requirements. I hope that you will take this
information into account in your preparation for
your next sales meeting. Thank you.

         Sincerely,


         Dom Lombardi,
         Product Manager
```

```
Mr. Jerry Jacobs
Sales Manager
Hilter Corporation
Bayside, California 98761

Dear Mr. Jacobs:

    I want to make a few comments about the
unsatisfactory performance of your sales staff in
dealing with our firm. First, your salespersons
have shown up very irregularly at our stores.
Second, they do not seem to know your products when
they do show up. Third, they do not seem to be aware
of our product needs. I hope that you will mention
this to them at your next sales meeting. Thank you.

            Sincerely,

            Dom Lombardi,
            Product Manager
```

The second letter has used simple, straightforward words to communicate the same message as the first letter. When we read the first letter, we do get the message (Mr. Jacobs' staff is not performing up to expectations), but it is a struggle. In the second letter, the message comes through loud and clear.

Structural Factors

Unlike oral communication, writing makes a visual impact. Visually appealing writing attracts the reader's interest. There are things you can do to make your message look appealing. Examine the three letters in figure 9–4. Which one makes the reader want to read further? If you are like most readers, you will probably prefer Example 3, because it looks the easiest to read. Journalists usually write in short paragraphs, because long paragraphs do not encourage the reader to read on. We want our letters to hold the interest of the reader. Short, compact paragraphs generally do this. It is a simple task to emphasize important ideas by stating them in the lead sentence of each paragraph. In the passage with longer paragraphs, it is hard for the reader to pick out the main ideas, because the structure suggests that everything is equally important. The letters in exhibits 9–6 and 9–7 demonstrate this difference.

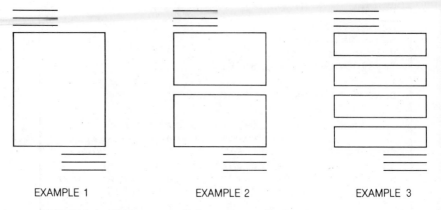

EXAMPLE 1   EXAMPLE 2   EXAMPLE 3

FIGURE 9–4   Which message is the most appealing?

EXHIBIT 9–6   Letter With One Long Paragraph

John Jones
1266 E. Second St.
Centerville, Calif. 92699

Dear Mr. Smith:

It has come to our attention that you are quite
delinquent on your revolving charge account at our
store. At last accounting, your bill was "past
due" nearly $700.00, and it has been nearly three
months since you paid anything on your account.
Normally when an account becomes past due for over a
three-month period, we turn it over to the
Centerville Collection Company for follow-up.
However, since you have been a regular customer
here at the Centerville Department Store and have
maintained a good credit record in the past, we want
to give you one last opportunity to take care of
this matter. In order to maintain a good credit
record, it is necessary that you immediately pay 10
percent (or $70.00) on your account to demonstrate
your good faith in meeting this obligation. If you
do not do this, we will have no recourse but to take
other action.

Sincerely,

George Thomas,
Credit Manager

EXHIBIT 9–7   Letter With Several Short Paragraphs

Mr. John Jones
1266 E. Second Street
Centerville, California 92699

Dear Mr. Jones:

    It has come to our attention that you are quite
delinquent on your revolving charge account at our
store.

    At last accounting, your account was "past due"
nearly $700.00, and it has been nearly three months
since you paid anything on your account.

    Normally when an account becomes past due for
over a three-month period, we turn it over to the
Centerville Collection Company for follow-up.
However, since you have been a good customer here at
the Centerville Department Store and have
maintained a good credit record in the past, we want
to give you one last opportunity to take care of
this matter.

    In order to maintain a good credit record, it is
necessary that you immediately pay 10 percent (or
$70.00) on your account to show us your good faith
in meeting this obligation. If you do not do this,
we will have no recourse but to take other action.

                Sincerely,

                George Thomas,
                Credit Manager

Notice how much easier to read the second letter looks, although the two letters say exactly the same thing.

Another structural factor is *format,* or the way in which paragraphs are styled. The two usual formats are as follows:

BLOCK STYLE

As a matter of tradition, the Trim Department will hold its annual Christmas party on the Friday before Christmas day. All members of the department and their families are invited to attend. Refreshments will be served, and gifts will be provided to all children.

INDENT STYLE

As a matter of tradition, the Trim Department will hold its annual Christmas party on the Friday before Christmas day. All members of the department and their families are invited to attend. Refreshments will be served, and gifts will be provided to all children.

Most organizations use the block style for internal memoranda and the indent style for correspondence. But this varies. Some organizations use one standardized format; others leave the choice of format up to the writer. Often writers will adopt the format that they feel makes the best impression on the reader.

Precision

In organizational writing, *precision* means saying what you have to say in the fewest and clearest possible words. In the following memorandum, the writer has not practiced precision. The editorial corrections show how he could have said approximately the same thing in far fewer words.

October 12, 1978

To: Members of the Sales Staff
From: Keven Locker, Sales Manager
Re: Redistricting of Sales Territories

~~Gentlemen and ladies~~ *Salespersons* it has come to my attention

~~from many sources~~ that we need to ~~think about~~

redistrict~~ing~~ our sales territories. After ~~giving~~

~~this matter~~ much thought ~~and analysis~~, I have ~~come~~

~~to the important~~ conclu~~sion~~*ded* that we should base the

sales territory on the salesperson's *yearly* record ~~of last~~

~~year~~. The salesperson with the highest dollar

volume *will* ~~in sales should be given the opportunity to~~

select the territory that he or she ~~thinks he or she~~

wants. The second highest salesperson ~~would~~ *will* select

and so forth ⊙
next ~~until every salesperson has selected his or~~

you approve of this plan ⊙
~~her territory~~, I hope that ~~this plan meets with all~~

~~of your approval.~~

Good communicators form the habit of going back over their writing to insure that it says what they intended, and that all of the unnecessary words and confusing ideas have been removed. This is just as important as getting the ideas down in the first draft.

Organization

Organization means deciding what goes where and which ideas should be treated with which other ideas. Organization was discussed in chapters seven and eight, and what applies to oral communication also applies to writing. If you will follow the following three guidelines, you should have no trouble organizing your message.

- Ideas that are related to each other should be grouped together.
- Supporting ideas should closely follow the main ideas that they are intended to document.
- Use stylistic and structural elements (e.g., numbers, hyphens, bullets—as used in this list) to set off lists and other items intended for equal treatment.

Let us examine each of these guidelines individually.

IDEAS SHOULD BE GROUPED   It is easier to follow written communication when ideas follow a logical sequence. If ideas jump all over the place, the reader has a difficult time relating them. The following memorandum illustrates what happens when ideas are transmitted with no apparent logic:

289

```
To: Production Supervisors

From: Hal Stowe, Foreman

Re: Maintenance

We have been having problems with the cleanup of the
work area again. Tools have been left out, and the
most expensive ones at that. We must help to keep
the area clean. We have been having safety problems
at the machinists' station because the bars are
extended at eye level. Oil has been left on the
floor. Workers could hurt their eyes if they run
into the bars. The tools have to be replaced. If
they are lost, it will take a lot of time to replace
them. Oil creates a very dangerous situation. We
must clean up the area. Maintenance is everyone's
business, not just the maintenance department's.
Let's get with it.
```

Although it is not impossible to get the main ideas out of this memorandum, the reader has to do a lot of work. Let us look at the same memo after it has been organized a bit more effectively.

```
To: Production Supervisors

From: Hal Stowe, Foreman

Re: Maintenance

We are having problems with the maintenance of the
work area again. There are three important safety
problems that we must solve immediately.

At the machinists' station, the bars have been left
extended at eye level. If someone should run into
one of them, he could be badly hurt. When not in use
the bars must be retracted.

In the storage area, tools have been left out.
People could trip and fall on them, or the tools
could be lost. Tools that are not being used should
be replaced. In the shop we have had oil left on the
floor. We could easily slide on the oil and go
```

> crashing into a machine. We have sand to absorb
> spilled oil. All of us are responsible for
> maintenance. It is not just the maintenance crew's
> job to keep the area clean. Let's get with it.

The second memorandium organizes the ideas in such a way that the reader knows at once what the problems are, how to solve them, and what will happen if they are not solved.

SUPPORTING MATERIAL SHOULD FOLLOW MAIN IDEAS CLOSELY When an idea needs clarification, the material used to clarify it should follow closely after the idea itself. Readers should not have to work through a lot of intervening material in search of supporting data. In the following example, the supporting material is easy to find:

> Fellow Employees!!
>
> You must join our labor union because management is
> unfair to us. Look what they have done to your
> co-workers over the past four years:
>
> -Refused to give us a cost of living raise
> -Fired three employees for union activities
> -Promoted only antiunion people to supervision
> -Refused to settle grievances fairly
>
> For these reasons you must join our union today. It
> is not only important for you, but important for all
> of us.
>
> Union Organizing Committee

The supporting material—in this case, examples of alleged mistreatment by management—is immediately apparent.

USE STRUCTURAL ELEMENTS The foregoing example used hyphens to set off each piece of supporting material. This structural device helps clarify important ideas for the reader. Numbering the paragraphs would have also been effective. Other symbols, including asterisks (*) and **boldface** type, can be used to alert the reader that important information is coming up.

291

forms of written communication

Reports

A *report* is a written status update on a particular project or job. It tells how things are going or how they went. One example would be an affirmative action report for the federal government to provide a status update on actions taken by the organization to insure equal employment of women and minorites. Another example would a report by the foreman to the plant superintendent on the number of units produced by the previous production shift. A report may be a brief paragraph describing one isolated event, or a thick volume, or anything in between. The report is an important written device because it documents events, provides critical information for decision making, and establishes the history of the organization through its inclusion in company filing systems. Reports must be accurate and concise because eventually nearly every level of management will review them.

Proposals

When someone in an organization has an idea that he or she wants to see adopted, that person develops a proposal. A *proposal* is a written document that presents a rationale for implementing an idea. Normally a proposal has five parts:

- *Background,* which provides the history of the situation that caused the person to suggest a change
- *Problem description,* which identifies the problem and establishes the parameters for the change strategy
- *Program objectives,* which lays out the change program and its objectives for the reader
- *Evaluation design,* which describes in some detail how the recommended program will be assessed
- *Budget,* which specifies what the change program will cost in money and man-hours

Although not all proposals will have these five specific parts, most proposals will contain this information in some form.

Memoranda

A *memorandum* is a written technique to transmit information within the organization. Almost all organizations use memoranda in some form. This chapter contained many examples of memoranda.

Correspondence

Probably the most widely used form of business writing is the letter. Business letters appear throughout this chapter as examples. They often *represent* the organization in terms of their appearance, style, and format.

Manuals

Organizations must often publish technical data related to their products or services. This is usually done in the form of *manuals.* Some manuals are volumes of highly technical messages that can only be interpreted by experts. Other manuals are developed for the lay audience. An example would be the guide used to complete income tax each spring.

Newsletters, House Organs

Some organizations put out *newspapers* and *newsletters* for both in-house and outside readers. These publications often conform in style and format to the local daily newspaper. Organizations often use their house organs as public relations vehicles. When this happens, the reader's need for information and organization's desire for good public relations may conflict. If the publication is highly oriented to the needs of the organization's members and contains much up-to-the-minute information, it may lose some of its public relations value because outside readers rarely care about very specific in-house information that is meaningful only to people who work for the organization. The ratio of current to noncurrent information often indicates which audience the publication is aimed at.

Resumes and Cover Letters

Resumes and cover letters are written when a personnel decision (to hire, to promote, to transfer) must be made. *Resumes,* which are also called vitae or personal data sheets, are brief outlines of an individual's background and experience. An example of a resume appears as exhibit 9–8. The *cover letter* accompanies the resume. It asks that the writer be considered for the available position. The research summarized in exhibit 9–9 tells what corporate leaders look for in a cover letter or resume. If you need to construct a resume, you would do well to consult the list to see if you have included everything that most personnel executives want to know.

EXHIBIT 9–8

William E. Stewart

Address: Personal Data:
1124 E. 11th Street   Born: April 2, 1950 in
El Cajon, Calif. 96431   San Diego, Calif.
Phone: 714/876-9192   Health: Good

Objective:
To further my career in marketing by gaining
experience in international trade and sales
management

Education:
B.S. 1972—San Diego State University- Major:
                                      Marketing
                                      Minor:
                                      Communication

A.A. 1970—Grossmont Community College
Diploma: 1968—El Cajon High School
Additional Graduate Work: 12 units toward M.B.A. at
                          United States
                          International
                          University

Experience:

Sales Representative, Hobard Manufacturing Co.,
San Diego, California, 1974-present. Assigned to
three southern counties of California to represent
Hobart trailers, truck beds, and campers. Contact
primarily with dealers and distributors. Acted as
southern sales manager when permanent manager is
out of town.

Sales Trainee, Gerpson Corporation, National City,
California. 1972-1974. "Inside" sales position
required follow-up on orders initiated in field.
After one year, was only trainee given backup
territory to support regular salesperson.

Salesman, Nikom Men's Shop, San Diego, California.
1970-1972. Part-time position selling men's
clothes while in college. Was responsible for
opening and closing store on weekends.

Store Boy, Alpha Beta Market, Lakeview,
California. 1966-1970. Part-time position while

EXHIBIT 9–8 Cont.

finishing high school and attending community college. Job included: stacking groceries, helping with store maintenance, and bagging grocery orders for customers.

Other Activities and Honors:

Salesman of year (1976) Hobart Manufacturing Co. Given to salesman with the highest dollar amount of sales for the year.

President, Alpha Chi Social Fraternity (1972), San Diego State University. Supervised fraternity activities for year.

Business Student Award, Grossmont College (1970). Award given to marketing student with the highest grade point average.

Senior Class President, El Cajon, California High School (1968). Elected to direct activities of senior class, which included senior recognition day, senior prom, and graduation.

References Available upon Request

EXHIBIT 9–9   What Should Be in Cover Letter and Resume*

A survey of the nation's largest corporations (500 surveyed) indicates the following, with regard to being contacted about a job:

I.   In the initial contact with the company
     98% preferred both a cover letter and a resume.
     67% wanted it typewritten.
     15% wanted it handwritten.
II. The following material was desired on the resume:
     98% wanted to know the military status or draft classification.
     92% wanted personal information such as date of birth, marital status, number of dependents, etc.
     91% wanted to know the personal interests of the applicant such as accounting, sales, statistics, finance, economics.
     87% wanted general as well as specific education (majors and minors in college).

*Source: Summarized from "The Cover Letter and Resume" by H. D. Jones. Reprinted with permission of Personnel Journal Copyright September 1969.

EXHIBIT 0-9 Cont.

        86% wanted to know if the applicant would be willing to relocate.

        86% wanted a list of scholarships or outstanding awards.

        82% wanted to know previous work experience and the reason for leaving.

        80% wanted to know the health status of the person applying.

        76% were interested in social data such as fraternity or sorority memberships, clubs, and organizations, along with a list of offices held in such.

        57% wanted to know salary requirements of applicants.

        57% wanted to know the major source of financing of college.

        48% desired to know the high school attended and rank in graduating class,

        46% wanted a list of college grades.

        41% wanted to know of any special aptitudes such as being able to type, run computers, etc.

        33% desired references.

        32% would like a photograph, even though they could not request it legally.

III.   Length of resume should be short

        35% did not want more than two-page resume, and preferred one.

        30% wanted one page only.

IV.   The cover letter should be short, to the point, and clearly stated. It should tell why the company has been selected and what the applicant desires in terms of a job. It should be used to amplify the resume, such as explaining about some low grades or other information that might harm the applicant.

The letter should list special interest in the company. It should not take the form of a "run of the mill" form letter. Neatness and clarity is essential to even getting noticed, but avoid the "canned" professional format. An honest, forthright, individual approach is not only effective, but refreshing. The letter should be viewed as an introduction, not a comprehensive report; that is the purpose of later interviews.

FOR STUDY

1 Identify six different situations where writing might be used in an organization.

2 Compare written to oral communication in the organization. What are the advantages and disadvantages of each?

3 Name some of the biggest problems in organizational writing. Have you encountered any of these problems in your experience with organizations?

4 This chapter has suggested that sloppy writing may well reflect sloppy thinking. Offer some examples of problems in thinking.

5 Name three ways to improve organizational writing.

case nine

The Freight Business

The Littleton Corporation is in the freight-forwarding business. It moves freight by truck and by railroad car. To operate effectively, Littleton must maintain an extensive network of branch offices and stations throughout the country. Cargo is checked as it moves through each of these branches. With the help of some industrial engineers and computer programmers, Littleton has established a sophisticated system for tracking cargo. Each piece of cargo, no matter how small, is computerized as it travels to its destination. If the piece is lost or misplaced, a map appears on the screen to trace its route over the last few days.

To keep the Littleton network working properly, it is necessary for each branch to write many memoranda to other branches. Since the freight-forwarding business is tightly regulated by both the state and federal commerce agencies, much information must be disseminated on such matters as tariffs and taxes. There are 11 major stations and 23 minor offices in the Littleton network. These 34 units must exchange information among themselves and with the home office in Phoenix.

Dave Keller is the vice-president of operations for Littleton. He is responsible for seeing to it that everything moves along rapidly and no cargo is lost. In the course of his day, he must read a large stack of memos and respond to numerous telephone messages from assistants out in the field. When a customer phones the head office to track down a pierce of cargo, the call will eventually reach Dave if no one can find the missing shipment. So most of Dave's job consists of reading correspondence and handling crises as they occur.

Dave recently became concerned about the quality of the memoranda he was receiving from Littleton employees out in the field. For example, he received this memo about three weeks ago:

To: Management Staff

From: Hector Salazar, Albuquerque Office

Re: New Tariff Regulations

It has come to my attention from a very reliable source that state legislators here in the state capital here in New Mexico are considering a "state through" tax which would very greatly pertain to Littleton trucks as they pass through New Mexico on their way to their destinations in both easterly and westerly directions. As I have been told, here

---

is how the tax will work in actual operation. When the truck arrives in the state, the driver would have to report the number of days he expects to be in the state, the number of miles he is planning to travel within the state, and he would be asked to drive on the scales which have been provided there. After all of these things, a tax is then computed which the driver would have to pay on the spot if he is an independent or he would be billed if he works for a major company like ours. Although the specific mechanism for this terrible tax is still being worked out, it would appear that the tax is going to work out to being something like $.03 per mile. We must do all that we can do to fight this because as you know New Mexico is one of the primary routes for our trucks moving both east and west. If this tax is approved, it would raise our operating cost at the Albuquerque terminal at least 10% (including the cost of the tax and the costs for administering it). I hope the supervisors of our company will come to New Mexico to talk with members of the New Mexico House of Representatives to make their views known on this subject. We must fight this if we are going to continue to move freight cheaply west and east. I would appreciate your thoughtful and helpful ideas on this issue. Please contact me with your remarks.

It took Dave nearly 20 minutes to plow through the Salazar memorandum. He was not particularily angry at Hec Salazar, because this memorandum was no worse than most of the others he received. People at branch terminals, and even at the home office, were taking far too many words to say simple things. They seemed to be spending their time cranking out memos to let everyone know how busy they were. Since there were at least 34 people at the various terminals and another 20 at the home office—all turning out memoranda that everyone was supposed to read—Dave determined that many employee hours were devoted to reading and writing memoranda. This problem was getting out of hand.

   To see how extensive the memorandum issue had become, Dave asked his fellow upper-level managers at the home office to keep track of the amount of correspondence they received each day for a week. To his amazement, some managers were receiving over 50 pieces of written material a day, and most were averaging nearly 25. About half of these required some kind of response, so at a rough calculation each manager at the home office was spending two to three hours a day on correspondence. The problem was intensified because many of the managers felt that most items did not *deserve* a response, but their jobs obliged them to write one anyway. As they began to study the issue further, they realized that they themselves were sending out written messages when it would have been much quicker to telephone.

Fortunately, the entire Littleton staff was meeting that week in Phoenix for the home office quarterly planning session. Dave asked for time on the agenda and suggested the following four rules:

1. Each writer should ask himself or herself whether this memorandum should be written in the first place.

2. If it should be written, it should be written as clearly as possible.

3. It should then be reviewed to see whether it could be cut in half.

4. Finally, instead of sending copies to everyone, the writer should only send copies to those who *must have* the information.

After these rules were implemented, efficiency at both the home office and the branch offices improved.

FOR STUDY

1 Why do you think people in an organization choose to write things rather than say them?

2 As an exercise, rewrite Hector Salazar's memorandum, using only half as many words.

3 What do you think of Dave's four rules? Would they be appropriate for most organizations?

4 What do you see as the relationship between writing and efficiency in an organization? If you force writers to take fewer words to say the same thing, do you necessarily improve efficiency?

5 Do you think that it costs an organization money to have writers who turn out memoranda like Hec Salazar's? Does cleaning up writing necessarily save money?

improving communication skills

PART FIVE

training:
Improving Communication Through Intervention

The final chapter of this book will be devoted to ways of improving communication in the organization. So far, we have considered various communication skills, but not how people acquire and improve these skills. This chapter will focus on some of the methods that an organization can use to train its members to communicate.

what is training?

David King defined *training* as "providing the conditions under which people can learn effectively."[1] Taking King's definition one step further, we might define training as *teaching members of an organization information and skills that they can use in their jobs.*

To improve the performance of its members, an organization will design a wide variety of educational programs, some formal, others informal. Usually, training programs are designed to meet a particular need (e.g., a workshop for first-line foremen who have been having trouble scheduling a production line). Occasionally, a program will be developed to meet more general needs. For example, many organizations offer programs to train people to become managers.

Training programs provide people with specific skills that enable them to become proficient in their jobs. In large metropolitian areas, those chosen to become fire fighters attend a six-month training school. Skill-training can be formalized, as in the fire academy, or it can be rather casual, such as a new service station attendant watching the veteran attendant pump gasoline.

[1]D. King, *Training Within the Organization* (London: Tavistock, 1964), p. 125.

chapter ten

Training may also deal with the attitudes of the trainees. In the early 1960s, a group of social scientists developed techniques for teaching people to become more sensitive to other people's needs. For many years, they attempted to teach these techniques through programs called T-groups or sensitivity sessions. Although the general goal of this movement was noble, later researchers have criticized it as ineffectual. Apparently, the results were often short-lived.[2] Nonetheless, many training programs in today's organizations emphasize changing the attitudes of trainees. Sometimes they do this by means of orientation sessions that focus on the history of the company, the benefits of membership, and the company's concern for its members' welfare. The idea is to develop the trainees' loyalty.

This chapter begins by examining some basic assumptions about training. Next, some representative models of the training process are examined. Training techniques are then discussed from the perspective of improving communication skills. The next section covers common training strategies. The following section is particularly important; it outlines the steps in designing a training program. Problem areas in training are considered next, and the chapter concludes with five sample communication training programs. These demonstrate how trainees can be taught some of the material on communication that was presented in the first nine chapters of this book.

some assumptions about training

Let us begin this discussion of training in the organization by considering five common assumptions about the training process. These assumptions will be stated in the form or preconditions that must be present for training to be successful.

1. *Training must have the support of upper management.* There is an old saying in some organizations that "the only good training is training that starts at the top." While this idea may be a bit oversimplified, it contains a kernel of truth. Unless upper-level management is sold on the potential benefits of a program, it will not succeed.

Management's feelings on this subject are easily assessed. Are employees allowed to attend training programs during work time? If so, management probably supports these programs. When management does not support training programs, trainees must usually attend on their own time, either after their regular shift or on weekends. Another

[2]J. Campbell and others, *Managerial Behavior, Performance, and Effectiveness* (New York: McGraw-Hill Book Company, 1970).

index of administrative support is the organization's willingness to pay for outside training programs. It tells employees a good deal when their organization says, in effect, "Training is important, but you must do it on your own time and pay for it with your own money." Finally, is training available on every level of the hierarchy? Some organizations strongly support training for *management* but are less than enthusiastic about providing training for nonmanagement personnel. In these organizations, the qualified become more qualified, but the unqualified never get anywhere.

2. *Training works best when it is developed in response to a particular problem.* Occasionally an organization will practice "training for training's sake." This kind of training may enrich the trainees' lives, but it is probably not the best use of the training dollar. Training appears to work best when it is designed to help solve a particular problem.

Two different training programs will serve as examples here. The first program teaches employees how to invest their money for retirement. While this program may improve their general outlook, it does nothing to improve their work performance. The second program is a management workshop for employees who have been selected for promotion to first-line foreman. It covers such things as motivation, communication skills, budgeting, Affirmative Action, and management theory. This program was developed to solve an immediate problem— getting the new supervisors ready for their upcoming promotion. Unlike the first program, it offers the organization some immediate payoffs.

3. *Training does not guarantee solutions to an organization's problems.* Training is no panacea. It cannot solve all of an organization's problems. Training is not the proverbial black magic box where you put the problem in one side and the solution comes out the other. The trainee who does not *want to* implement the ideas covered in the program probably will not implement them. The trainee who cannot *understand* and *see the relationships among* these ideas will not be interested in them. And finally, the trainee who cannot see an idea's inherent *value to him or her* may not do much to implement it. Another factor that helps to determine whether the training will be implemented is the quality of the relationship between the trainer and the trainee. A good relationship with the trainer will lead to greater changes in the trainee's work behavior. Training leads to solutions when the trainee is motivated to apply what he or she has learned.

4. *Training is sometimes costly, but it is usually worth the money.* Any training program is going to cost money. In terms of salaries and personnel fees, the generation of materials, and real work time lost,

training would have to be considered a fairly expensive activity. As was already suggested, most training programs will not guarantee an immediate profit or cut production costs right away. However, *in the long run,* training will contribute to the overall improvement of production and service.

In most cases, training should be thought of as an investment in the future of the organization. Organizations spend thousands of dollars each year on new machinery and capital improvements. They see this as a hedge against the future. They should take the same attitude with respect to their employees.[3] Organizations must have people who, in the future, will be capable of assuming leadership roles. These leaders can be hired away from the organization's competitors, or they can be developed from the talent within. Considering the organizational loyalty of members, the knowledge they already possess, and the time it takes to orient new employees, it makes good sense to develop leaders from within. While training may seem to be of limited value and costly in the short run, in the long run it is money well spent.

5. *Training must be considered as part of an ongoing people development program.* Traditionally, most of the "people functions" in an organization are centralized in the personnel department. It is personnel that handles wages, benefits, recreation, and promotions. But personnel departments are often less than personal, providing only the basics, and showing little concern for quality.

In some countries, the organization is considered responsible for the development of the whole person. This may seem a bit paternalistic at first, but it can be very effective. One man, for example, worked for several years in a manufacturing plant in Japan before coming to the United States to continue his career. To him, the biggest difference between the work climate here and in Japan was that in Japan, the firm assumed much more responsibility for the employee's total welfare. It was not uncommon for the firm to have its own flag, its own song, its own community recreational centers for employees, and various after-work activities for workers and their families. Employees often vacationed together, played in sports leagues, and generally depended on each other for support in emergencies. The Japanese man noticed none of these things at his American job. He liked his work and his weekly paycheck, but he commented, "This place really does not care very much about me. I think that I am only thought of as body to fill a space at a work station." He attributed what he considered to be huge differ-

---

[3]For an extensive treatment of this idea, see A. Sanford, G. Hunt, and H. Bracey, *Communication Behavior in Organizations* (Columbus, Ohio: Charles E. Merrill Publishing Company, 1976), pp. 265–79.

ences in the quality of manufacturing between Japan and the United States to this difference in the treatment of employees. While the United States and Japan may represent two extremes, the difference between them illustrates a very real problem in contemporary American industry. Many people feel a genuine part of their organization only on payday. At other times, there is no relationship between the member and the organization.

Earlier in this chapter it was suggested that the best training is developed in response to specific problems. Some organizations have begun to offer general training and growth opportunities with the assumption that these opportunities will enable people to make an increased contribution eventually. They do not expect the member to have an immediate impact on his or her job because of this training. If a secretary gains the ability to become a computer programmer through the organization's tuition reimbursement plan, the organization will benefit from the increased skill (assuming that the skill is utilized). In this way training is part of a "people development" program within the organization.

models of the training process

Every training program has four essential elements: (1) the participants, (2) the curriculum, (3) the intended short-term goals, and (4) the intended long-term goals. The relationship among these four elements is illustrated in figure 10–1. The participants are members of the organization who have been chosen or who have elected to participate. The curriculum or content is what is being taught. Almost all organizational training has as its short-term goals changing the participants' attitudes,

FIGURE 10–1   Basic training model

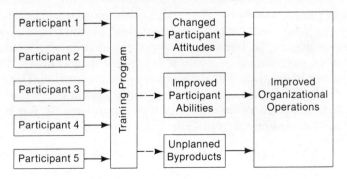

or developing skills that can be used immediately, or both. Other benefits, such as an improved social climate or increased understanding of the organization's objectives, may sometimes result from training. Theoretically, the main purpose of any training effort is to improve the overall operation of the work environment. This is the implied long-term goal of training. Different types of programs will concentrate on different aspects of these objectives.

The model in figure 10–1 may suggest that there is a direct relationship among the respective parts. This is not really the case. Training does not guarantee improved skills or changed attitudes. It is difficult to determine whether attitudes change because of the training program, in spite of it, or independently of it. Nor does the model allow for unplanned events. This model is merely a simple diagram of what is sometimes a complex process.

Spiral Model of Training

Let us turn to the more sophisticated model developed by Rolf Lynton and Udai Pareek.[4] The spiral model reproduced as figure 10–2 outlines many of the chronological phases of the training experience. It demonstrates that training is a complicated function, comprising many feedback loops and interrelationships. Some of the important components of the Lynton and Pareek model are discussed in the following pages.

INITIAL EXPECTATIONS AND READINESS The organization, the training staff, and the trainees all have certain expectations of and attitudes toward the program. These are referred to here as *initial expectations and readiness*. Stated differently, these indicate how ready the trainees are for training. If eager participants are given a solid program, training will probably be successful.

People enter social situations with some beginning perception of what they think will happen. They make calculations based on previous experience. Thus they have their "minds set" by the time the actual experience begins. An important component of these expectations is the level of pretraining motivation represented in trainees. People enter a training program with different levels of motivation. Their level of motivation will be strongly influenced by the way in which they were selected. If you have volunteered for a program because you believe that it applies directly to your job or to your own life, you will be

[4]R. Lynton and V. Pareek, *Training for Development* (Homewood, Ill.: Richard D. Irwin, Inc., 1967).

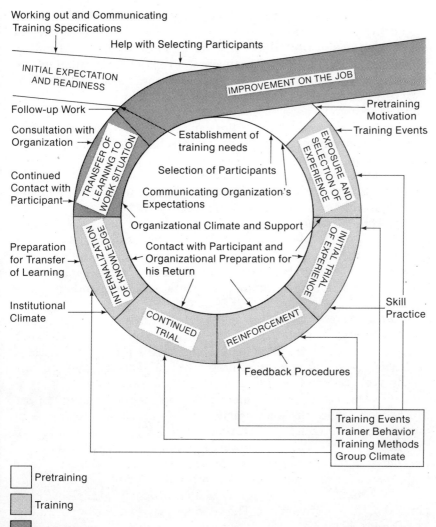

Working out and Communicating
Training Specifications

Help with Selecting Participants

INITIAL EXPECTATION
AND READINESS

IMPROVEMENT ON THE JOB

Follow-up Work

Consultation with
Organization

Continued
Contact with
Participant

Preparation
for Transfer
of Learning

Institutional
Climate

TRANSFER OF
LEARNING TO
WORK SITUATION

INTERNALIZATION
OF KNOWLEDGE

Establishment of
training needs

Selection of Participants

Communicating Organization's
Expectations

Organizational Climate and Support

Contact with Participant and
Organizational Preparation for
his Return

CONTINUED
TRIAL

REINFORCEMENT

EXPOSURE AND
SELECTION OF
EXPERIENCE

INITIAL TRIAL
OF EXPERIENCE

Pretraining
Motivation

Training Events

Skill
Practice

Feedback Procedures

Training Events
Trainer Behavior
Training Methods
Group Climate

Pretraining

Training

Posttraining

FIGURE 10-2 Spiral model of training process. From R. Lynton and V. Pareek, *Training for Development* (Homewood, Ill.: Richard D. Irwin, Inc., 1967), p. 19. Used by permission.

motivated to learn. If you have been ordered to attend by someone else, and you have no idea how you will use the information in the program, you may not be highly motivated. This is not to imply that only volunteers are motivated; if this were so, a few people would wind up getting all the training. It is occasionally necessary to build a fire under potential trainees by showing them what this program has to offer them personally.

Fair selection procedures help to establish interest in training. Fair procedures go beyond the person's current job description to consider where he or she will be in five years. Also, organizational members must feel that they have a fair opportunity to qualify for training. More will be said about selection later in this chapter.

The trainees' initial expectations and readiness become important when the program begins. If motivation is high, little time need by spent building it during the early phases of the training.

PHASES OF THE TRAINING PROGRAM As you can see from the model, the actual training consists of five phases.

Exposure and selection of experience. In any training program, a feeling-out process takes place over the first few sessions between the trainer and the trainees. The climate of the program is established, and the various methods to be used are introduced to the participants. This first phase may last a few minutes or several hours, depending on the program.

Initial trial of experience. In the second phase, the program gets down to the serious business of presenting content material to the trainee. In most training situations, this entails the use of teaching materials (e.g., lectures, films, printed material). This provides the basis for the skill practice included in most training programs.

Reinforcement. After trainees have had the opportunity to practice relevant skills, this skill practice is reinforced and reviewed by means of such activities as structured role playing and simulations. As the trainee attempts to gain skill by participating in simulated events, the trainer and the other trainees observe his or her behavior to see if it approximates successful behavior in the real world.

Continued trial. The spiral model proposes a trial-and-error method of skill improvement. The trainee is given many opportunities to test out specific behavior, to determine which approach works best for him or her. During this phase, trainees' apply the constructive criticism that they received during the previous phase. The longer this trial-and-error phase lasts, the more chance the trainee has to practice the desired skills.

Internalization of knowledge. While knowledge should be internalized throughout, it is assumed that internalization of knowledge will be the final phase of the training program, although it should have gone on throughout. During this phase, trainees try to abstract those things from the program which they can apply to their jobs. This constitutes the *transfer of learning,* which is an implied goal of most organizational training programs.

POST TRAINING The ultimate success or failure of all training is determined after the trainee has gone back to work. If the trainees do not apply what they have learned, or if the material is useless to the organization, the program was a waste of money. As you can see from the model, close contact, consultation, and follow-up should continue after the training program has ended. This insures that the efficacy of the program will be evaluated, which in turn helps managers of training make decisions on future training objectives. More will be said later about the evaluation of training.

One of the strengths of the spiral model is that it shows training as a process that closely monitors its own results and continually assesses training needs. An organization that is able to view training in this way will thereafter consider it a crucial tool—one that helps the organization to maintain good operations.

training techniques

In this section, we will consider some of the training techniques that are commonly used in organizations. All of the techniques discussed here can be used in training to improve communication skills.

On-the-Job Training

Sometimes an employee is given instruction, whether formal or informal, as a regular part of a new job. This instruction is called *on-the-job training* or *OJT.* For many entry level positions, which require little skill, OJT is the method of preference. The advantages are apparent: (1) The trainee is given immediate experience doing the exact job for which he or she was hired. (2) The training is realistic. (3) The trainee's level of motivation should be high. (4) It is easy to determine whether or not the trainee has the potential to do the job.

Even with these advantages, OJT often breaks down. This occurs, not because of limitations in the technique, but rather because of human limitations. For OJT to work, the supervisor of training must understand exactly how the job should be done, and there must be close and free communication between the trainer and the trainee. The following example shows what can happen otherwise.

John Younger was hired by the Selecter Corporation as an assembly line worker. He reported the first day to the personnel department, where he heard an hour lecture on the company and its benefit package. He was then led to his work station in the plant. His boss came up, introduced himself, and took about 15 minutes to explain what John was supposed to do as each part rolled by on the line. The boss then left, having completed John's OJT.

John worked for four hours with no problems and then left the station for his lunch break. When he came back from lunch, the shape and size of the object rolling down the line had changed drastically. He did not know what to do with the part, and there was no time to ask anyone, so he kept doing the same thing he had been doing before lunch. Twenty minutes later, the boss came running down the aisle directly to John, telling him that he had messed up the whole line, and that it was going to have to be stopped for 15 minutes for repairs. The boss told John that when the second unit started down the line after lunch, he was supposed to reverse the process and add his component to the other side of the unit. All John said was "But you never told me."

People make errors of omission, distortion, and filtering in their communication behavior. These errors are what often make OJT less than effective.

OJT may be used to improve communication skills. For example, suppose you are selected to make a presentation to a group of other employees. The training would consist of having the trainer listen to your talk and then offer constructive criticism that you could use the next time you were assigned the same task. This situation, like most situations where OJT is used, assumes that a person is capable of doing a particular job from the moment he or she is assigned to do it. The learn-by-doing approach can be effective, but it does depend on the trainer's ability to offer sound guidance in a nonthreatening way.

Workshops

A *workshop* is a session where a group of people who want to (or are told to) learn something come together to learn it. Workshops are often designed with a variety of activities—such as lectures, demonstrations, and exercises—around a single theme. Some workshops can be given in two hours; others last as long as three days, though rarely longer. Workshops differ from lecture forums and symposia in that they encourage widespread participation by trainees.

One important question that supervisors of training must ask themselves is whether a program should be conducted in-house, using only personnel from the organization, or whether members of the organization should be sent elsewhere to participate in outside workshops. Each choice has its own advantages and disadvantages.

IN-HOUSE WORKSHOPS The primary advantage of an in-house workshop is that the organization maintains fairly tight control over the material and over the way in which it is presented. This means that the curriculum can be oriented to the immediate situation, and all of the exercises and activities can be designed to simulate actual problems in the organization. This guarantees that the workshop will do something, at least, toward solving the problems that caused it to be planned in the first place. The primary disadvantage of an in-house workshop is that it offers little opportunity for fresh insights and new approaches. Old problems and old solutions are generally rehashed. Grudges and memories of old battles are often resurrected at inopportune moments.

OUTSIDE WORKSHOPS   Outside agencies offer a wide range of workshops to members of organizations. Generally these are one- or two-day functions held in hotels or conference facilities. They are sometimes associated with the continuing education department of universities. Often open to anyone who is interested, these workshops are usually advertised in the business section of the local newspaper or in professional journals. College instructors, consultants, or training firms sponsor these public workshops.

Outside workshops have certain disadvantages. When a workshop is held within the organization, the content can be carefully controlled, but this is not the case when it is held outside. Since it is not generally possible to tell the group putting on the workshop that you want certain material covered, it becomes a matter of chance whether you can use the material they provide. The advantage of outside workshops is that they offer members the opportunity to interact with people from different groups and agencies. In this way, members pick up much new and sometimes useful information. This cross-fertilization of ideas is one of the important by-products of outside training. Normally communication skills are taught in workshop format by a trainer who presents content material in lecture form. After the lecture, the participants have the opportunity to practice what they have learned in relevant exercises.

Classroom

Some organizations operate their own training schools. The range of programs varies. Some organizations take hard-core unemployables and teach them basic skills, such as reading and writing, while giving them a regular job. At the other extreme, the new Xerox University, in Virginia, offers a wide variety of educational programs for company employees.

The classroom approach differs from other kinds of training in that it normally places a heavy emphasis on content. Over the years high schools and, to some extent colleges, have been criticized for not teaching students basic skills. Almost weekly, the popular media depict the plight of graduating high school seniors who cannot complete a simple application for employment or handle elementary mathematics. Yet almost all semiskilled and most unskilled positions require the ability to read and to make rudimentary business decisions. It is within this context that many large organizations, especially those in big cities, have begun to offer programs in basic skills. This training makes good sense. The new employees will make a greater contribution after they have had the opportunity to improve.

Some jobs require considerable specialized knowledge. The fire fighter must learn how to deal with different types of fires. The police officer must learn the law. The pilot must learn flight mechanics. Often this material is taught in the classroom as a part of the employee's regular training. Organizations often give classroom instruction on such communication variables as listening, small group leadership, and writing.

Internships and Apprenticeships

Apprenticeship is the oldest of all forms of training. Traditionally, when a young man had completed the basic school requirements in his community, he returned to the family farm to learn the business of raising food. It was probably his father who established a regular program for him, one that would expose him to all aspects of farming. This apprenticeship might last for many years, sometimes until the father died.

Today's apprenticeship programs are highly sophisticated. Most apprenticeships consist of several years of preparatory work under the close supervision of a master. After the preparatory years have been completed, the apprentice advances to the rank of master, either by vote of a committee who know his or her work or by passing a skills examination. It is harder to get a place in the apprenticeship programs of some popular skill crafts unions today than it is to get into Harvard Law School.

The intern, like the apprentice, works under the guidance of a master. The master shows the intern various tasks, so that he or she gets a sense of the whole job. But while the apprentice often practices the same tasks as the master, the intern's duties are sometimes limited. (For example, the intern physician cannot perform surgery.) The apprentice assumes that he or she will eventually become a master, but the intern cannot always make this assumption. Some organizations use the internship to weed out unpromising candidates. In some organizations, the intern is on probation in the sense that he or she has few job security rights. In other words, the intern can be fired at any time for little cause.

In the field of communication, internships are becoming increasingly popular.[5] Some students in college and university communication programs spend time working at a communication job for academic credit. The student's work is monitored by both the university and the organization.

Internships and apprenticeships, like OJT, depend on a good communication relationship between the trainee and the master. There must be a lot of give and take, and the master must be concerned about the growth and development of the trainee. If their relationship does not allow the trainee to ask for clarification in a psychologically safe environment, training using this format will be difficult.

Laboratory

Like OJT and the apprenticeship, the laboratory method emphasizes learning by doing, but in a simulated environment where failure does not really count. For a baseball team, batting practice would be an example of the laboratory method of training. For a new school teacher, it would be a practice teaching assignment in front of a videotape machine. In the organization, the laboratory method has significant advantages over some other training techniques because it enables one to try out one's emerging skills under the critical eye of peers who have one's welfare at heart.

A number of communication skills can be taught using the lab approach. Suppose you have been assigned to train your peers in listening. The best method, perhaps, would be to use a training room that duplicates real-life conditions in the organization. You might develop a simulated business conference in which all of the participants had to pick up all of a certain type of information. It would be possible to test their retention to determine how well they had listened. If their listening was unsatisfactory, you could give them guidelines for improving it. After this, you could run another simulated business conference to ascertain whether their listening skills had, in fact, improved.

For the laboratory method to work efficiently, the trainer must be highly skilled. He or she must be able to identify areas within the simulations that need improvement. The lab method also works well when it is combined with other techniques.

[5]See C. Downs, P. Harper, and G. Hunt, "Internships in Speech Communication," *Communication Education*, 25, no. 4 (1976), 276–82.

training information strategies

Once the training technique has been selected, it is necessary to decide how information is going to be transferred. Many training sessions use a wide variety of strategies. In this section, let us examine some of the best of them.

Lecture

The lecture method is still widely used. It is popular because it is functional and cost-effective in terms of man-hours and materials. It has, however, three major limitations. (1) Trainees do not always retain the most important information. (2) Trainees are sometimes bored. (3) Not all trainers are good lecturers. Assuming that these limitations can be overcome—and this may be a tenuous assumption—the lecture technique can be effective.

Most training includes some form of lecture presentation. However, a single training session that depends entirely on the lecture method may ask too much of the trainee, since the typical listener will retain only about 25 percent of the information presented by a lecturer.[6]

For communication skills training, the lecture method is good for such content topics as the steps in listening correctly, types of leadership behavior, and the methods used to organize a report. But we normally sharpen our communication skills by means of some form of *participation*. Since the lecture method is a one-way strategy, it is difficult to assess whether the listener has learned enough to improve his or her communication skills.

One-on-One

Although it is extremely costly in terms of man-hours, the one-on-one method is the most effective training strategy. The father who teaches his son how to run the family farm is using this method, and supervisors often use it to train subordinates. The one-on-one method is a special application of two-person communication in which there must be considerable exchange between the participants. Its obvious

---

[6]See D. Yoder, *Personnel Management and Industrial Relations* (Englewood Cliffs, N.J.: Prentice-Hall, Inc., 1962), and Sanford, Hunt, and Bracey, *Communication Behavior*, pp. 289–90, for a treatment of the advantages of the lecture method of training.

advantage is that the trainer can easily use dialogue to determine the trainee has picked up the information that is being transmitted. This form of training can also improve the social-emotional climate of work environment. The trainee is receiving a great deal of special attention, which may stroke his or her ego. Given this opportunity to work directly with an influential person, the trainee may also be more than usually motivated. Probably you have already guessed the major disadvantage of one-on-one training. This is the cost factor. Most organizations simply cannot afford to train people by this method. Usually, they will trade off individualized attention for reduced costs and compromise by training their employees in small groups.

In communication skill training, the one-on-one method may be effective. When an expert trainer is able to sit down with a trainee, he or she is able to diagnose and solve any communication problems present. The trainer can give direct feedback to the trainee's writing or method of conducting a group meeting. Trainees' communication skills generally improve through the individualized counseling approach.

Printed Material

Organizations use printed material extensively in training. Perhaps you remember being hired for a job and visiting the personnel office on your first day for orientation. There, you received a packet of printed material that explained the firm's various employee benefits. But probably nobody ever followed up to find out if you had read and understood this information.

Printed material is an economical medium for transmitting information because once the intitial cost has been met, there is little additional outlay, assuming that the copy does not change. However, it has several disadvantages. "Training" via this medium may consist of nothing more than having an assistant hand out the printed material to the trainees. It is more effective to use printed material in combination with lectures or group discussions. Also (as is true of some other strategies) there is no built-in mechanism for checking out the effectiveness of the transmission. Think back to that time when you were sent to the personnel office to pick up your orientation packet. You probably did not *actually read* that printed material until you needed the answer to a specific question. Even then, if you are like most people, you probably called the personnel office first and asked the question orally. A trainee must be highly motivated to sit down and plow through a huge stack of printed material. If the trainee is unwilling to do this, no training has taken place.

Simulation, Role Playing

Many trainees and professional trainers believe that role playing is the most effective training strategy available.[7] It is certainly a good strategy for training people in communication skills.

Role playing works as follows. The trainer presents certain information, using one of the strategies already described, and then asks the trainee to apply this information by assuming a role in a hypothetical incident. For example, if the trainee is being taught how to be open in conducting interviews, he or she may be asked to simulate an interview, the details of which are provided by the trainer. The trainer can tell whether the trainee has learned the information previously presented by observing the trainee's behavior in the simulation. This is the great advantage of role playing—it brings the content material to life. However, it must be used in conjunction with other strategies. Role playing cannot be used alone to transmit training information because different people will learn different things from role playing, depending on their individual experience. Since the experience of the players is limited, the information transmitted is limited, too.

Most communication training includes some form of role playing. This strategy can be used effectively for that skill practice which was mentioned earlier in this chapter. Getting trainees on their feet to demonstrate a communication principle can teach them to test out, through activity, the material they have learned.

Group Discussion

Group discussion gives trainees the opportunity to talk over the implications of what they have learned. The success of this strategy depends on the trainer's skill in leading group discussions. Topics should be structured to enable trainees to develop an insight into the problem. Group discussion sessions must be specific if they are to meet the needs of the trainees. The trainer must be perceptive enough to apply the information being discussed to the trainees' work situation. Given an experienced and skillful trainer and sophisticated, articulate trainees, group discussion can be a fairly effective training strategy.

Group discussion has one advantage over some other strategies—trainees seem to *prefer* it. Since most of us like to give our opinion, group discussion tends to build interest and keep trainees "with" the program. There is some intrinsic value in group discussion because it

---

[7]S. Carroll, F. Paine, and J. Ivancevich, "The Relative Effectiveness of Alternative Training Methods for Various Training Objectives," *Personnel Psychology*, 25 (1972), 497.

gives people the opportunity to speak out. Discussants generally benefit from sharing ideas—and gripes—with others.

Group discussion can be useful in training people to improve their communication skills, because it gives the trainer a means of assessing their skills prior to training. Later, it gives the trainer the chance to see if the trainees have applied the information presented to their own communication behavior—a measure of the success of any training program. Like role playing, group discussion can be used effectively in combination with the lecture method.

Practice–Critique

In the practice–critique method the trainer watches the trainee's behavior and then offers a critique. It is assumed that the trainee will follow the critic's suggestions. An example of this strategy might be an earthquake drill in which all the city's emergency units must respond as they would in a real earthquake. The exercise is closely monitored by the trainer, an expert in emergency response. After the exercise, the expert evaluates the drill and offers suggestions for improvement.

The important advantage of the practice–critique is that it does not interrupt the organization's routine. People can be observed while they go about their usual business. The critique itself can be scheduled at the convenience of the trainer and the trainees. The disadvantage of this strategy is that the critic may tend to focus only on the trainees' mistakes. This is the danger of most kinds of evaluation. The session can turn into a long list of things that the trainee did wrong. If the trainees are too overwhelmed by their errors, they may lose their motivation to improve.

The practice–critique can be used effectively in training to improve communication skills. Once the trainer has some impression of the trainees' present skills, he or she can design a critique that identifies their problems and encourages the trainees to overcome them. To do this, the trainer must understand what constitutes good or poor communication.

steps in designing a training program

Now let us consider the steps in designing a training program. These steps are the same, regardless of the content of the program and whether it is long or short.

1. *Assessing problems and needs.* At the beginning of this chap-

ter, we suggested that training should be done in response to specific needs. The first step in designing a training program is to determine what those needs are. This can be done in many ways. One of the most common techniques is the *needs assessment questionnaire*. This is a formal procedure to gain perceptions of needs for training from people within the organization. The results are tabulated to ascertain how strong these needs are. Other sources for assessing problems and needs include informal discussions in the lunchroom and company records. Records are generally kept to provide information, normally in statistical form, about potential problem areas. It is sometimes possible for older, more perceptive employees to identify problems for the training staff or to judge the severity of these problems. Once the general needs have been identified, it is necessary to formulate strong and specific problem statements about them. These will be used later to develop the training objectives and to design the evaluation plan for the training program.

2. *Deciding what type of program is needed.* After they have assessed the organization's needs, the training staff should consult with representatives of management, of supervisory staff, and of the units to be trained. To decide what type of program is needed, it is necessary to know what types of programs are available. These may include prepackaged programs offered by outside firms, which are made available to organizations for a fee. In the long run, the prepackaged program will be more cost-effective than a program that must be developed from scratch. If a prepackaged program exists that can meet the organization's identified needs, there is no reason to consider time and money constraints and the competence of the in-house training staff. If the organization has the right personnel in-house, it will be ahead of the game. If not, it must hire staff from an outside talent pool.

3. *Formulating specific objectives.* The next step is to formulate the specific objectives of the training program. In doing this, the results of the needs assessment, the program logistics, and the staff must all be taken into consideration. Most of the discussion up to now has revolved around a general question such as, "What do we really want this program to accomplish for us?" The most fruitful approach would be to determine what specific skills and attitudes one wants the trainees to acquire. One can then formulate specific objectives based on these desired results. For example, "At the end of the training session, we want our first-line foremen to be able to: (1) conduct a satisfactory appraisal interview, (2) identify their own strengths and weaknesses as appraisal interviewers, and (3) write a report on the results of their appraisal interviews with subordinates." These objectives are stated in simple language, and it is easy to tell whether they have been achieved by observing the trainees' behavior.

4. *Determining the best methods for reaching the objectives.* Some people feel that determining the objectives and the methods for reaching them should be the first two steps. These decisions cannot be made until the "housekeeping" matters just discussed have been resolved. Determining methods means selecting the most appropriate training technique and strategies to meet your objectives. If the organization is purchasing a prepackaged program with the objectives and methods already spelled out, this program must now be refined. If it is designing a new program in response to a particular need, the training staff must now choose the most appropriate technique. Under certain conditions, on-the-job training may be best; under others, workshops; under still others, a laboratory approach. Close contact among everyone concerned—trainer, training staff, representatives of units affected, and trainees—will help the staff to make the right choice here.

5. *Designing the program.* The next step is to lay out the schedule, content, and activities carefully. A one-day workshop on persuasive techniques for salespersons might look like this:

8:00–8:30	Rolls and coffee
8:30–9:30	Getting reacquainted and discussion on company sales policies
9:30–9:45	Coffee break
9:45–10:45	Presentation on understanding the customer
10:45–12:00	Training exercises on creating customer confidence
12:00–1:30	Lunch Address: "What Our Company Expects from the Salesperson," by George Thomas, Vice-President, Sales and Marketing
1:30–2:30	Training exercise on meeting the customer's needs
2:30–3:30	Presentation on overcoming customer resistance
3:30–4:30	Role-playing exercise on sales interviewing
4:30–5:00	Wrap-up and debriefing
5:00–6:30	Cocktails and dinner

In training, regardless of the techniques employed, it is imperative to develop a schedule for the program. During the course of the program the schedule may be changed slightly, but it is still the foundation of the program. In long-term training, the schedule should include conference periods and meetings to determine the progress of the trainee. In short-term training, the schedule should provide for some variety by alternating lecture presentations with exercises and activities.

6. *Choosing the participants.* At first it may seem like a rather simple task—picking those members of the organization who are most

able to benefit from the program. Unfortunately, this is not as easy as it looks. The difficulty is that an organization is a social system, so that what happens in one area eventually influences what happens somewhere else.

Suppose you are working side by side with a friend in the office of a large organization. When the notice for a new program on management training comes out, your friend's name is on it but yours is not. You will probably be hurt and disappointed. Doesn't your organization feel that you are worth training for management? Your feelings of rejection may intensify if you ask your friend how he came to be selected and he tells you that he has no idea. Under these conditions, the climate in your office is likely to degenerate.

In the best of all worlds, everyone who wanted special training would receive it. However, in real life, organizations must follow the cardinal rule of training: *The members selected for training should be the members who can use it most.* This being so, the best way to prevent bad feelings from developing is to announce clearly what criteria were used to choose trainees—why some people were chosen and why others were not.

7. *Orienting the participants.* Orientation takes place between the time that the trainees are selected and the time that the program begins. It consists of telling the trainees what to expect. Obviously, it will cover the logistics (e.g., where the program will be given, how long it will last, how to dress). More subtly, the staff must try to reduce the feelings of threat and tension that may be bothering the trainees. During the orientation period, through close contact and communication with the staff, all of the trainees' initial concerns can be met. Thus when the first day of the actual program arrives, the trainees will be present and ready to go.

8. *Conducting the program.* Once all of the preliminary planning has been completed, the actual operation of the program should go smoothly. Ideally, the program will go as planned, and no wholesale changes will be necessary. In any training situation, the staff must be perceptive of the trainees' developing orientations. The staff must make sure that the trainees have gained at least the minimum level of knowledge. They do this by paying close attention to the information being fed back by the trainees. Sometimes minor adjustments must be made in the overall plan, but they should be made carefully and only in response to a specific problem.

9. *Evaluating the program.* All training must be carefully evaluated. There are two general approaches to evaluation. The first deals with the program in its own right. Was it interesting? Useful? Worth-

while? Was it a good program in and of itself? The second deals with the application of the program. Was it a good tool? Will it help the trainees to do their job more effectively? In a training program on ways to improve one's listening abilities, for example, the first approach to evaluation would be to ask the trainees whether the program was interesting. They might be asked if they enjoyed it, learned from it, and would recommend it to a friend. In the second approach to evaluation, the trainees might be asked what they learned in the program that will make them better listeners on their jobs. Both approaches are important; both provide useful data for further training.

But evaluation of a training program does not stop here. It is necessary to go one step further to determine if the program had any effect on the total work situation. Remember, *training is best done to solve a specific problem.* Part of the evaluation process consists of determining whether the program has, in fact, solved the problem it was designed to solve. This part of the evaluation may take months to accomplish. Sometimes it is necessary to monitor the trainees' work behavior to find out if they have implemented the content of the program. With some kinds of training—for example, teaching a new employee to operate a machine—this can be determined in an hour or so. Either the person can handle the machine, or he cannot. With other kinds of training—for example, training in management development, communication, planning, and leadership—it may take much longer— sometimes many months.

Everyone who is involved in the training program is responsible for evaluating it. The trainer or the training staff may evaluate it from one perspective and the trainee's immediate supervisor from another. Evaluators should also allow for unforseen results. A trainee who is exposed to new ideas and information may behave in an entirely unexpected way. The director of training of a large organization once told the following story. A long-time employee had been giving his supervisors problems on the job. His record of attendance was poor, and he had twice come close to being fired for incompetence. Almost as a last resort, this employee was selected for a training program to learn a new manufacturing process that was being implemented in the work unit. Instead of giving the program his usual halfhearted effort, this employee took full advantage of the information and became the work unit's expert on the new process. When someone had a question or an idea about the process, he went to this previously marginal employee. When the program was expanded, the employee began to train others. Within a year, he was promoted to assistant foreman. At this point, the personnel manager could no longer restrain his curiosity. He asked the employee what had happened after that initial program to make him change. The employee replied that the training program was the first opportunity that his organization had ever given him to better himself. When it came, he wanted to prove that he was just as capable as anyone. These side effects of training can never be predicted, but they should be included in any evaluation.

10. *Determining new directions for training.* Training should be thought of as an ongoing process that continually identifies and attempts to solve problems. The final step, then, is to use the data that were generated in the evaluation to build new and innovative programs for this purpose. To keep up to date, trainers must be aware of new developments in training. These new developments include the recognition that employees are living longer and have more leisure time. Training programs in retirement planning and the creative use of leisure time are no longer unusual in organizations. Although such programs have little direct impact on the employee's current job, they do recognize that a person who is well rounded and comfortable is more likely to contribute to the organization than one who is not.

problem areas in training

Perhaps you think that if only you follow the steps outlined, your training program will automatically succeed. Not necessarily. In this part, we will briefly consider six of the most common problem areas in training.

Resistance to Change

Change comes slowly. People tend to resist innovations, preferring to stick with the status quo. In fact, in some organizations, things get rejected *just because* they are new. This resistance to change takes two important forms. First, some conservative organizations will not engage in any training they consider unproven. This is the old "if we haven't done it before, we are not going to do it now" principle. Second, within organizations that are willing to train people in new areas, there are individuals who will not attend training sessions voluntarily. When they are forced to attend, they will not apply what they learn. To overcome this resistance, it is sometimes necessary to ease people into training slowly by demonstrating what it can do for them. When the organization itself is resistant, it is usually pressure from competitors that forces it to offer new training programs.

Training Halo Effect

Sometimes just the fact that one has been exposed to training will improve one's job performance. Paying special attention to any person puts that person under the spotlight. It is not always possible to determine whether it is the training or the special attention that causes the improvement. Sometimes we can find out by examining the group data. If everyone's performance seems to have improved, and the improvement lasts after the training has stopped, it may be attributable to the program. If the improvement is temporary and spotty, the program probably did not have its intended effect.

Poor Climate

Training takes place within the total climate of the organization. If the climate is poor, training will probably not be successful. People must *want to* improve their work performance before any type of training will work. If people and departments are not getting along well, they will not be motivated to improve. The best climates for training are open, flexible, and creative.[8] If training is not working, check out the psychological conditions in the organization.

Unclear Objectives

This chapter has emphasized the need for clearly defined objectives in any training program. Training programs are normally designed to produce specific outcomes. If these have not been developed carefully beforehand, training may not succeed. In any work situation, you need to know what is expected of you before you can judge whether you have done it. The same holds true in training. You know if you have achieved the purpose of the program only when that purpose has been clearly defined.

Limited Administrative Support

The first assumption in the beginning of this chapter was that *training must have the support of upper management.* Without this support, training will encounter huge roadblocks. Support means that administrators are willing to go out of their way to insure that the program will be successful by encouraging employees to participate. If employees feel that they must be trained "in spite" of management, there is little chance that the program will succeed.

---

[8]L. James and A. Jones, "Organizational Climate: A Review of Theory and Research," *Psychological Bulletin,* 81, no. 12 (1974), p. 1098.

Low Participant Motivation

Low motivation on the part of the trainees can be caused by a number of things that have already been discussed. Low motivation, whatever the cause, deals with a death blow to any organized training effort. The "why should I learn this stuff" attitude is frequently reflected in trainees before a training program. The organization should be honest in describing to potential trainees the payoff they can expect if they complete a program. This should solve the problem of low motivation, assuming that the trainees think the payoff is worthwhile.

No Work Carry-Over

This chapter has emphasized that training should carry over into the trainee's work. If the material in the program has only limited application, there may be problems. The trainer should continually refer to the link between the training curriculum and the work setting, and the material itself should be designed so as to allow the trainee to make this application.

communication training programs

So far we have concentrated on training in general. Now let us apply this material specifically to communication. Six training outlines follow. These outlines do not represent definitive approaches to training. They only demonstrate what can be done in the area of communication skills.

IMPROVING INTERVIEWING SKILLS

Goals:
1. To allow each participant the opportunity to examine his own skills in communicating with superiors and subordinates.
2. To provide each participant with materials and advice to encourage him to improve his own interviewing communication.
Overview: Since nearly 60% of all business communication takes place in groups of two's and three's, the executive should understand the important dimensions of interviewing. The effective manager must be able to ask questions, answer questions, and listen carefully to be a dynamic communicator. Unfortunately, few managers ever receive training in interviewing. This workshop will suggest methods to help each manager develop and refine his "interviewing style."
Topics Covered:
1. Establishing Goals in the Interview
2. Listening
3. Asking and Answering Questions

4. Conducting Appraisals
5. The Manager as Counselor
6. Rapport-Building in the Interview
7. Termination Interviews
8. Understanding Nonverbal Communication
9. The Interview for Motivating Subordinates

Activities: Each workshop participant will be expected to conduct a simulated interview under "real-life" conditions. Case studies of successful and unsuccessful interviews will be studied. Advice and suggestions will be provided each participant by the training staff.

GIVING THE ORAL TECHNICAL REPORT

Goals:
1. To guide each participant to be an articulate speaker who can communicate with clarity and soundness to others in his/her area of specialization.
2. To help each participant communicate with maximum meaning to an audience unfamiliar with the technical area of the speaker.

Overview: Many technically competent managers find themselves having difficulty when they must communicate with the non-technical audience. Along with providing essential information about controlling anxiety and message delivery, this workshop will focus on "sizing up" the audience and determining a realistic goal for the technical report. Also included will be a discussion of building the message, the use of clear concise language, developing speaker credibility, the use of visual materials, and techniques for responding to questions from the audience.

Topics Covered:
1. Goals for the Technical Report
2. Self Confidence and Meaningful Delivery
3. Audience Analysis
4. Collecting and Organizing Information
5. Language for Accuracy and Clarity
6. Making the Technical Report Interesting
7. Using Visual Aids
8. Answering Audience Questions

Activities: Each participant will be provided "hand-out" guides during a two-hour lecture period. He/She will be asked to use the principles discussed by presenting a ten-minute simulated technical report in a subject from his/her area of expertise. Each report will be evaluated by the training staff who will provide both a written and oral critique.

PREVENTING FAILURES IN ORGANIZATIONAL COMMUNICATION

Goals:
1. To provide participants with the opportunity to develop abilities to detect possible breakdowns in communication within their own organization.
2. To encourage participants to develop creative solutions to communication failures.

Overview: Communication failures costs, organizations thousands of dollars every year. One department begins a project without proper consultation with other concerned groups. The hourly employee is often forced to act upon distorted or inaccurate information because he never "gets the word." Through proper training, these and other breakdowns can be avoided. It is very important that the manager understand why communications fail in organizations. This workshop will expose the participant to some of the current thinking on organizational communication and provide a number of specific solutions to typical communication problems.

Topics Covered:
1. Improving Upward Communication
2. The Nature of Downward Communication
3. Types of Communication Breakdown
4. Utilizing Human Resources
5. Improving the Organizational Climate
6. Suggestions and Suggestion Systems
7. Encouraging Feedback from Subordinates
8. Developing Solutions for Communication Problems
9. Developing Workable Communication Programs

Activities: A number of short case studies have been developed for use in this workshop. The cases are designed to sharpen the participant's skill in diagnosing communication problems.

DEVELOPING ABILITIES IN SMALL GROUP COMMUNICATION

Goals:
1. To provide each participant with the content to allow him/her to improve his/her knowledge of small groups.
2. To develop and nurture leadership skills in each participant.

Overview: Managers are continually called upon to make decisions in small groups. Often these same managers find themselves unfamiliar with the complexities of how small groups work. This workshop will provide each participant with materials to help him/her improve skills both as a leader and member of small groups. Since even the most well-planned meetings sometimes degenerate into extremely unproductive sessions, it is necessary for the resourceful executive to know how to bring the meeting "back on track." After this workshop, each participant will be able to conduct a successful small group meeting where good decisions are made and members feel good about the group's process.

Topics Covered:
1. Leadership
2. Resolving Conflict
3. Cohesion in Small Groups
4. Establishing Goals in Groups
5. Satisfactory Group Climates
6. Communication Networks
7. Parliamentary Procedure
8. Formal Business Meetings

Activities: Participants will take part in a simulated small group meeting which will require them to implement many of the principles discussed in the workshop. The training staff will be responsible for evaluating and offering advice about the small group meeting.

MAKING THE PERSUASIVE PRESENTATION

Goals:

1. To guide each participant to win support for his/her ideas from an audience in his/her department when an oral presentation is necessary.

2. To effectively influence an audience outside the organization for public relations or marketing goals.

Overview: Increasingly, today's manager is forced to "sell" himself or his company in an oral presentation. He/She may have to win approval for a proposal such as a budget for his/her department or present his/her company's plan for expansion to the local Chamber of Commerce. Many executives have never had any practical training in this important kind of communication activity. This workshop will include the essential principles of controlling communication anxiety and delivery to meet specific persuasive challenges. Training will also be provided to encourage each participant to focus on motive analysis of the audience in the persuasive presentation. The "motivated sequence" for speech construction and methods for leading an audience to the speaker's proposition will be considered at length.

Topics Covered:

1. The Realities of Persuasion
2. Persuasive Purpose
3. Coping with Speech Tension in Persuasive Settings
4. Motive Analysis and the Audience
5. Strategic Organization
6. Physical and Vocal Force
7. "Winning Acceptance"
8. Additional Elements of Persuasion for Effectiveness

Activities: Each participant will be provided "hand-out" guides during the two-hour lecture period. He/She will be asked to use the principles discussed by presenting a ten-minute simulated persuasive speech. Each presentation will be evaluated and written/oral suggestions for improvement will be given by the training staff.

IMPROVING THE MANAGER'S WRITING ABILITIES

Goals:

1. To develop in the manager a sensitivity to effective business writing.

2. To help the improve his own writing habits.

Overview: Far too many man-hours are wasted because the manager is forced to plow through high stacks of poorly written letters, notices, and memoranda. In today's organizations, the memorandum has become the major medium of managerial communication. Unfortunately few managers have acquired the skills to write clearly and succinctly. Too often, the harried executive will simply turn out a memo or letter without first thinking about the effect he/she wants his/her writing to have upon the reader. The purpose of this workshop is to encourage each participant to improve his/her writing during the actual training session.

Topics Covered:

1. Effective Language Usage

2. Organizing Your Ideas
3. When to Write It; When to Say It
4. Developing Persuasive Arguments in Writing
5. Editing Skills
6. Methods for Improving Subordinates' Writing

Activities: Each participant will take part in a series of exercises which are designed to improve business writing.[9]

final words about training

Training was made the topic of this last chapter because it is through training that we improve our communication skills. Let us conclude this chapter with two ideas related to training philosophy.

1. Training may appropriately affect the private life of the trainee. When given the opportunity to learn, some people bloom. Training is one of those things in the organization that can make a difference in a member's private life. Of course, this is true of training in personal areas, such as retirement planning or personal investment, but it is equally true of work-related training. Training in interpersonal communication, for example, can make one not only more effective at work, but more effective with one's family and friends as well. Good organizational training exposes people to things that can improve their lives.

2. Training should implement the principles of good communication. This means that information about training opportunities must be communicated widely, in a language that people can understand. It also means that training programs should be designed with a specific audience in mind. Finally, it means that training should be followed up through continual feedback and monitoring of activities. Training and good communication go hand in hand.

FOR STUDY

1 Identify four situations that require some form of training within an organization.
2 Do you see a relationship between morale and good training? Is it possible that good training might contribute to good morale?
3 What communication techniques can be used to improve training?
4 Consider the training techniques (e.g., lecture, role playing) presented in this chapter. Which of these techniques require good communication to be used effectively?
5 How would you evaluate the success of a training program? Would you expect a program to contribute to the increased productivity of the organization?

[9]Reprinted by permission of Gary T. Hunt.

case ten

The Director of Training

Helen Arlen works as the director of training for the State of Nevada Department of Economic and Community Development (NDECD). This agency has offices in Carson City, the state capital, and Las Vegas, the state's urban and commercial center. About 900 employees work for NDECD in Nevada, and another 200 are stationed in Nevada Centers in large cities throughout the world. People who work in these offices promote tourism and orderly economic development within the state and encourage businesses to hold their meetings and expand their organizations in Nevada. Thus most of the duties of NDECD involve some form of sales and public relations.

It is Helen Arlen's job to make sure that all new employees are oriented to NDECD's mission, and that all employees, new and old, have the tools they need to do their jobs. Helen runs an eight-week orientation program for new employees, which is held alternately at the Carson City office and the Las Vegas office. Normally about eight or nine people are hired each month at each office, and Helen takes these new employees one day a week for eight weeks. Here is her program:

Day One:	The department and its history
Day Two:	Nevada and what it offers
Day Three:	Policies, rules, and regulations of the department
Day Four:	Structure and organization of the department
Day Five:	The department and its mission
Day Six:	Being public relations minded
Day Seven:	How to sell Nevada
Day Eight:	Wrap-up and final discussion

Helen has designed this program to serve two purposes: (1) to make sure that each employee understands his or her new agency, and (2) to encourage all employees to be sales conscious. It occurred to Helen, as she was developing materials for this training program, that selling Nevada was the business of everybody who worked at the agency, from the receptionist to the director. So Helen has been pushing courtesy and public relations ever since. This effort has paid off. A number of people have commented that of all of the state agencies, they get the best treatment at NDECD. Local residents always get a friendly response when they call with a question. Visitors who stop at the office are given the red-carpet treatment. And organizations that request convention information are provided with a complete packet of materials.

Helen has also developed a public relations approach to training old employees. She has implemented programs in (1) convention management, (2) new trends in marketing, (3) innovative approaches to personnel management, (4) conducting marketing interviews, (5) publicity and advertising techniques, (6) improving oral communication, and (7) retirement planning—to name but a few. It is the agency's policy to give employees work time to complete these training courses, so Helen wants to insure that they get the most out of their participation. Helen conducts some of the programs herself and contracts others out with consultants. To make sure that the training time is well spent, Helen monitors the programs carefully. She wants them to reflect a balance between theoretical and practical material. By this she means that there should be some information that enables the trainee to understand *why* something should be done, but that emphasis should be on *what* should be done. During the actual training, Helen sees to it that there is a good balance between lecture materials and participation activities. She likes programs that give trainees something new to do at least every two hours. A recent one-day workshop on publicity and public relations for department heads illustrates Helen's philosophy on training:

8:00–8:15	Coffee and rolls
8:15–9:00	Lecture: Current trends in publicity and public relations
9:00–11:00	Problem identification (PI) session on public relations problems in NDECD
11:00–11:30	Lecture: Improving organizational image through public relations
11:30–12:00	Group discussion on improving the image of the State of Nevada for business growth
12:00–1:00	Lunch
1:00–2:00	Case study on public relations
2:00–3:00	Reports on case study
3:00–4:00	Lecture: Public relations from a manager's perspective
4:00–4:30	Exercise on writing public relations releases
4:30–5:00	Debriefing and evaluation

Since Helen has taken over the training effort at NDECD, employees who never before considered training to be important find themselves looking forward to attending sessions. In fact, they compete for the few available spaces in the training workshops. After attending a few sessions, employees have said that they have learned a lot of things that have enabled them to improve their work performance. Her supervisors at NDECD consider Helen to be one of their most important executives. They have done all that they can to make her happy in her job, because they are afraid that she will be lured away from NDECD to accept a higher paying position in private industry.

FOR STUDY

1 What do you consider to be the major strengths of Helen's training programs?

2 In developing a successful training program, what assumptions did Helen make about her fellow employees at NDECD? How did these assumptions affect her training efforts?

3 If you were an employee at NDECD, do you think that you would enjoy participating in one of these programs? Why?

4 How might Helen have used good communication principles in structuring her programs? What do you see as the relationship between good communication and good training?

5 What do you consider to be the three essentials of effective training? List the essentials and the reasons why you think that each is important.

references

ANDERSEN, K., and T. CLEVENGER, "A Summary of Experimental Research of Ethos," *Speech Monographs*, 30 (1968), 59–78.

ANDERSEN, M., W. LEWIS, and J. MURRAY, *The Speaker and His Audience.* New York: Harper & Row, Publishers, Inc., 1964.

ARMSTRONG, H., "The Relationship of Auditory and Visual Vocabularies of Children" (unpublished Ph.D. dissertation, Stanford University, 1953).

ATKINSON, J., *An Introduction to Motivation.* New York: Van Nostrand Reinhold Company, 1964.

BALES, R., and R. STRODTBECK, *Interaction Process Analysis: A Method for the Study of Small Groups.* Reading, Mass.: Addison-Wesley Publishing Co., Inc., 1950.

BARNLUND, D., "A Transactional Model of Communication," in *Foundations of Communication Theory,* eds. D. Sereno and C. Mortensen. New York: Harper & Row, Publishers, Inc., 1970.

————, and F. HAIMAN, *The Dynamics of Discussion.* Boston: Houghton Mifflin Company, 1960.

BECKHARD, R., *Organizational Development: Strategies and Models.* Reading, Mass.: Addison-Wesley Publishing Co., Inc., 1969.

BENNE, K., and P. SHEATS, "Functional Roles of Group Members," *Journal of Social Issues,* 4, no. 1 (1948), 41–49.

BIRDWHISTELL, R., *Kinesics and Context.* Philadelphia: University of Pennsylvania Press, 1970.

BRILHART, J., *Effective Group Discussion* (2nd ed.). Dubuque: William C. Brown Company, Publishers, 1974.

BROOKS, W., *Speech Communication* (3rd ed.). Dubuque: William C. Brown Company, Publishers, 1978.

CAMPBELL, J., M. DUNNETTE, E. LAWLER, and K. WEICK, *Managerial Behavior, Performance, and Effectiveness.* New York: McGraw-Hill Book Company, 1970.

CANNELL, C., and R. KAHN, "Interviewing," in *The Handbook of Social Psychology,* vol. II, eds. G. Lindzey and E. Aronson. Reading, Mass.: Addison-Wesley Publishing Co., Inc., 1968.

CARROLL, S., F. PAINE, and J. IVANCEVICH, "The Relative Effectiveness of Alternative Training Methods for Various Training Objectives," *Personnel Psychology,* 25 (1972), 29.

COLLINS, B., and B. RAVEN, "Group Structure: Attraction, Coalitions, Communication, and Power," in *The Handbook of Social Psychology*, vol. IV, eds. G. Lindzey and E. Aronson. Reading, Mass.: Addison-Wesley Publishing Co., Inc., 1968.

COOPER, L., *The Rhetoric of Aristotle*. New York: Appleton-Century-Crofts, 1932.

DAHLE, T., "Transmitting Information to Employees: A Study of Five Methods," *Personnel*, 31, no. 2 (1954), 243–46.

DANCE, F., "Toward a Theory of Human Communication," in *Human Communication Theory*, ed. F. Dance. New York: Holt, Rinehart and Winston, 1967.

DAVIS, K., *Human Behavior at Work* (4th ed.). New York: McGraw-Hill Book Company, 1972.

DISALVO, V., C. MONROE, and B. MORSE, *Business and Professional Communication*. Columbus, Ohio: Charles E. Merrill Publishing Company, 1977.

DOVER, C., "Listening—The Missing Link in Communication," *General Electric Review*, 61, no. 3 (May 1958), 7–10.

DOWNS, C., P. HARPER, and G. HUNT, "Internships in Speech Communication," *Communication Education*, 25, no. 4 (1976), 276–82.

DUNNETTE, M., J. CAMPBELL, and K. JAASTAD, "The Effects of Group Participation on Brainstorming Effectiveness for Two Industrial Samples," *Journal of Applied Psychology*, 47, no. 3 (1963), 30–37.

EWING, D., "Who Wants Corporate Democracy?" *Harvard Business Review*, 49, no. 6 (November/December 1971), 12–28, 148–49.

FARACE, R., P. MONGE, and H. RUSSELL, *Communicating and Organizing*. Reading, Mass.: Addison-Wesley Publishing Co., Inc., 1977.

FESSENDEN, S., *Listening 75*. Indianapolis: The Bobbs-Merrill Co., Inc., 1955.

FESTINGER, L., *A Theory of Cognitive Dissonance*. Evanston, Ill.: Row, Peterson, 1957.

FIEDLER, F., "A Comparison of Therapeutic Relationships in Psychoanalytic, Non Directive, and Adlerian Therapy," *Journal of Consulting Psychology*, 14, no. 4 (1950), 436–45.

———, *A Theory of Leadership Effectiveness*. New York: McGraw-Hill Book Company, 1967.

FILLEY, A., *Interpersonal Conflict Resolution*. Glenview, Ill.: Scott, Foresman & Company, 1975.

FISHER, A., *Small Group Decision-Making: Communication and the Group Process*. New York: McGraw-Hill Book Company, 1974.

FREDERIKSEN, N., "Administrative Performance in Relation to Organizational Climate" (paper presented at the annual meeting of the American Psychological Association, 1966, in San Francisco).

FRENCH, W., and C. BELL, *Organizational Development.* Englewood Cliffs, N.J.: Prentice-Hall, Inc., 1974.

GANTT, H., *Work, Wages, and Profits.* New York: The Engineering Magazine Co., 1916.

GIBB, J., "Defensive Communication," *Journal of Communication,* 11, no. 2 (1961), 141–48.

GIBSON, J., J. IVANCEVICH, and J. DONNELLY, *Organizations: Structure, Processes, and Behavior.* Dallas: Business Publications, Inc., 1973.

GIFFIN, K., "The Contribution of Studies of Source Credibility to a Theory of Interpersonal Trust in Communication," *Psychological Bulletin,* 68, no. 2 (1967), 104–20.

———, "Interpersonal Trust in Small Group Communication," *Quarterly Journal of Speech,* 53, no. 3 (1967), 224–34.

GILBRETH, L., *The Psychology of Management.* New York: Macmillan Publishing Co., Inc., 1914.

GUETZKOW, H., "Communication in Organizations," in *Handbook of Organizations,* ed. J. March. Chicago: Rand McNally & Co., 1965.

HALL, R., *Organizations: Structure and Process.* Englewood Cliffs, N.J.: Prentice-Hall, Inc., 1972.

HAMPTON, D., C. SUMMER, and R. WEBBER, *Organizational Behavior and the Practice of Management.* Glenview, Ill.: Scott, Foresman & Company, 1973.

HEIDER, F., *The Psychology of Interpersonal Relations.* New York: John Wiley & Sons, Inc., 1958.

HERZBERG, F., B. MAUSNER, and B. SNYDERMAN, *Motivation to Work.* New York: John Wiley & Sons, Inc., 1967.

HICKS, H., *The Management of Organizations: A Systems and Human Resources Approach* (2nd ed.). New York: McGraw-Hill Book Company, 1972.

HOXIE, R., *Scientific Management and Labor.* New York: Appleton-Century Crofts, 1915.

HUNT, G., and C. LEE, "The Effects of Leadership Style on Group Performance and Member Satisfaction" (paper presented at the annual meeting of the Western Speech Communication Association, 1976, in San Francisco).

———, "Organizational Climate: A Laboratory Approach" (paper presented at the annual meeting of the International Communication Association, 1976, in Portland).

JACKIM, H., "Scoring the Committee Game," *The Chronicle of Higher Education,* 10 (July 21, 1975), 18.

JAIN, H., "Supervisory Communication and Performance in Urban Hospitals," *Journal of Communication,* 23, no. 1 (1973), 103–17.

JAMES, L., and A. JONES, "Organizational Climate: A Review of Theory and Research," *Psychological Bulletin*, 81, no. 12 (1974), 1096–1112.

JOHNSON, B., *Communication: The Process of Organizing*. Boston: Allyn & Bacon, Inc., 1977.

KAHN, R., and C. CANNELL, "Interviewing," in *The Handbook of Social Psychology*, vol. II, pp. 536–95, eds. G. Lindzey and E. Aronson. Reading, Mass.: Addison-Wesley Publishing Co., Inc., 1968.

KELLY, C., "Actual Listening Behavior of Industrial Supervisors as Related to 'Listening Ability,' General Mental Ability, Selected Personality Factors, and Supervising Effectiveness" (unpublished Ph.D. dissertation, Purdue University, 1962).

———, "Empathic Listening," in *Small Group Communication*, eds. R. Cathcart and L. Samovar. Dubuque: William C. Brown Company, Publishers, 1974.

KIESLER, C., B. COLLINS, and N. MILLER, *Attitude Change: A Critical Analysis of Theoretical Approaches*. New York: John Wiley & Sons, Inc., 1969.

KING, D., *Training Within the Organization*. London: Tavistock, 1964.

KORZYBSKI, A., *Science and Sanity: An Introduction to Non-Aristotelian Systems and General Semantics* (3rd ed.). Garden City, N.Y.: Country Life Publishing Co., 1948.

LAFOLLETTE, W., and H. SIMS, "Is Satisfaction Redundant with Climate?" *Organizational Behavior and Human Performance*, 13, no. 2 (1975), 252–78.

LAWLER, E., and L. PORTER, "Antecedent Job Attitudes of Effective Managerial Performance," *Organizational Behavior and Human Performance*, 2, no. 2 (1967), 139–55.

LEAVITT, H., *Managerial Psychology* (3rd ed.). Chicago: University of Chicago Press, 1972.

LEE, C., "An Experimental Study of Organizational Climate" (unpublished Master's thesis, Ohio State University, 1975).

LEE, I., *Language Habits in Human Affairs*. New York: Harper & Row, Publishers, Inc., 1941.

LESIKAR, R., *Business Communication Theory and Practice*. Homewood, Ill.: Richard D. Irwin, Inc., 1967.

LIKERT, R., *The Human Organization*. New York: McGraw-Hill Book Company, 1967.

LOWIN, A., "Participative Decision-Making: A Model, Literature Critique, and Prescriptions for Research," *Organizational Behavior and Human Performance*, 3, no. 1 (1968), 68–106.

LYNTON, R., and V. PAREEK, *Training for Development*. Homewood, Ill.: Richard D. Irwin., Inc., 1967.

McCLELLAND, D., D. ATKINSON, R. CLARK, and E. LOWELL, *The Achievement Motive*. New York: Appleton-Century-Crofts, 1953.

McGregor, D., *The Human Side of Enterprise.* New York: McGraw-Hill Book Company, 1960.

McGuire, W., "The Current Status of Cognitive Consistency Theories," in *Cognitive Consistency: Motivational Antecedents and Behavior Consequents,* ed. S. Feldman. New York: Academic Press, Inc., 1966.

Maslow, A. *Motivation and Personality.* New York: Harper & Row, Publishers, Inc., 1954.

Miles, R., *Theories of Management.* New York: McGraw-Hill Book Company, 1975.

Miller, G., *Language and Communication.* New York: McGraw-Hill Book Company, 1951.

Moe, I., "Auding as a Predictive Measure of Reading Performance in Primary Grades" (unpublished Ph.D. dissertation, University of Florida, 1957).

Monroe, A., and D. Ehninger, *Principles and Types of Speeches.* Glenview, Ill.: Scott, Foresman & Company, 1967.

Mortensen, C. D., *Communication.* New York: McGraw-Hill Book Company, 1972.

Newcomb, T., *The Acquaintance Process.* New York: Holt, Rinehart and Winston, 1961.

Nichols, R., "Do We Know How to Listen? Practical Helps in a Modern Age," *Speech Teacher,* 10, no. 29 (1961), 118–24.

————, and L. Stevens, *Are You Listening?* New York: McGraw-Hill Book Company, 1957.

Osgood, C., and P. Tannenbaum, "The Principle of Congruity in the Prediction of Attitude Change," *Psychological Review,* 62 (1955), 42–55.

Patton, B., and K. Giffin, *Interpersonal Communication.* New York: Harper and Row, Publishers, Inc., 1974.

Perrow, C., "Hospitals: Technology, Structure, and Goals," in *Handbook of Organizations,* ed. J. March. Chicago: Rand McNally & Co., 1965.

Potter, D., and M. Andersen, *Discussion: A Guide to Effective Practice.* Belmont, Calif.: Wadsworth Publishing Co., Inc., 1970.

Rankin, P., "The Measurement of the Ability to Understand Spoken Language" (unpublished Ph.D. dissertation, University of Michigan, 1926).

Read, W., "Upward Communication in Industrial Hierarchies," *Human Relations,* 15, no. 1 (1962), 3–15.

Redding, W., *Communication Within Organizations.* New York: Industrial Communication Council, 1972.

Roberts, K., and C. O'Reilly, "Failures in Upward Communication: Three

Possible Culprits," *Academy of Management Journal,* 17, no. 3 (1974), 205–15.

———, "Measuring Upward Communication," *Journal of Applied Psychology,* 69, no. 3 (1974), 321–26.

ROETHLISBERGER, F., and W. DICKSON, *Management and the Worker.* Cambridge, Mass.: Harvard University Press, 1939.

ROGERS, C., *Client-Centered Therapy: Its Current Practice, Implications, and Theory.* Boston: Houghton Mifflin Company, 1951.

———, "A Theory of Therapy, Personality, and Interpersonal Relationships as Developed in Client-Centered Framework," in *Psychology: The Study of a Science,* vol. III, ed. C. Rogers. New York: McGraw-Hill Book Company, 1959.

———, and R. FARSON, *Active Listening.* Chicago: Industrial Relations Center, University of Chicago, 1955.

ROSS, R., *Speech Communication* (4th ed.). Englewood Cliffs, N.J.: Prentice-Hall, Inc., 1977.

RUESCH, J., and G. BATESON, *Communication: The Social Matrix of Psychiatry.* New York: W. W. Norton & Co., Inc., 1951.

SANFORD, A., *Human Relations Theory and Practice* (2nd ed.). Columbus, Ohio: Charles E. Merrill Publishing Company, 1977.

———, G. HUNT, and H. BRACEY, *Communication Behavior in Organizations.* Columbus, Ohio: Charles E. Merrill Publishing Company, Inc., 1976.

SCHRAMM, W., "How Communication Works," in *The Process and Effects of Communication,* ed. W. Schramm, Urbana: University of Illinois Press, 1954.

SCRANTON, W., *U.S. President's Commission on Campus Unrest.* Washington, D.C.: U.S. Government Printing Office, 1970.

SERENO, K., and C. MORTENSEN, *Foundations of Communication Theory.* New York: Harper & Row Publishers, Inc., 1970.

SHANNON, C., and W. WEAVER, *The Mathematical Theory of Communication.* Urbana: University of Illinois Press, 1949.

SHERIFF, C., M. SHERIFF, and R. NEBERGALL, *Attitude and Attitude Change: The Social Judgement-Involvement Approach.* Philadelphia: W. B. Saunders Company, 1965.

SIGBAND, N., *Communication for Management.* Glenview, Ill.: Scott, Foresman & Company, 1969.

STEWART, C., and W. CASH, *Interviewing Principles and Practice.* Dubuque: William C. Brown Company, Publishers, 1974.

STOGDILL, R., and A. COONS, *Leader Behavior: Its Description and Measurement,* Monograph 88. Columbus: Ohio State University, Bureau of Educational Research, 1957.

TANNENBAUM, R., and G. MASSARIK, "Leadership: A Frame of Reference," in *Organizational Behavior and Management*, ed. D. Porter. Scranton, Pa.: International Textbook Company, 1968.

TAYLOR, F., *Scientific Management*. New York: Harper & Row, Publishers, Inc., 1947.

THAYER, L., *Communication and Communication Systems*. Homewood, Ill.: Richard D. Irwin, Inc., 1968.

———, "On Theory-Building in Communication: I. Some Conceptual Problems," *Journal of Communication*, 13, no. 3 (1963), 217–35.

THOMPSON, J., *Organizations in Action*. New York: McGraw-Hill Book Company, 1967.

TIFFIN, J., and E. McCORMICK, *Industrial Psychology*. Englewood Cliffs, N.J.: Prentice-Hall, Inc., 1973.

TOWNSEND, R., *Up the Organization*. New York: Alfred A. Knopf, Inc., 1970.

TURNER, A., "A Conceptual Scheme for Describing Work Group Behavior," in *Organizational Behavior and Administration*, ed. P. Lawrence. Homewood, Ill.: Richard D. Irwin, Inc., 1961.

VROOM, V., "Industrial Social Psychology," in *The Handbook of Social Psychology*, vol. IV, eds. G. Lindzey and E. Aronson. Reading, Mass.: Addison-Wesley Publishing Co., Inc., 1968.

———, *Work and Motivation*. New York: John Wiley & Sons, Inc., 1964.

WALKER, D., *Rights in Conflict*. Chicago: National Commission on the Causes and Prevention of Violence, 1968.

WEAVER, C., *Human Listening: Process and Behavior*. Indianapolis: The Bobbs-Merrill Co., Inc., 1972.

WEBER, M., *Essays in Sociology*, trans. H. Gerth and C. Mills. London: Oxford University Press, 1946.

WEICK, K., *The Social Psychology of Organizing*. Reading, Mass.: Addison-Wesley Publishing Co., Inc., 1969.

YODER, D., *Personnel Management and Industrial Relations*. Englewood Cliffs, N.J.: Prentice-Hall, Inc., 1962.

author index

subject index